Food and Beverage Management

John Cousins, David Foskett and David Shortt

Thames Valley University
Ealing, London and Slough, Berkshire

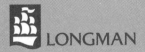 LONGMAN

Pearson Education Limited
Edinburgh Gate, Harlow
Essex CM20 2JE, England
and Associated Companies throughout the world

First published 1995
Third impression 1999

British Library Cataloguing in Publication Data
A catalogue entry for this title is available from the British Library

ISBN 0-582-27543-1

Set by 8 in 9/13pt Palatino
Printed in Malaysia, TCP

Food and Beverage Management

Contents

Contents

Preface

The aim of this book is to provide supporting information for those involved or likely to be involved in a variety of levels of food and beverage management. This is an introductory text for students and practitioners and also provides a framework on which to build further knowledge and skill.

In preparing this book we have taken into account the various changes in examining and awarding body syllabuses and in particular the British National Vocational Qualification standards. The book is specifically intended to cover the underpinning, knowledge and skill required by those wishing to be assessed up to level four. However, the book has also been written to meet the broader study requirements of a range of other programmes of study including Higher National Diploma, HCIMA and degree programmes.

The hospitality industry in Britain consists of over 250 000 establishments (HCTC estimate) and provides employment for 2.4 million people or 10 per cent of the workforce. This is a large and diverse industry. This book aims to cover aspects of the management of food and beverage operations which are applicable to a wide variety of sectors. In preparing this book we have had though, to be selective in its content and we have assumed that those using this text will have already acquired knowledge and skills in food and beverage operations.

Food and beverage operations within Britain have seen some remarkable changes over the last few years. The general quality of food, drink and service has increased and the professionalism of those employed has improved with better training and a greater understanding of customer needs.

The recent recessionary influences which created, for the first time in Britain, a highly competitive market environment caused many to reassess their business approaches. There is now a general understanding that in order to attract business, meeting the customers' needs becomes important. Also, it has become realized that as well as the food and drink on offer there are other needs of customers to be met, the quality of service now becoming a key differentiating factor when customers are choosing between different establishments. It is also recognized that existing regular customers are worth looking after, maintaining customer loyalty being far cheaper than seeking new customers. It is to support these approaches that this text has been written. Our view is that good food and beverage operations have a clear understanding of their customers' needs and continually seek to meet them.

Although the content of this book is reflective of current industrial practice it should not be seen as a prescriptive book. It is more a collection of information on various aspects of food and beverage management and the consideration of various approaches which students and the food and beverage manager may find useful.

1995   John Cousins, David Foskett and David Shortt

Acknowledgements

The preparation of this text has drawn upon a variety of research and experience. We would like to express our grateful thanks to all the organizations and individuals who gave us assistance and support.

In particular we would like to thank: The food and beverage lecturing teams of The School of Hospitality Studies at Thames Valley University, London; Linda Brosnan of Thames Valley University, London; Croner's Catering, Croner Publications, London; Andrew Durkan, wine and service lecturer and hotel and restaurant consultant; Griersons Wine Merchants Ltd, London; The Hotel and Catering Training Company, London; The Hotel and Catering International Management Association (HCIMA), London; IFS Publications, Bedford; Dennis Lillicrap, Senior Lecturer in Food and Beverage Service; Penelope Woolf of Pitman Publishing; Gardner Merchant Ltd.

1 An overview of food and beverage operations and management

Aim   This chapter aims to set the scene for the rest of the text.

Objective   The objective for this chapter is to enable you to:

- set the contents of this book in context
- develop an approach towards the categorization of the industry and the nature of the food and beverage product
- gain an insight into service quality issues and the legal framework in which the food service industry operates

Food and beverage operations

Food and beverage operations are concerned with the provision of food and drink within business. The various elements which comprise food and beverage operations can be summarized in the catering cycle shown in Fig. 1.1. Food and beverage operations are therefore concerned with:

(a)   The **markets** served by the various sectors of the industry and **consumer** needs.

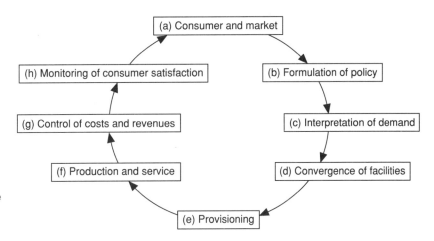

Fig. 1.1 The catering cycle (*after* Cracknell *et al.*, 1983)

(b) The range and **formulation of policies** and business objectives of the various sectors and how these affect the methods adopted.

(c) The **interpretation of demand** of the sectors for food and drink to be provided as well as other services.

(d) The planning and design to create a **convergence of facilities** required for food and beverage operations and the plant and equipment required.

(e) The development of appropriate **provisioning** methods to meet the needs of the production and service methods used within given operational settings.

(f) Operational knowledge of technical methods and processes and ability in the **production and service** processes and methods available to the caterer, understanding the varying resources required for their operation, as well as decision-making on the appropriateness of the various processes and methods to meet sectoral requirements.

(g) **Controlling the costs** of materials as well as the costs associated with the operation of production and service and **controlling the revenue**.

(h) The **monitoring of customer satisfaction**.

The catering cycle is not just a statement of what food and beverage operations are concerned with. It is also a dynamic model in the sense that difficulties in one area of the cycle will cause difficulties in the elements of the cycle which follow. Thus, for instance, difficulties with purchasing will have effects on production and service and control. Similarly, difficulties experienced under one element of the cycle will have their causes in preceding elements.

The catering cycle has been used to form the basis for this book as follows:

*   Stage 1 The market: This is considered in Chapter 2 'Customers'.
*   Stage 2 Policies and Stage 3 Interpretation of demand: These are considered in Chapter 3 'Food production', Chapter 4 'Wine and drink' and Chapter 6 'Food and beverage service'.
*   Stage 4 Facilities: This is considered in Chapter 5 'Food and beverage areas and equipment'.
*   Stage 5 Provisioning: This is considered under the relevant chapters on food (Chapter 3) and beverages (Chapter 4).
*   Stage 6 Production and service: This is considered for production in Chapter 3 and for service in Chapter 6.
*   Stage 7 Control of costs and revenue: This is introduced in Chapters 3–6 and is consolidated in Chapter 7 'Operations performance appraisal'.
*   Stage 8 Monitoring customer satisfaction: This is also considered in Chapter 7.

Chapter 8 'Cases in food and beverage management' aims to bringing the cycle together through the examples of case studies.

This re-presentation of the catering cycle for the structure of this book can be shown as in Fig. 1.2.

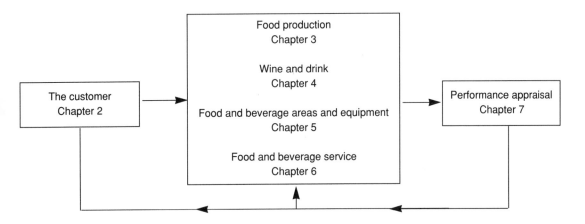

Fig. 1.2 Re-presentation of catering cycle for the structure of this book

A systems approach

The underlying thinking behind much of this text relies on a systems approach to the management of food and beverage operations. There are, however, two dimensions to this approach. The first is concerned with being systematic in the design, planning and control of food and beverage operations and the second is the management of the operating systems within food and beverage operations.

The systems approach for the management of service is summarized in Table 1.1. The operating systems which are managed within food and beverage operations have traditionally been seen as first a system for production and second a system for service. The service element is primarily seen as a delivery system. However, for the purpose of this text, three systems are recognized within food and beverage operations. These are:

1. the system for food production
2. the system of delivery or the service sequence
3. the system of customer management or the customer process

Table 1.1   Comparison of traditional and system approaches

Traditional approach	Systems approach
Based on assumptions of linearity in the market-place	Sensitive to changes in business conditions
Depends on the experience of key people	Depends on staff experience and good data
Information not readily available	Information available as needed
Intuitive	Quantitative
Reactive in nature	Pro-active in nature
Service driven	Cost and service driven
Vulnerable to turnover of key people	Less vulnerable to turnover of key people
Weak in accountability	Strong in accountability

Source: Records and Glennie (1991)

The food and beverage operation may therefore be summarized in Fig. 1.3. This approach is based on the recognition that the management of any operating system is concerned with three elements (Morris and Johnston, 1987):

1. the management of materials
2. the management of information
3. the management of people (customers)

This approach is reflected in the separation of the consideration of food and beverage service in Chapter 6 into the management of the service sequence and the management of the customer processes. This can be further clarified by reference to the operations hierarchy in Table 1.2.

This book is primarily concerned with the management of methods and operations under the definitions given in Table 1.2.

Table 1.2   Operations hierarchy

Element of operation	Description
Skills and knowledge	Knowledge of food accompaniments, handling a spoon and fork
Task	Group of skills, e.g. glasswashing
Duty	Group of tasks, e.g. preparing bar for service
Method	Group of duties combined to achieve a particular service, e.g. silver service
Operation	Combination of various methods, e.g. production, service, billing, thus creating a complete system for the provision of food and beverages within a specific type of outlet
Sector	Business environment in which the operation exists

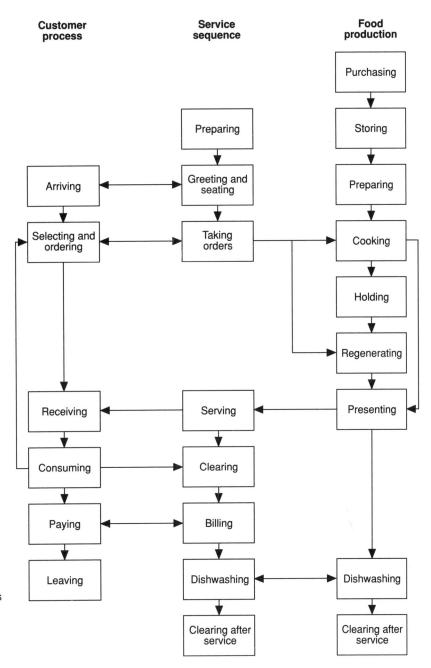

Fig. 1.3 The three systems of food and beverage operations and their inter-relationship (*after* Lockwood, 1994 and Cousins, 1988)

The hospitality industry and its products

The hospitality industry is usually identified by its output of products which satisfy the demand for food, drink and accommodation away from home. The industry is normally split into the accommodation and food service industry.

The food service industry tends to be separated into two sets of sectors: the profit-orientated sectors and the cost provision sectors (e.g. welfare catering). In the profit sectors marketing is aimed at meeting customer demand, usually in competition with other organizations, for profit. The profit motivation does not appear in the cost-orientated sectors, however the need to satisfy customer demand does, albeit within the constraints of a given budget. It is generally now recognized for instance that better-fed workers work better and better-satisfied patients recover more quickly.

There are many different kinds of food and drink operations which are designed to meet a wide range of types of demand. It is perhaps important, though, to recognize that it is the needs people have at the time, rather than the type of people they are, that these different operations are designed for. The same person may be a business customer during the week, but a member of a family at the weekend; he or she may want a quick lunch on one occasion, a snack while travelling on another or a meal for the family at a further time. Additionally the same person may be booking a wedding or organizing some other special occasion. Clearly there are numerous reasons for eating out, other examples being: to do something different, to try different foods or for sheer convenience because one is already away from the home – out shopping, at the cinema, a conference or an exhibition.

The reasons for eating out vary and with this, the types of operation that may be appropriate. Differing establishments offer different service, in both range and price as well as service levels. Also the choice offered may be restricted or wide. Basically there are three types of markets in which operations may be meeting demand. These are:

1. Captive markets where the customer has no choice, e.g. hospital patients.
2. Non-captive markets, e.g. those people who have a free choice of establishments.
3. Semi-captive markets where there is some restriction, e.g. people travelling by air who have a choice of airline but once the choice is made, are restricted to the food and drink on offer. This category also applies, for instance, to railways, some inclusive-term holidays and people travelling on motorways.

To every product (and food service is no exception) there are two dimensions: features and benefits. Features are the physical characteristics of the product but marketers tend to stress benefits because of the realization that products are bought for the satisfaction they provide.

The food service industry's products may be defined as the set of satisfactions or dissatisfactions which customer receives from a food service experience. The satisfaction may be physiological, economic, social or psychological or convenience as follows:

• Physiological needs, e.g. to satisfy hunger and thirst, or to satisfy the need for special foods.

• Economic needs, e.g. staying within a certain budget, wanting good value, a convenient location or fast service.

• Social needs, e.g. being out with friends, business colleagues or attending special functions such as weddings.

• Psychological needs, e.g. responding to advertising, wanting to try something new or simply fulfilling life-style needs.

• Convenience needs, for example it may not be possible to return home or the desire may be there for someone else to prepare, serve and wash up.

Dissatisfaction falls into two categories:

1. Controllable by the establishment, e.g. scruffy, unhelpful staff, cramped conditions.

2. Uncontrollable, e.g. behaviour of other customers, the weather, transport problems.

Customers may be wanting to satisfy all or some of these needs and it is important to recognize that it is the reason behind wanting or having to eat out, rather than the food and drink by themselves, that will play an important part in determining the resulting satisfaction or dissatisfaction with the experience. It is quite possible that the motivation to eat out is not to satisfy basic physiological needs at all.

Product augmentation

Sometimes the product delivered to the customer is different from that received by the customer. In other words, the reason for the customer buying the product may determine the satisfaction rather than specifically the product itself (e.g. out with friends).

Distinctions are often drawn between the core, tangible and augmented concepts of the product: for example, the core is the food and drink provision itself; the tangible methods of delivery (silver service restaurant or vending machine) or portions of a certain size; augmentation takes into account the complete package. Differing sectors of the food service industry are essentially meeting similar customer demands, i.e. offering the same core product. However, this can be modified and enhanced in cost-effective ways to make the product more attractive. Competition within specific sectors largely takes place at the augmented level. In the food service industry this might include:

- speed of service
- ordering/booking convenience
- reliability
- provision of special foods
- cooking to order
- home deliveries
- availability of non-menu items
- entertainment
- privacy/discretion
- acceptance of credit cards
- availability of account facilities

These various elements are often drawn together with the core and tangible elements under the heading the 'meal experience' concept (Jones, 1988).

The meal experience concept

If people have decided to eat out then it follows that there has been choice to do this in preference to some other course of action. In other words, the caterer has attracted the customer to buy his/her product as against some other, for example theatre, cinema or simply staying at home.

Reasons for eating out may be summarized under seven headings:

1. Convenience, for example being unable to return home as in the case of shoppers or people at work or involved in some leisure activity.
2. Variety, for example trying new experiences or as a break from home cooking.
3. Labour, for example getting someone else to prepare, serve food and wash up or simply the physical impossibilities to house special events at home.
4. Status, for example business lunches or people eating out because others of their socio-economic group do so.
5. Culture/tradition, for example special events or simply because it is a way of getting to know people.
6. Impulse, for example simply spur-of-the-moment buying.
7. No choice, for example those in welfare, hospitals or other forms of semi or captive markets.

People are, however, a collection of different types as any demographic break-down would show. While it is true that some types of food service operation might attract certain types of customers this is by no means true all the time; for example, McDonalds is marketed to the whole population and attract customers depending on their needs at the time.

The decision to eat out may also be split into two parts: first, the decision to do so for the reasons given above and then the decision as to what type of experience is to be undertaken. It is generally agreed that there are a number of factors influencing this latter decision. These factors extend the core, tangible and augmented distinctions drawn earlier. The factors that affect the meal experience may be summarized as follows:

Food and drink on offer

The range of foods, choice, availability, flexibility for special orders and the quality of the food and drink.

Level of service

Depending on the needs people have at the time, the level of service sought should be appropriate to these needs. For example, a romantic night out may call for a quiet table in a top-end restaurant, whereas a group of young friends might be seeking more informal service. This factor also takes into account services such as booking and account facilities, acceptance of credit cards and also the reliability of the operation's product.

Level of cleanliness and hygiene

This relates to the premises, equipment and staff. Over the last few years this factor has increased in importance in the customers' minds. The recent media focus on food production and the risks involved in buying food have heightened awareness of health and hygiene aspects.

Perceived value for money and price

Customers have perceptions of the amount they are prepared to spend and relate these to differing types of establishments and operations. However, many people will spend more if the value gained is perceived as greater than that obtained by spending slightly less. (Also see the notes on price, cost, value and worth on page 23.)

Atmosphere of the establishment

This is difficult to quantify as it is an intangible concept. However, it is composed of a number of factors such as: décor, lighting, heating, furnishings, acoustics and noise levels, the other customers and the attitude of the staff.

Identifying the factors above is important because it considers the product from the point of view of the customer. All too often food service operators can get caught up in the provision of food and drink, spend several thousands on décor, equipment, etc. but ignore the actual experience the customer undertakes. Untrained service staff are a good example of this problem. Operations tend to concentrate on the core product and forget the total package. A better understanding of the customer's viewpoint or the nature of customer demand leads to a better product being developed to meet it.

The food service industry sectors

There are many types of eating out premises but differing premises do not necessarily indicate the nature of the demand being met. For instance, a cafeteria may be found in industrial catering, motorway service stations, hospitals and retail operations. For marketing purposes, sectors are better identified based upon customer demand and not on the type of operation. The list of sectors given in Table 1.3 is based upon the purpose of the sector, i.e. the nature of demand being met. This method of classification of sectors by purpose provides for either the small company to identify its immediate competitors or for the larger company – which may be operating in a number of markets – to specifically identify immediate competitors within a specific sector. It also provides for the identification of other sectors where competition might exist for the specific sector under consideration, i.e. alternatives (hotels, popular caterers, fast food) may attract the same customers.

The legal framework

Within food service operations there are a number of situations which are the subject of legal regulation. These are highlighted below. It should, however, be borne in mind that these are highly summarized guidelines and that many of the issues highlighted are affected by the particular circumstances at the time.

The provision of services

Food service operations are under no obligation to provide services unless the operation is an establishment covered by the Hotel Proprietors Act 1956 and the customers seeking services are classed as bona fide travellers. Establishments may refuse to serve people who do not meet the dress requirements of the establishments, e.g. the wearing of jackets or non-allowance of beachwear. Additionally, licensed establishments may refuse to serve people who are drunk or quarrelsome.

Establishments are, however, under the obligation to ensure that they do not breach the Sex Discrimination Act 1975 and the Race Relations Act 1976. These Acts, among other things, legislate against discrimination on the grounds of sex, race, creed or colour. Under these Acts, establishments may not refuse services, provide inferior services or set unreasonable conditions on the basis of these characteristics.

Describing services

Under the Sale of Goods Act 1979 the customer can refuse to pay for a meal or demand a replacement if:

* The goods supplied do not correspond to the description.

Table 1.3   Sectors of the food service industry (Lillicrap D and Cousins J, 1994)

Sector	Purpose of sector
Hotels (and other tourist accommodation)	Provision of food and drink together with accommodation
Restaurants Including: conventional specialist and 'carveries'	Provision of food and drink generally at high price with high levels of service
Popular catering Including: cafes, pizza, Wimpy, grills, specialist coffee shops, Little Chefs, steak houses	Provision of food and drink, low/medium price with limited levels of service
Fast food e.g. McDonalds, Burger King	Provision of food and drink in highly specialized environment characterized by high investment, high labour costs and vast customer throughput
Take-away including: ethnic, spuds, KFC snacks, fish and chips, sandwich bars, kiosks	Provision of food and drinks quickly
Retail stores	Provision of food and drink as adjunct to provision of retailing
Banqueting/conferences/exhibitions	Provision of food and drink on large scale, usually pre-booked
Leisure attractions e.g. theme parks, galleries, theatres, airline terminals	Provision of food and drink for people engaged in another leisure pursuit
Motorway service stations	Provision of food together with retail and petrol services for motorway travellers, often in isolated locations
Industrial catering Either in-house operations or provided by catering contractor	Provision of food and drink to people at work
Welfare Including: hospitals, schools, prisons, other welfare	Provision of food and drink to colleges, universities, forces, to people through social need, primarily determined by an authority
Licensed trade Including: public houses, wine bars, licensed clubs, members' clubs	Provision of food and drink in environment dominated by licensing requirements
Transport Including: railways, airline, marine	Provision of food and drink to people on the move
Outdoor catering ('off premises' catering)	Provision of food and drink away from home base and suppliers

- A displayed item is not what it seems: for example, a sweet where the cream which would reasonably be expected to be fresh is in fact artificial.
- The food is inedible or the drink undrinkable.

Additionally, the Trades Description Acts 1968/1972 make it a criminal offence to misdescribe goods or services.

Customer payment

If the customer is without the means to pay and this is a pure mistake, then the operation can seek proof of identity and take a name and address. However, if fraud is suspected, then the police may be called in. The operation may not take personal items as security unless the customer is staying in a hotel covered by the Hotel Proprietors Act 1956. In this case the proprietor has the right to lien; in other words, luggage may be taken pending payment.

The customer and their property

If an establishment is covered by the Hotel Proprietors Act 1956, then it is liable for customers' property while they are staying there. Other than this, there is no automatic liability unless the damage to, or loss of, the customer's property has resulted from negligence on behalf of the establishment, which would have to be proved. Under the health and safety legislation (1974 and other) there is a duty on the part of the establishment to care for all lawful visitors, and negligence is a criminal offence. Establishments are, therefore, legally bound to look after the customers' (and all the lawful visitors') health and safety while they are on their premises.

The health and safety issues are of particular importance within food service operations. The Food Safety Act 1990 is a piece of wide-ranging legislation designed to ensure that all food (and in this context it includes beverages) produced and offered by sale is safe to eat and is not misleadingly advertised or presented.

Price lists, service and minimum charges

Restaurants are required to display food and drink priced (Price Marketing Order 1979) so they can be seen by customers before entering the premises or, in the case of a complex, before entering the dining area. If service and cover charges are stated on menus and price lists, then they should normally be paid unless, in the case of service charges, the customer considers that the service has been poor.

Under the Food Labelling (Amendment) Regulations 1989 there is a requirement that the alcoholic strength (given as a percentage of alcohol by volume) of a representative sample of dispensed drinks be displayed on price lists, wine lists and menus.

In 1989 Part III of the Consumer Protection Act 1987 came into force. This part of the Act deals with misleading prices and among the provisions it states that it is an offence to give misleading price information. It recommends that, where the customer has to pay a non-optional charge, it should be incorporated into the total price or should not be charged at all. It also states that cover charges and minimum charges should be prominently displayed. Compliance with these provisions is not obligatory, but failure to do so could be used as evidence by the Office of Fair Trading that an offence has been committed.

Other legal issues are considered under the appropriate section (licensing in Chapter 4 for example). For further information see for instance: *Croner's Catering* and A. Pannett, *Principles of Hotel and Catering Law*, Cassell (1989).

Service standards

Within food and beverage operations service standards may be seen under two headings:

1. technical standards
2. service standards

Technical standards refer to the items on offer, the portion size or measure, the cooking method, the degree of cooking, the method of presentation, the cover, accompaniments, the cleanliness of items, etc.

Service standards refer to two aspects: first, the procedures for service and second, the way in which the procedures are carried out. Procedures include meeting and greeting, order taking, seeking customer comment, dealing with complaints, payment, special needs of customers. The method in which service is carried out includes attention to the attitude of staff, attentiveness, tone of voice, body language, etc.

Accepting that any standard must be achievable and measurable then this is quite possible with technical standards and with some aspects of service standards. However, it becomes increasingly difficult to set actual standards for the way that the service should be carried out.

Below are a number of possible aims for the service to achieve but is it arguable whether all of these are in fact standards or simply intentions:

*   The supervisor should be visible in the room.
*   The supervisor will visit all tables at least once during the customers' meal.
*   Service employees should have positive attitudes.
*   Servers should be noticeably comfortable in their respective roles.
*   Co-operation between staff should be noticeable.
*   Customers should be addressed by name.

- All customers should be addressed by name at least once during the meal.
- Customers' needs will be met.
- Ninety per cent of customer requests will be met.
- Menu items can be substituted or combined.

The other difficulty is that the intentions may not suit all customers all the time and therefore the service staff in endeavouring to meet these intentions may not be providing good service when considered from the customer perspective.

An alternative to this approach is first to recognize that the product is the totality of what the customer receives. The customer makes no real distinction between the physical product and the intangible aspects of service. It is probable in this context that the manager should also view the product as a whole, setting standards only where it is actually possible.

Customer service and resource productivity

On the one hand a food and beverage operation is designed to provide customer service and on the other the achievement of profit is largely determined by the efficiency of the use of resources. Customer service can be defined as being a combination of five characteristics. These are:

1. Service level: the style of service, e.g. self-service, tray service, silver service.
2. Availability of service: e.g. the opening times, variations in the menus and drinks lists on offer.
3. Level of standards: e.g. food quality, décor, equipment cost, staffing professionalism.
4. Reliability of the service: the extent to which the product is intended to be consistent in practice.
5. Flexibility of the service: the provision of alternatives, variations in the standard product on offer.

The resources used in food service operations are:

- Materials: commodities and equipment.
- Labour: staffing costs.
- Facilities: basically the premises and the volume of business which the premises are able to support.

This can be seen as a model, as shown in Fig. 1.4. The management of the operation must therefore take account of the effect that the level of business has on the ability of the operation to maintain the service while at the same time ensuring a high productivity in all the resources being used.

An approach to service standards

If it is difficult to set meaningful service standards then the natural question is: what else can be done?

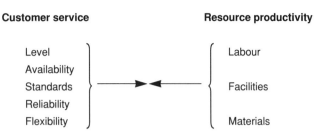

Fig. 1.4 Customer service versus resource productivity

If a customer service specification is drawn up based on the five factors indicated above then the next step is first to check that the specification can be met by the capabilities of the operation and also that the specification can be delivered through the service system. This can be seen as a six-stage process as follows:

1. Determine service specification in terms of level, availability, standards, reliability and flexibility.
2. Check that operation is physically capable of supporting the service specification at a given volume of business.
3. Check that the service systems and the service staff are able to deliver to the customer the totality of the service specification.
4. Monitor operational aspects.
5. Monitor customer satisfaction.
6. Feedback to original service specification and alter as appropriate.

This approach ties in with the systems approach and also follows the philosophy of the various approaches to total quality management.

Quality in the management of food and beverage operations

The term 'quality' is currently used in a variety of ways to mean a variety of things. To support the approach of this book the term 'quality' relies on the approach of the British Standard Institute which bases the Quality Award BS 5750 on an assessment: 'in the fitness for purpose and safe in use sense: is the service provided or product designed and constructed to satisfy the customer's needs'.

This process, however, does not include some external measure of the customer's satisfaction with a particular operation. It is primarily concerned with evidence of systematic processes which are employed within an operation which can demonstrate that there is a link between customer demand and the services and products on offer. In this respect the catering cycle can provide a useful model on which to base this approach.

The approach to the assessment of quality is also becoming recognized within the rest of Europe and the USA. The European Quality Award (1993) and in the USA the National Quality Award (based on the Baldridge criteria as one example) take similar approaches.

In effect all these awards support the systems approaches, intended to achieve total quality management. This is summarized by the European Foundation for Quality Management in the publication *Total Quality Management: The European Model for Self-Appraisal, 1993* shown graphically in Fig. 1.5.

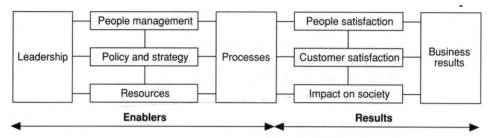

Fig. 1.5 Framework for the European Quality Award

Processes are the means by which the organization harnesses and releases the talents of its people to produce *business results*. In other words, the processes and the people are the *enablers* which provide the *results*. This model was developed as a framework for the European Quality Award. Essentially the model tells us that customer satisfaction, people (employee) satisfaction and impact on society are achieved through *leadership* driving policy and strategy, people management, resources and *processes*, leading ultimately to excellence in *business results*.

Each of the nine elements shown in the model is a criterion that can be used to appraise an organization's progress towards total quality management. The results aspects are concerned with what the organization has achieved and is achieving. The enablers aspects are concerned with how results are being achieved.

The overall objective of a comprehensive self-appraisal and self-improvement programme is to regularly review each of these nine criteria and, thereafter, to adopt relevant improvement strategies.

British Standard 5750

BS 5750 is the British national system for indicating that an organization operates a quality-orientated system, sometimes described as a total quality management system. It relates to the International Organization for Standardization (ISO) standard 9000. BS 5750 identifies the systems, procedures and criteria which ensure that a product or service meets a customer's requirements.

The key elements in quality management for most organizations in the hospitality industry include:

- Management responsibility; policy, objectives, key personnel.
- Quality system procedures; all functions must be covered.
- Auditing the system; it must be audited internally.
- Quality in marketing; honest promotional activities.
- Material control and traceability; supplies must be traceable.
- Nonconformity; ensuring that faulty products/service do not reach the customer.
- Corrective action; identifying reasons for faults, measures taken and records to be kept.
- After-sales service; procedures for monitoring quality of after-sales service.
- Documentation and records; records of checks and inspections, action taken, audit reports.
- Personnel and training; identification of needs, provision and verification of training.
- Product safety and liability; procedures for handling, storing and processing materials, e.g. foods.

BS 5750 can be important to caterers for two reasons. Firstly, when purchasing goods and services BS 5750 indicates that a supplier operates a quality system of a high standard. Secondly, caterers, such as contract caterers, may find that they will not be considered as potential tenderers if they have not achieved BS 5750. In addition, BS 5750 may even provide useful evidence that due diligence had been exercised, for example, in the event of a caterer being prosecuted under the Food Safety Act.

In an increasingly competitive market-place, and with increasing uniformity between operations, the level of service provided and its quality become ever more important. It is the front-line staff that offer this service, hence their training and development are crucial to the successful running of an operation. Total quality management offers a framework by which staff are given the scope to treat guests as individuals, and thereby offer superior service.

However, the costs involved can be high and therefore, the introduction of BS 5750 needs to be carefully assessed before implementation takes place. However, the reviews from many of the organizations moving towards BS 5750 have suggested that it is cost-effective.

Further information on quality matters can be obtained from:

The Malcolm Baldridge National Quality Award
National Institute of Standards and Technology,
Administration Building, Room A537
Gaithersburg, Maryland MD 20899 USA

The European Quality Award
The European Foundation for Quality Management,
Building 'Reaal', Fellinoord 47A,
5612 AA Eindhoven, The Netherlands

BS 5750
BSI Standards
389, Chiswick High Road
London W4 4AL

Also see the following publications:

East J 1993 *Managing Quality in the Catering Industry,* Croner's Publications.
HCIMA Technical Brief Sheet No. 20.

Summary

This chapter has provided information on the basis for the rest of the text. The catering cycle is identified as providing a tool for the systematic examination of food service operations. The nature of the food service industry has been examined and sectors identified, as well as a range of differences between customer needs and the range of operations designed to meet their needs. Customer service issues have also been highlighted, including the possible trade-off between the maintenance of customer service and the efficient management of resources. Lastly, quality management approaches have been briefly examined as being relevant to the management of food service operations.

References

Cousins J 1988 Curriculum development in operational management teaching in catering education. In Johnson R (ed) *The management of service operations* IFS Publications, Bedford: pp. 437–59

Cracknell H L, Kaufman R J and Nobis G 1983 *Practical professional catering* Macmillan, London

Jones P 1988 *Food service operations* Cassell, London

Lillicrap D and Cousins J 1994 *Food and beverage service* Hodder and Stoughton, London

Lockwood A 1994 Developing operating standards. In Jones P (ed) *The management of foodservice operations* Cassell, London: p. 103

Morris B and Johnston R 1987 *Dealing with the inherent variability – the difference between manufacturing and service.* Paper given at the Operations Management Association International Conference, Warwick University

Records H and Glennie M 1991 Service management and quality assurance. *The Cornell HRA Quarterly*, **32**(1) May 1991: pp. 26–35

2 The food and beverage consumer and the consumer–product relationship

Aim This chapter aims to explore the nature of demand for food and beverage products and the consumer–product relationship.

Objective The objective of this chapter is to enable you to identify and appraise key issues associated with the nature of demand for food and beverage products and the consumer–product relationship.

Development of a consumer–product relationship framework

In order to achieve the aim and objective of this chapter it is considered helpful to apply a framework identifying the key issues which shape the nature of demand for food and beverage products and create the consumer–product relationship. Literature concerning consumers and markets is readily available, much of which applies specifically to food and beverage operations. The literature explores the nature of demand for products from different viewpoints. These viewpoints include marketing, psychology, anthropology, economics, sociology, geography and social psychology. Other points of view or subjects appear as these sciences develop into new disciplines, i.e. consumer behaviour.

The key issues concerning the nature of demand for food and beverage products are identified using a well-validated if somewhat oversimplified list of questions: Who are the consumers of the food and beverage product? What food and beverage product do they want? Why do they want a food and beverage product? When do they want a food and beverage product? Where do they want a food and beverage product? and How do they obtain a food and beverage product? These questions can be explored individually, but only one is key: What products do consumers want? The who, why, where, when and how are all part of the product and are inherent in answering the question as to which products consumers want. The first key issue in the framework will therefore be centred around the product.

Consumers of food and beverage products are sophisticated, complex and dynamic. Psychology, sociology, social psychology, geography and anthropology identify the behaviour of individuals and groups in an attempt to understand the human condition, and relate to the consumer through the examination of human needs, wants, demands, goals and values. Economics focuses on the examination of the human condition as it relates to the commercial and business world through the examination of the allocation of scarce resources and the link between supply and demand. Marketing focuses on the human condition as it relates to products, i.e. the study of the consumer. Kotler (1984, p. 4) argues that 'Marketing attempts to serve as a link between society's needs and its pattern of industrial response.' The consumer is the actual link. Without the consumer there is no link between human needs and food and beverage products. A product is simply a consumer's satisfied need.

People who do not consume are not consumers. However obvious or trite this statement might appear it does eliminate the possible confusion between a consumer and a non-consumer. For example, families who eat four times a year in a motorway service area when they visit their daughter, but otherwise never eat anywhere *en famille* except in private seclusion (i.e. their family home or a relative's home), are consumers of the motorway service area food and beverage product, even if they consume relatively little of this product. They are potential consumers of many existing and future food and beverage products but at present are consumers of only one product from a vast range available, but are not consumers of the rest. They are consumers of many other products but are consumers of only one food and beverage product. They may have an unsatisfied food and beverage need, but a product is unavailable to them as yet which may satisfy this need.

When 'consumers' are discussed they are often addressed as large groups comprising millions of people, which they are when all added together. But when they are examined in detail they are certainly not homogeneous, because they consume, or not consume, millions of products in a very dynamic and rapidly changing way. They are individuals who group together to form a market for a particular product. This market grouping may range from 300 people, as in a small rural exclusive restaurant, up to and beyond 300 million people for world-branded products like McDonalds. The question for managers in the food and beverage industry is: Who do we want our consumers to be? Managers may say that their consumers are the same as the consumers they want them to be, i.e. 'We have achieved our objective of creating a consumer that fits our product.' However, even if such a desirable state exists, the nature of the consumer is continually changing and as such management need to understand their consumers and how changes are taking place which affect consumers. It is a clear argument for the establishment of a customer-oriented business. The second key issue in the framework is therefore centred around consumers.

The two key issues can be expanded to identify their component parts as in

Fig. 2.1. The component parts are tasks listed chronologically both culminating in a product–consumer relationship. These parts may be merged to form a framework (Fig. 2.2) which makes possible a systematic approach to the development of a consumer–product relationship.

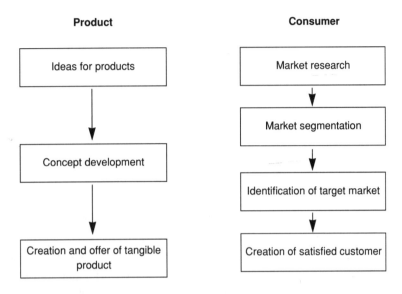

Fig. 2.1 Product and consumer issues

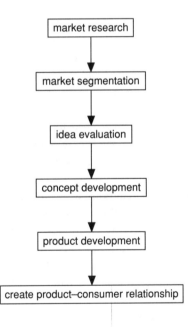

Fig. 2.2 Product–consumer relationship development framework

The framework in Fig. 2.2 may be viewed as a list of tasks to be performed chronologically, but in practice some of these tasks will be performed simultaneously as the process of creating a product–consumer relationship is a process in which food and beverage operations continually engage. However, in order to explore and evaluate the nature of demand and the product–consumer relationship, each part of the framework will be addressed in turn.

Market research

Researching into the food and beverage market can be performed at various levels. Large food and beverage businesses may invest considerable resources in acquiring market information. Marketing departments will use consumer panels, questionnaires, interviews, sales analyses, market information from specialist publications, specifically commissioned market information and other generally available data. Small food and beverage businesses do not usually have a marketing department and in these instances the unit manager or owner-operator will perform the market research function. In all types of operation the focus of market research is concerned with human needs, wants, demands, goals and values.

Food and beverage needs are a state of felt deprivation for basic satisfactions including shelter, safety, belonging and esteem, as well as food and drink. 'These needs are not created by society or by marketers; they exist in the very texture of human biology and the human condition' (Kotler, 1984, p. 5). These needs coexist in the human condition so that a food and drink need may coexist with a belonging and esteem need.

Food and beverage wants are desires for satisfiers of these needs. A hamburger can be a want for food *and* a want for belonging and esteem. Seven-year-old children may want to go to McDonalds to satisfy their need for belonging to their peer group, to satisfy their need for esteem within their peer group and to satisfy their need for food and drink. Wanting to satisfy their belonging and esteem needs may outweigh their food and drink needs. A food and beverage product may satisfy needs not initially stimulated by hunger and thirst.

Food and beverage demands are wants for specific food and beverage products supported by the capability to buy them. The Pizza Hut product may be demanded and purchased by customers wanting to satisfy their need for belonging to their peer group, to satisfy their need for esteem within their peer group and to satisfy their need for food and drink. Food and beverage operators should try to influence demand by making their product desirable, valuable and available.

Consumers have goals when they decide to choose a food and beverage product. The goals in purchasing a food and beverage product can include esteem, belonging, status, attention, entertainment, privilege, relaxation, intimacy, romance, convenience, physiological and psychological comfort, and satisfying hunger and thirst. Sometimes satisfying hunger and thirst are not always goals needing to be achieved. The collection of goals an individual has when choosing a food and beverage product may be referred to as the *goal set*. Each food and beverage product has the capacity to satisfy different goal sets. Accordingly, a consumer may perceive a take-away as providing greater convenience and as being less expensive than an up-market à la carte restaurant, but the restaurant may be perceived as providing greater attention (level of service) and a higher level of esteem and status. The consumer will make a choice as to which is the most satisfying product for their particular goal set at the time.

Value is identified by Kotler (1984, p. 6), as the 'consumer's estimate of a product's capacity to satisfy a set of goals'. If a consumer's goal set is prioritized as food, convenience and variety, they may be satisfied by different food and beverage products. A consumer with this goal set may satisfy these goals with a fish and chip shop product, whereas another consumer may satisfy the same goal set with a public house meal product. The choice as to which product to choose is made by a consideration of price, cost, worth and value. Price is the amount of money required to purchase the product. Costs include the cost of not going somewhere else, the cost of transport and time, the cost of potential embarrassment, the cost of having to look and behave in a required manner and the cost in terms of effort at work to earn the money. Worth is a perception of the balance between satisfied goals and the costs involved in satisfying those goals. Good value is where the worth is perceived as greater than the costs, and poor value is where the costs are perceived as greater than the worth.

Individual consumers will value food and beverage products in different ways. An individual may value convenience when purchasing coffee and croissants on the way to work in the morning, value a low price at lunchtime when purchasing a meal in the workplace restaurant and value high levels of service and entertainment when purchasing a celebration meal in the evening. These values change during an individual's life cycle as his/her needs, wants and demands also change in relation to the circumstances. Individuals may value a night club product in their youth, may value a fast food restaurant when they have young children and may value a reduced price for pensioners product in their old age. Additionally, consumers may place different values on the same product or parts of a product. One individual may value silver service because it is perceived as increasing the status of the occasion, while others may not value silver service because it makes them feel uncomfortable in an unusual situation.

Researching the market will facilitate the identification of consumers' needs, wants, demands, goals and values as they relate to food and beverage products. Having identified these it is possible to group them using a mix of criteria. These groupings are termed *market segments*.

Market segmentation

There are many different ways to segment a market. Food and beverage operators will try different segmentation variables in the attempt to identify the needs, wants and demands of possible market groupings. These variables are most usually grouped into geographic, demographic, psychographic and behavioural elements.

Geographic segmentation will involve dividing the market into geographical areas such as nations, regions, cities, districts and neighbourhoods. Food and beverage products such as Forte's Harvester and Whitbread's Beefeater target regions of the UK's food and beverage market. My Kinda Town restaurants target European capital cities. Up-market restaurants may target a district, and a fish and chip shop may only target a neighbourhood. A food and beverage product may operate in areas with different geographical needs, satisfying these different needs by making alterations to their product mix. Menu items vary between the My Kinda Town restaurants in different European cities. Well-known fast food restaurants operate discriminatory pricing by applying a different price to the same product in relation to location, i.e. higher price at airports than on high streets, and different prices in relation to different countries. The reason this is done is because the needs, wants and demands vary by geographical location, and the product/marketing mix will be altered in an attempt to exploit and accommodate the differences.

Demographic segmentation will involve dividing the market into groups using such variables as age, gender, stage in the family life cycle, income, occupation, education, religion, race and nationality. A public house may segment its market into single, 25–35-year-old men with average income, whose education finished at 16, and who are employed in manual skilled and semi-skilled professions. Another public house may segment its market in the same way but substitute married couples with two small children for 25–35-year-old singles. The first public house could be located in a city centre, and the second in a seaside holiday resort. The needs, wants and demands of these two segments are very different.

Psychographic segmentation is a stage further on from demographic grouping and identifies the social class, life style and personality characteristics of a consumer. Social class exists in all areas of our society with various individuals forming into sets whose patterns of behaviour and attitude vary widely. Food and beverage consumers may be segmented as to their social class with products designed specifically to satisfy their demands. Some social groupings will prefer seclusion and formality when consuming a food and beverage product while another group may prefer informal and crowded atmospheres. Further social groupings can be distinguished as captive and semi-captive markets, such as those in hospital or on board a channel ferry. Different social groupings exhibit preferences for particular food and beverage products. Life-style segmentation can be seen in the development of food and beverage products such as TGI Friday, appealing to consumers who see themselves as young, fashionable, informal and adventurous. Personality segmentation is used to develop beverage products such as beers, appealing to consumers who see themselves as sharp and quick-witted (Harp lager), or discerning traditionalists (real ale).

Behavioural segmentation divides the market into groups depending on the way in which customers use the product. The food and beverage product may be used as a place to meet others, or as a place of anonymity. The behaviour exhibited will relate to consumer needs which the product must try and satisfy, i.e. lots of open areas in the former, and booths in the latter. Behavioural segmentation also includes identifying the position of consumers in the hierarchy of usage, from having never used the product through regular users to ex-users. Consumers who have never used the product before may need to be made psychologically comfortable by a genuinely friendly welcome and introduction to the food and beverage product. Some steakhouse chains ask customers if it is their first visit to the brand as a standard practice, with different procedures for the two, yes and no, responses. Attracting first-time buyers necessitates the identification of how first-time buyers behave. How often the product is consumed is another behavioural variable. A consumer may use a bar every day, a take-away once a week, a pizza restaurant once a month or go to a dinner dance twice a year. Identifying the usage rate enables the identification of the needs, wants and demands of that segment, and will contribute to product design. A dinner dance may be perceived by consumers as a special occasion and they must therefore be made to feel special with personalized attention from senior staff. A bar may be perceived as a place to rest and unwind after work and may therefore be designed to be peaceful and comfortable. Loyalty is another behavioural variable which applies to food and beverage products. This is the ratio between the consumption of a range of products. If a customer only eats in one restaurant he/she is 100 per cent loyal to that restaurant. If a customer eats in a mix of six restaurants, he/she may be 50 per cent loyal to one, and 10 per cent loyal to the rest. The consumer's needs, wants and demands may be different at different loyalty levels.

Using segmentation variables allows a more objective view of food and beverage consumers, and facilitates the identification of consumers with similar needs, wants and demands. New groups are forming and old groups dying continually and therefore the need to make this identification is also continual. These groupings or market segments must be the focus of the food and beverage operators' business. Choosing which segments you will target your product on will depend on the resources available. These resources are usually grouped into financial, technological, material and human resources; management is the manipulation of these resources to achieve customer satisfaction and organizational satisfaction, the latter being primarily concerned with profitability. How segments are chosen, shaped, reached, targeted and satisfied, begins by generating ideas.

Idea evaluation

Ideas can be generated using a variety of techniques and sources. Having segmented a market it is possible to examine how the demands of these segments are being met by existing food and beverage products. Researching how well one's own and the competition's products satisfy customers' demands may stimulate ideas and identify key factors for success. Other methods of generating ideas are management and staff brainstorming and asking customers, with the focus clearly on customers' needs, wants and demands. It is a sad situation that many new food and beverage operations fail because only one idea has been generated and alternatives have not been considered. The generation of many ideas which need to be considered enables a more objective appraisal to be made. Idea generation should be sought from all parties in an open and supportive atmosphere. If one idea is criticized, other ideas may not be forthcoming for fear of ridicule. Food and beverage operators would benefit by formalizing the idea generation process and by giving their employees information about segmentation variables. This would lead to a continuous flow of good new ideas to meet customer needs.

A flow of product ideas focused on consumers' needs, wants and demands needs to be screened. Screening out ideas and progressing the remainder into the next stage of concept development can be achieved by setting up processes through which the idea must successfully pass. Screening processes will be drawn up by the stakeholder(s) and applied accordingly. An example idea-screening process is as follows:

- Does the idea meet consumers' needs?
- Is the group of consumers with these needs large enough to make the idea worth while?
- Does the food and beverage operator or potential operator have the necessary resources available to deliver the idea?
- Will the idea generate customer satisfaction?
- Will the idea generate a benefit to the operation, usually expressed in financial terms?

This idea-screening process asks questions which may be very difficult, and sometimes impossible, to answer, but trying to answer them will give indications of what will be needed to make the idea worth investing in further. This approach to idea screening should reduce the amount of ideas considerably, but is by no means a foolproof system. Good ideas may still be discarded and poor ones adopted no matter how sophisticated the screening processes are.

These approaches to market research, market segmentation and idea generation and screening apply to all situations where new products are being developed. A brand new restaurant concept like Planet Hollywood will have gone through this development process, as will a change in the opening times, service methods and décor of an existing food and beverage product. All ideas need to be screened according to the stakeholder's objectives and resources. Screening processes should be individually tailored to suit the objectives of the business. It is also necessary to review the screening process periodically as business objectives may change. If a successful food and beverage operation decides to expand and open other operations, the idea-screening process may need to be changed to accommodate product branding, continuity and consistency issues.

Concept development

It is helpful to consider the generated ideas which pass a screening process in terms of how they might be conceptualized as products or parts of products. An idea to introduce a self-service buffet operation could be conceptualized as (1) an informal continental-style all day restaurant, (2) a family meal occasion to satisfy all appetites or (3) an inexpensive, value for money, eat as much as you like concept. Turning the ideas into concepts allows for the identification of the competition were the concept to be converted into a product. Evaluating the competition, perhaps with a relative strengths and weaknesses analysis, will help position the new product. The position of the product is related to key consumer needs variables. These variables will be directly related to a particular market segment and should be clearly focused on customers' needs. For example, if speed of service and convenience are identified as key consumer needs for a particular target market, the perceptions of various products may be presented as in Fig. 2.3.

Other variables are also used to position a concept/product, including price, quantity, amount of choice, consumers' quality perceptions and amount of product usage. It is also possible to set up a three-dimensional model using three variables. Product positioning draws a map of the food and beverage market and places the various products in relation to each other.

Once the idea has been converted into a concept it should be tested in the identified market segment by asking consumers and potential consumers questions about the concept. These questions might include how they view the concept in relation to the competition, if they would purchase the product and how frequently, what price might they be prepared to pay, what they see as the benefits of the product and what improvements to the product could be made. This will help position the new concept more accurately.

Testing new product concepts is essential. Even if performed badly it is

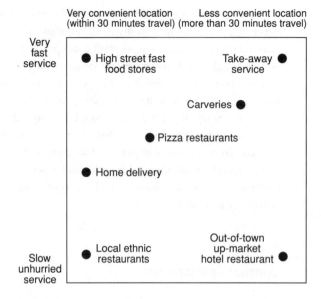

probably better than not testing at all. Large operations will test their new concepts thoroughly using consumer panels and sometimes actually create the real product in selected areas to test consumer reaction. Smaller operations with fewer resources to test the concept can still be thorough by talking, and most importantly, listening, to existing customers and likely competitors' customers. Well-structured interviews relating to a product's benefits and image will produce valuable data to inform the development of the new concept. Well-tested food and beverage concepts have a reduced risk of failure.

Product development

This stage of developing a consumer–product relationship considers the nature of a food and beverage product, and the questions and decisions which need to be addressed to turn a consumer focus (the abstract concept that consumers purchase), into an operational focus.

The food and beverage product may be viewed by consumers as a quick snack, a night out, a celebration, an indulgent extravagance or an absolute necessity. These concepts are what customers purchase, but the food and beverage product is what operators construct and manufacture. Like many service industry products, the food and beverage product is highly perishable although preserving and regeneration techniques have given operators more flexibility. The availability of food and beverage commodities in a variety of states from live ingredients through semi-prepared to ready to serve, influences not only the development of the concept but also gives the operator more control over costs.

Marketers will identify the product as: a central consumer concept known as the core product; a surrounding layer of tangible features; and an outer layer of augmentation. Placing the framework on a food and beverage product might show that the core product is a wedding celebration, the tangible product is a full wedding banquet, and the augmented product is the opportunity to pay in instalments. It is helpful to apply this product framework to the development of concepts.

Having sifted through the ideas and identified and tested product concepts (the core product), the tangible product must be addressed. This part of the food and beverage product is often known as the *meal experience*, comprising the food and beverage itself, the service, the price and the atmosphere. (A fifth element, that of cleanliness and hygiene, can be included in the atmosphere.) As there are four elements to consider, the inevitable question arises as to which one should be addressed first. Most food and beverage operators immediately explore the food and beverages, with the construction of a menu and beverage list. However, it might be more appropriate to explore the price first, or the style of service that will be provided, or the atmosphere and ambience to be created. The core concept in the form of benefits to the consumer will guide an operator to rank the meal experience factors in order of priority to the consumer. Table 2.1 gives some examples.

It is appropriate therefore to consider the core concept when setting out to design a tangible product in order to establish the weighting of the meal experience elements. In order to continue to explore the development of the

Table 2.1

Core concept	Possible factor ranking
Night out	Atmosphere
	Price
	Service
	Food and drink
Gourmet event	Food and drink
	Service
	Atmosphere
	Price
Cheap Meal	Price
	Food and drink
	Service
	Atmosphere
State banquet	Service
	Food and drink
	Atmosphere
	Price

tangible product, each of the meal experience elements will be addressed separately as if they were the element with the highest ranking.

Atmosphere   Atmosphere development leads to the creation of emotions. There are happy atmospheres, gloomy, stressful, joyful, cheerful, angry, bustling, sedate, calming, invigorating, indulgent, peaceful, comfortable, uncomfortable, boring and inviting atmospheres. These atmospheres can be created, and examples abound. The bright, young, clean atmosphere of McDonalds; the farmhouse atmosphere of Forte's Harvester, the luxurious atmosphere in the main restaurant on the QE2, the cosy and informal atmosphere of a local French bistro; are all created. With so much control available, food and beverage operators must try to match the atmosphere with the customer's core concept. There are always structural and cost constraints to atmosphere creation, but operators should invest in atmosphere to their best ability. If the right atmosphere is not created, in the hope that business success will finance further atmosphere development, success might not come at all. It might be better to consider targeting a different market for which atmosphere creation is less expensive, and then moving on to the original target market when the atmosphere-creation funds are available.

Atmosphere is sensed through sight, sound, touch, taste and smell. Food and beverage operators use the sense of sight through furniture and textures, colours, employees, shapes, spaces and their own customers. The sense of sound can be controlled through acoustics, the use of materials and shapes which alter sound and the use of music and operational sounds including speech. The sense of touch will include the quality of the air, the fabrics with which customers come into contact, the texture of the foods and drinks and the touching of other people. The sense of taste has great volumes of documentation dedicated to it through recipe and wine books and the variations are almost infinite. The sense of smell is used by many food and beverage operators to attract customers through coffee, bread, roast meat, etc. and any other aromas which may be associated with the core consumer concept.

Some consumers want hot, sweaty, noisy, dark, vibrant and exciting atmospheres, while others will prefer quiet, comfortable, light, relaxing atmospheres. Specialist designers are available to construct an atmosphere for a food and beverage operation, and some large businesses employ their own design teams. These designs can be used to test the concept further by showing them to consumer panels and recording the reaction. At whatever level a food and beverage operator is resourced, investing in a part of the product which so closely relates to the core concept should be made a priority.

Price   Price is that element of the meal experience which relates to value. Price is also directly related to profitability. However, price is also very flexible and can be changed relatively easily, thereby changing value perceptions and possibly changing profitability. Chapter 7 on food and beverage operations appraisal covers profitability in more detail, and for the moment only the consumer's concept of value will be explored. Good value is where the worth is perceived as greater than the cost, and therefore a successful operator must add value to the consumer into the product. Price should also be set in relation to the value perception that operators want consumers to have. A high-priced product might be perceived as either good quality or a rip-off, and a low-priced product as poor quality or good value, indicating that it is more than just the absolute price which determines value, but rather price relative to worth. Price is also used to stimulate demand by using special offers and happy hours, and to attract custom from the competition.

When developing, changing or supporting a product concept it is good practice to establish a price range within which the consumer will be prepared to pay. Another price range can be established within which the operator is prepared to offer the product. The overlap is the range available to the operator. Setting prices within ranges which consumers will pay should be accomplished with reference to the particular market segment and the core concept. Market research can determine a range within which families travelling on motorways are prepared to stop and pay for food and drink, and will also be able to determine a price range for a particular menu item. This is accomplished by setting up consumer panels and asking them about price and product. The information to be gained from researching customers' attitudes and behaviour towards price will reveal that lowest price is far from always the main consideration, as Table 2.1 (page 29) showed.

Pricing methods used by operators vary in their appropriateness and sophistication. The most common method is *cost plus*, where the ingredient cost is established – not always very accurately – and the required profit (referred to as gross profit) is added. The result is a selling price which gives the operator the required profit for that dish. It should be noted that this required profit will only be realized when that dish is sold. This method is attractive because of its simplicity, but it ignores price sensitivity and demand, makes the assumption that the required profit can be established by making it a set percentage of the selling price (usually between 65 and 75 per cent), fails to account for different restaurant types and different menu categories and does not take into account that each dish/drink is only part of a collection of items purchased to produce the meal experience. This method fails to take into account that price is a determinant of demand, and that value for money must be factored into the pricing decision.

Prime costing methods   These attempt to factor-in the labour cost of a dish, and *actual cost* pricing attempts to include fixed and variable costs as well as labour. These additional costs are also established as a percentage of the final selling price (e.g. labour at 25 per cent and variable costs at 10 per cent). These methods are flawed in the same way as cost plus: labour is a factor related to the time needed to prepare a dish, not to the value of the ingredients used to prepare it; no account is taken of volume of business or item popularity in assessing the labour content of a dish, therefore not taking into account economies and diseconomies of scale; and allocating fixed and variable costs to each menu item should at least be related to the volume of each dish sold rather than a fixed percentage figure to be used for each menu item.

Backward pricing This attempts to match costs to a price previously established for a desired potential market. This market-driven approach – which is not really backwards – is a good starting point in new product development, but it is still difficult to establish the necessary gross profit, ingredient and labour costs, and care must be taken to avoid the problems of using percentages.

Rate of return pricing This tries to establish price based on a forecast of sales and costs and may be used to produce a break-even matrix for the operation. This may help give a guide to the price range but will not itself establish individual selling prices.

Profit-per-customer pricing This establishes the total profit required and allocates this to a forecast demand resulting in an average profit per customer. This 'profit' is then added to the material and/or other costs to produce a selling price for each dish. Again this may be used to produce a break-even matrix, but caution should be exercised because profit is a factor of demand, which is a factor of price, which is a factor of demand, and so on.

Elasticity pricing This asks how sensitive a market is to price changes. In order to determine menu prices the operator will try to determine the effect a price change may have on demand. It should be remembered that it is possible to increase demand and profitability through price decreases. However, it is very difficult to predict market responses to price changes, but considering elasticity may inform the pricing decisions.

Competition pricing This is copying the competitors' price. However, their cost structure may be different, enabling them to produce higher profits at a particular market price. Copying the competition may also take the form of discounting, premium promotions, happy hours, special meals, free wine and children's toys, all short-term tactics which can lead to increasing costs and fierce competition. There are more types of menu pricing methods including: marginal analysis (Buttle, 1988); break-even analysis (Miller, 1980; Buttle, 1988; Jones and Lockwood, 1989; Greenburg, 1986); cost margin analysis (Pavesic, 1985); individual menu item profit and loss (Hayes and Huffman, 1985); and frequency distribution pricing (Miller, 1988). Whichever methods are used, an operator should always have a clear pricing policy or objective in mind. Some of these pricing objectives might include:

- Sales volume maximization, where the pricing objective is to achieve the highest sales possible.
- Market share gain, where the objective is to increase your number of customers relative to the total possible market and the competition.
- Profit maximization, where the pricing objective is to achieve the highest profit possible.
- Market penetration, where the pricing objective is to move from a position of a zero or low market share to a significant market share.

Once a clear pricing objective is established, the pricing methods most suitable to that particular objective can be drawn from the available pool.

Service

Service is a part of the tangible product and may be considered the human (usually) interface between the product and the consumer. The exception is vending operations where the machine is the interface. Food and beverage operators usually identify service as different service methods, such as silver service, buffet service, cafeteria service and so on, from which can be selected the most appropriate to meet the demands of their customers. Quick service when the customer is in a hurry, slower service for an intimate dinner, and stylish service for customers who want to be entertained are examples of service methods meeting demand. However, service also involves a personal interaction between customers and service personnel. This interaction can deliver benefits to the customer, such as feeling valued, and should therefore be designed into the product rather than just hoping these benefits will be delivered. William Martin (1986) identified two factors which shape food and beverage service. One factor is 'procedural', which includes how timely, consistent and organized the service is, and the second is 'conviviality', which includes the friendliness and attitude of the staff. These two factors can be used to construct a framework into which service styles can be placed. Figure 2.4 shows what consumers may think and say about particular styles of service.

It is hoped that all operators would wish to be in the 'We care and deliver' quadrant. However, the two factors are interdependent and if the procedural element of the service is poorly designed and delivered resulting in overworked and poorly motivated staff, it is more likely that conviviality will deteriorate. A food and beverage operator must ensure that both elements are addressed and considered and design them into the product. Training and feedback concerning service performance should also be built into the product to ensure the standards required by consumers are delivered.

Food and drink

The food and drink itself, usually in the form of a menu and drinks list, must also clearly focus on the needs and demands of the consumer. Operators must ask themselves what food and drinks do market segments want. The permutations of range, tastes, textures and presentations of food and drink are

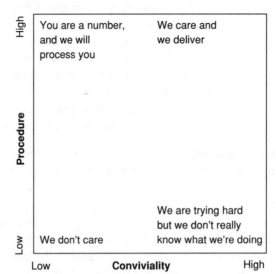

High

Procedure

Low

| You are a number, and we will process you | We care and we deliver |

| We don't care | We are trying hard but we don't really know what we're doing |

Low   **Conviviality**   High

Fig. 2.4 Service framework (*after* Martin, 1986)

almost endless. However, the menu and drinks offerings are a list from which customers construct a package to suit their own needs, and therefore the range of food and drink offered should be considered in this light. There may be vegetarians, dieters, customers who are hungry and ones who are not, ones who like seafood and those who do not, ones who like steaks and not much else, all part of your market segment. If there are a wide variety of demands in your market segment it may be appropriate to consider further segmenting. Trying to satisfy everyone can lead to satisfying no one.

Many operators are identified by the type of food and drink that they offer. Chinese, Greek, Italian, pizza, souchi, steakhouse, seafood, French, Jamaican, Creole, American, Old English, Indian and Thai food and beverage operations are identified by their cuisine. The food and drink offering will play a considerable part in a market segment's perception and expectations of the product and again a consideration of the market's needs, wants and demands in terms of the food and drink on offer is important. Ideas can be generated and tested on consumer panels to identify these demands rather than relying on instinct and a propensity to deliver what the operator knows how to deliver as opposed to what the customer wants.

These factors which make up the tangible product are designed to deliver the core consumer concept. The augmented product can also have a considerable influence in an operator's success. Being able to reserve a table, pay by various credit cards, vary portion size, access health information and availability of highchairs, for example, will be factors which will influence consumer choice. They may be factors which particular market segments value highly and should be researched, and if thought worth while introduced as additions to the tangible product.

Once products to satisfy particular market segments have been designed it is necessary to identify the steps to be taken to create the product–consumer relationship.

Creating the product–consumer relationship

This final element in the process may be viewed as a four-stage sequence.

1. determine promotional channels
2. estimate profitability
3. plan product launch
4. offer product and appraise performance

Determining promotional channels

Determining promotional channels is important because it will identify how consumers will be reached and attracted to the product. Food and beverage operators should identify and monitor consumers in order to be informed as to which promotional channels are best for their product. When choosing promotional channels the target market segment variables are considered in relation to the product message and the medium through which it may be delivered. The message to be delivered should relate to the consumer's needs, wants and demands, and be delivered through a medium used by the target consumers, reflecting their life styles and self-images. Table 2.2 shows possible messages and media for different food and beverage products.

Choosing the message and the medium is a critical element in promoting the product. Large businesses will spend millions of pounds promoting their product through national television, radio, press and billboards. Small operations may only spend hundreds of pounds but the criterion is the same,

Table 2.2 Possible message and media for food and beverage products

Product	Message	Media
Branded pizza restaurant	Meet friends and have fun	Television, local radio and press, mailshots
New Year's Eve dinner dance	Celebrate in style and spoil yourself	Local radio and press, in-house literature, direct suggestive selling to existing customer base
Local bistro	A touch of continental style	Word of mouth
Public house	Traditional British hospitality	Word of mouth, local press, *Good Food Guide*

namely is it effective? Regular reviewing of promotional activity and spending and how it relates to increased sales and profits, will enable effective evaluation of the process to take place. Consumers' responses to promotional activities should be researched.

Estimating profitability

Estimating profitability is a case of budgeting costs and sales. How these budgets might be set is addressed in Chapter 7 on operations appraisal, but when launching new products and changing existing ones the art of predicting outcomes is extremely indefinite. Methods used can be very sophisticated. Some operators will measure the size of their selected target and segmented market, apply usage or uptake measures between competing products and multiply the resultant number of customers for their product by an estimated average spend per head. This may be performed for each hour, day and month to produce the sales budget. Applying a 'profitability on sales percentage' will determine the budget profit. However, the measures used cannot be guaranteed correct, and therefore a best and worst scenario should be considered. This may take the form of a break-even chart to show an operator what the profitability levels are for various numbers of customers.

Having said this, outcomes are usually different from those expected. Estimating profitability will at least give some indication as to what might happen, and progress after launch can be evaluated against the estimates.

Planning the product launch

Planning the product launch is an operational as well as a promotional issue. Operationally, the new food and beverage product will need testing. This will involve staff scheduling and training, specifying and sourcing the necessary ingredients and equipment and if possible testing full-scale production. If a full-scale test production run is not possible, perhaps due to cost restraints, a reduced-scale test should be performed. There will always be elements of the product which do not take place as planned, and finding out before the product launch enables matters to be rectified. Not being able to deliver the product as promoted will result in consumers' expectations not being met, and could negatively affect the market segment's uptake of the product. Customers seem to remember bad experiences more than good ones.

The launch of a new product gives rise to promotional opportunities. Special sessions can be organized by offering the product free to selected groups on a one-off basis, thus gaining good public relations exposure. This would also be a good operational test of the product without the repercussions of not meeting customers' expectations. Special offers can also be introduced to initially attract customers to the product, such as two items for the price of one, or free bottles of wine with a meal. However, special consideration must be given to the market segment's perception of the promotion, as free offers or reduced prices may not project the required image.

The timing of the product launch is also an important consideration. There are two issues regarding timing; one is getting the time right, and the other is having enough time available to get the product right. Getting the time right involves choosing a launch date which provides the best advantage to the operator. This will mean investigating other possible events which may detract or enhance the launch. If demand is expected to fluctuate, and demand for food and beverage products does fluctuate between time of day, week, month and year, launch time should take this into account. It may be appropriate to launch before a busy period, in order to build up to full capacity. Operations which do not give themselves enough time to develop and launch their product can find themselves offering products which are not successful, and the time available to develop a product may often be seen as not enough. If the product is not ready to be introduced in time, it is probably worth considering delaying the launch.

Offering the product   Offering the product and appraising performance are now a question of putting the plan into action and monitoring the result. Operations performance appraisal and product performance appraisal are covered in Chapter 7.

The consumer–product relationship as a dynamic process

Having explored the nature of the consumer and the development of a consumer–product relationship, it may be helpful to conceptualize the issues as the management of change. As consumers' needs, wants and demands change, and as the competition increases and technology offers new opportunities, the process of creating a consumer–product relationship is also the process of managing change. It is suggested that the most desirable management skill for the future will be the ability to manage change.

This chapter has explored the issues surrounding the consumer–product relationship, and has suggested some frameworks to help evaluate and develop the relationship. These frameworks may be viewed as tools to be applied when required, but they are really tools which need to be applied continually. As already mentioned, a food and beverage operation will engage in different stages of developing a consumer–product relationship at the same time. Market research should be an ongoing commitment; generating ideas and concepts should be built into the management of an operation; and searches for new and developing market segments is a major management responsibility. With so many variables changing all the time, including the operator's own personal and business objectives, it can be seen how promoting the status quo and relying on consumers to remain fixed over time is a dangerous assumption. As product life cycles continue to shrink the importance of managing these changes, both threats and opportunities, is increased.

Managing change effectively and profitably in a food and beverage environment is as complex and as difficult as in any other type of business. In order really to embrace change there must be a management vision of where they want to be. The focus of this vision will be satisfying the consumers of the food and beverage product. Management's first commitment is to communicate this vision with their staff, for without staff who are convinced of the need to change and of the need to do things differently, the vision will not happen. Managing relationships within food and beverage operations, between groups of personnel, will play an ever-increasing role for senior management in the successful development of changing consumer–product relationships.

Summary

This chapter has developed a framework to investigate the consumer–product relationship. The importance of satisfying consumers' needs, want and demands, and understanding their goals and values, has been addressed. Component parts of the consumer–product development process have been identified and explored, and the management of change is seen to be a key skill.

References

Buttle F 1988 *Hotel and foodservice marketing – a managerial approach* Cassell, London

Greenburg C 1986 Analyzing restaurant performance, relating cost and volume to profit. *The Cornell Hotel and Restaurant Administration Quarterly*, **27**(1) May: pp. 6–11

Hayes D K and Huffman L 1985 Menu analysis, a better way. *Cornell Hotel and Restaurant Administration Quarterly*, **25**(4) February: pp. 64–9

Jones P and Lockwood A 1989 *The management of hotel operations* Cassell, London

Kotler P 1984 *An introduction to marketing* Prentice-Hall International, London

Martin W 1986 Defining what quality service is for you. *The Cornell Hotel and Restaurant Administration Quarterly*, **27**(1) February: pp. 32–8

Miller J 1980 *Menu pricing and strategy* Van Nostrand Reinhold, New York

Miller S G 1988 Fine tuning your menu with frequency distributions. *Cornell Hotel and Restaurant Administration Quarterly*, **29**(3) November: pp. 86–92

Pavesic D V 1985 Prime numbers, finding your menu's strengths. *Cornell Hotel and Restaurant Administration Quarterly*, **26**(3) November: pp. 56–7

3 Food production

Aim   This chapter aims to demonstrate the importance of sound menu planning and emphasize its importance to the planning and implementation of food production systems.

Objective   This chapter is intended to help you to:

- recognize that hygiene management is an implicit function in the food production process
- identify the main food production systems available to the caterer
- describe the purchasing function and its relationship in the total operational process
- develop an appreciation of the importance and significance of operational control procedures

Food production systems

A production system has to be organized to produce the right quantity of food at the correct standard, for the required number of people, on time, using the resources of staff, equipment and materials effectively and efficiently.

As costs of space, equipment, fuel, maintenance and labour continue to rise, more thought and time have to be given to the planning of a production system and to kitchen design. Research is often lacking in this area of the hotel and catering industry, although research from equipment manufacturers concentrating on new technology is increasing. New technology enables us to plan production systems more effectively.

The requirements of the production system have to be clearly identified with regard to the type of food that is to be prepared, cooked and served to the required market at the correct price. All areas of space and the different types of equipment available must be fully justified and the organization of the kitchen personnel must also be planned at the same time.

Many operations today are based on the process approach as opposed to the 'partie' system. The process approach concentrates on the specific techniques and processes of food production. The system places importance on the identification of these common techniques and processes across the full range of required dishes. In developing the production system, groupings are not then based on the types of dishes or foods, which is the basis of the 'partie' system, but on the clustering of similar production techniques and processes which apply a range of common skills and encourage flexible open-endedness.

Food production in the hospitality industry must be seen as an operating system. A whole range of different cuisines are able to fit more neatly into this approach, because the key elements focus on the process, the way the food is prepared, processed (cooked) stored and served.

Using this approach food production systems within the hospitality industry may be identified using the input/process/output model of systems and the basic process set out as in Fig 3.1. From this a general model of the production system can be shown as in Fig. 3.2 and nine production systems can be identified as shown in Table 3.1.

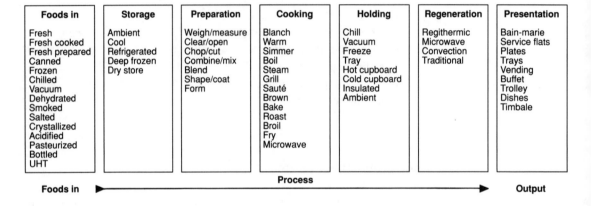

Foods in	Storage	Preparation	Cooking	Holding	Regeneration	Presentation
Fresh	Ambient	Weigh/measure	Blanch	Chill	Regithermic	Bain-marie
Fresh cooked	Cool	Clear/open	Warm	Vacuum	Microwave	Service flats
Fresh prepared	Refrigerated	Chop/cut	Simmer	Freeze	Convection	Plates
Canned	Deep frozen	Combine/mix	Boil	Tray	Traditional	Trays
Frozen	Dry store	Blend	Steam	Hot cupboard		Vending
Chilled		Shape/coat	Grill	Cold cupboard		Buffet
Vacuum		Form	Sauté	Insulated		Trolley
Dehydrated			Brown	Ambient		Dishes
Smoked			Bake			Timbale
Salted			Roast			
Crystallized			Broil			
Acidified			Fry			
Pasteurized			Microwave			
Bottled						
UHT						

Process

Foods in ▶ ——————————————————————————————————— ▶ Output

Fig. 3.1 Elements of food production

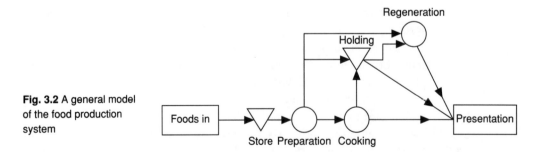

Fig. 3.2 A general model of the food production system

Regeneration

Holding

Foods in

Store Preparation Cooking

Presentation

Table 3.1   Methods of food production

No.	Method	Description
1	Conventional	Term used to describe production utilizing mainly fresh foods and traditional cooking methods
2	Convenience	Method of production utilizing mainly convenience foods
3	Call order	Method where food is cooked to order either from customer (as in cafeterias) or from waiter. Production area often open to customer area
4	Continuous flow	Method involving production line approach where different parts of the production process may be separated (eg. fast food)
5	Centralized	Production not directly linked to service. Foods are 'held' and distributed to separate service areas
6	Cook–chill	Food production storage and regeneration method utilizing principle of low temperature control to preserve qualities of processed foods
7	Cook–freeze	Production, storage and regeneration method utilizing principle of freezing to control and preserve qualities of processed foods. Requires special processes to assist freezing
8	Sous-vide	Method of production, storage and regeneration utilizing principle of sealed vacuum to control and preserve the quality of processed foods
9	Assembly kitchen	A system based on accepting and incorporating the latest technological development in manufacturing and conservation of food products

Centralized production systems

Centralized production has recently been considered by a large number of employers in the hospitality industry. Considerations have been based on:

- labour cost using staff more effectively and efficiently
- food costs, greater control over wastage and portion sizes linked to standardized recipes and standardized purchasing specifications
- equipment, more use of technology reducing commitment in individual units

Cook–chill system   Cook–chill is a catering system based on normal preparation and cooking of food followed by rapid chilling, storage in controlled low-temperature conditions above freezing point, 0–3 °C (32–37 °F), and subsequently reheating immediately before consumption. The chilled food is regenerated in finishing kitchens which require low capital investment and minimum staff.

The purpose of chilling food

The purpose of chilling food is to prolong its storage life. Under normal temperature conditions, food deteriorates rapidly through the action of micro-organisms and enzymic and chemical reactions. Reduction in the storage temperature inhibits the multiplication of bacteria and other micro-organisms and slows down the chemical and enzymic reactions. At normal refrigeration temperature reactions are still taking place but at a much slower rate and at frozen food storage temperatures (-20 °C (-4 °F) approx.) nearly all reactions cease. A temperature of 0–3 °C does not give a storage life comparable to frozen food but it does produce a good product.

It is generally accepted that, even when high standards of fast chilling practice are used and consistent refrigerated storage is maintained, product quality may be acceptable for only a few days (including day of production and consumption). The storage temperature of 0–3 °C is of extreme importance to ensure both full protection of the food from microbiological growth and the maintenance of maximum nutritional values in the food. It is generally accepted that a temperature of 10 °C (50 °F) should be regarded as the critical safety limit for the storage of refrigerated food. Above that temperature, growth of micro-organisms may render the food dangerous to health.

The cook–chill process

1. The food should be cooked sufficiently to ensure destruction of any pathogenic micro-organisms.
2. The chilling process must begin as soon as possible after completion of the cooking and portioning processes, within 30 minutes of leaving the cooker. The food should be chilled to 3 °C (37 °F) within a period of $1\frac{1}{2}$ hours. Most pathogenic organisms will not grow below 7 °C (45 °F), while a temperature below 3 °C (37 °F) is required to reduce growth of spoilage organisms and to achieve the required storage life. However, slow growth of spoilage organisms does take place at these temperatures and for this reason storage life cannot be greater than 5 days.
3. The food should be stored at a temperature between 0 and 3 °C (32–37 °F).
4. The chilled food should be distributed under such controlled conditions that any rise in temperature of the food during distribution is kept to a minimum.
5. For both safety and palatability the reheating (regeneration) of the food should follow immediately upon the removal of the food from chilled conditions and should raise the temperature to a level of at least 70 °C (158 °F).
6. The food should be consumed as soon as possible and not more than 2

hours after reheating. Food not intended for reheating should be consumed as soon as convenient and within 2 hours of removal from storage. It is essential that unconsumed reheated food is discarded.

7. A temperature of 10 °C (50 °F) should be regarded as the critical safety limit for chilled food. Should the temperature of the chilled food rise above this level during storage or distribution the food concerned should be discarded.

Cook–chill is generally planned within a purpose-designed, comprehensive, new central production unit to give small, medium or large-scale production along predefined flow lines, incorporating traditional catering/chilling/post-chilling packaging and storage for delivery to finishing kitchens.

Within an existing kitchen, where existing equipment is retained with possible minor additions and modifications, chilling/post-chilling packaging and additional storage for cooked chilled food are added.

Finishing kitchens
These can consist of purpose-built regeneration equipment plus refrigerated storage. Additional equipment, such as a chip fryer, boiling table and pressure steamer for chips, sauces, custard, vegetables, etc. can be added if required to give greater flexibility.

Where chilled food is produced to supply a service on the same premises, it is recommended that the meals should be supplied, stored and regenerated by exactly the same method as used for operations where the production unit and finishing kitchens are separated by some distance. Failure to adhere to just one procedure could result in disorganized production and reduce productivity. Once a decision is taken to sever production from service this method should be followed throughout the system.

Distribution of cook–chill
Distribution of the chilled food is an important part of the cook–chill operation. Fluctuations in storage temperature can affect the palatability and texture of food and lead to microbiological dangers requiring the food to be discarded.

The distribution method chosen must ensure that the required temperature below 3 °C (37 °F) is maintained throughout the period of transport. Should the temperature of the food exceed 5 °C (41 °F) during distribution the food ought to be consumed within 12 hours; if the temperature exceeds 10 °C (50 °F) it should be discarded (Department of Health guidelines). Because of this, refrigeration during distribution is to be encouraged in many circumstances.

In some cases the cook–chill production unit can also act as a centralized kitchen and distribution point. Food is regenerated in an area adjacent to the cook–chill production area and heat retention or insulated boxes are used for distribution. During transportation and service the food must not be allowed to fall below 62 °C (145 °F).

Quality control

All staff working in a cook–chill production unit must be trained to the highest standard and must work under skilled supervision. Adequate control of bacterial contamination and multiplication, which are hazards in any kitchen, can be achieved by a survey of the initial installation by a qualified analyst and batch checks thereafter. In a very large production kitchen, producing 10 000–15 000 meals, a full-time microbiologist would normally be employed.

Regeneration food service system for hospitals

In hospitals the system utilizes specially designed porcelain or stainless steel dishes with stainless steel covers. Centrally produced meals are chilled in a purpose-built chilling unit. The chilled meal packs are distributed for ward-level regeneration to service temperature in a purpose-designed trolley/oven unit. This thermal heating system is based on quartz radiant heaters, proportionally spaced to ensure even and simultaneous heat distribution on both the porcelain dish and the stainless steel cover.

Alternatively, regeneration may be carried out in convection ovens with steam injection; a humidifier oven will prevent the food drying out and counteract any loss of moisture that may have occurred during the chilling process.

Employee self-service

This system utilizes bulk stainless steel dishes into which cooked food is portioned prior to chilling and storage. At service time the food is batch regenerated behind service counter for self-help or self-service. One central kitchen can supply chilled meals to numerous satellite services where cooking operations are virtually eliminated.

Banqueting

This system utilizes ceramic banquet dishes, divided into ten to twelve portions, into which the food is normally placed after chilling. Banquet meals are stored in cold rooms prior to regeneration which can take place in portable thermal units; this is particularly suitable for hotels where banquets and seminars occur in different venues or on different floors.

Production

1. Skilled staff are employed in the production operation.
2. It is largely unskilled staff, under strict supervision, who carry out packaging, chilling, storage and regeneration.

Maximum efficiency should follow if the production area is set up in a new location, but, depending on circumstances, a simple layout can be established in an existing kitchen for possible use in room service, banqueting, small-scale staff catering (night shifts) and as a pilot scheme for a potentially larger operation.

Cook–freeze system   Blast freezers have increasingly been introduced with success into catering operations. The ability to freeze cooked dishes and prepared foods, as distinct from the storage of chilled foods in a refrigerator or already frozen commodities in a deep-freeze, allows a caterer to make more productive use of kitchen staff. It also enables economics to be introduced into the staffing of dining rooms and restaurants.

The cook–freeze process

Cook–freeze uses a production system similar to that used in cook–chill. The recipes used have to be modified, enabling products to be freezer-stable and modified starches are used in sauces so that on reheating and regeneration the sauce does not separate. Blast freezers are used in place of blast chillers. The freezing must be carried out very rapidly to retain freshness and to accelerate temperature loss through the latent heat barrier, thus preventing the formation of large ice crystals and rupturing of the cells.

Blast freezing takes place when low temperature air is passed over food at high speed, reducing food in batches to a temperature of at least $-20\,°C$ ($-4\,°F$) within 90 minutes. Blast freezers can hold from 20 to 400 kg (40 to 800 lb) per batch, the larger models being designed for trolley operation.

Preparation of food   The production menu for a month is drawn up and the total quantities of different foods required calculated. Supplies are then ordered, with special attention given to their being:

* of high quality
* delivered so that they can immediately be prepared and cooked without any possibility of deterioration during an enforced period of storage before being processed

The dishes included in the menu must be cooked to the highest standards with rigid attention to quality control and to hygiene. It will be remembered that deep-freeze temperatures prevent the multiplication of micro-organisms but do not destroy them. If, therefore, a dish were contaminated before being frozen, consumers would be put at risk months later when the food was prepared for consumption. The exact adjustment of recipes to produce the best results when the food is subsequently thawed and reheated is still in the process of being worked out by chefs, using numerous variations of the basic system. The single change needed in recipes involving sauces is the selection of an appropriate type of starch capable of resisting the effects of freezing. Normal starches will produce a curdled effect when subsequently thawed and reheated. In order to achieve rapid freezing with a quick reduction of temperature to −18 °C (0 °F) or below, the cooked food must be carefully portioned (close attention being paid to the attainment of uniform portion size). Each portion is placed into a disposable aluminium foil container, may be placed conveniently into aluminium trays holding from six to ten portions each, sealed and carefully labelled with their description and date of preparation.

Freezing   The food thus divided into portions and arranged in trays is immediately frozen. An effective procedure is to place the trays on racks in a blast-freezing tunnel and expose them to a vigorous flow of cold air until the cooked items are frozen solid and the temperature reduced to at least −5 °C (23 °F). The quality of the final product is to a significant degree dependent on the rapidity with which the temperature of hot cooked food at say 80 °C (176 °F) is reduced to below freezing. The capacity of the blast freezer should be designed to achieve this reduction in temperature within a period of 1–$1\frac{1}{4}$ hours.

Storage of frozen items   Once the food items are frozen they must at once be put into a deep-freeze store maintained at −18 °C (0 °F). For a catering operation involving several dining rooms and cafeterias, some of which may be situated at some distance from the kitchen and frozen store, a 4 weeks' supply of cooked dishes held at low temperature allows full use to be made of the facilities.

Transport of frozen items to the point of service   If satisfactory quality is to be maintained, it is important to keep food frozen in the cooked state, frozen until immediately prior to its being served. It should therefore be transported in insulated containers to peripheral kitchens, if such are to be used, where it will be reheated.

If frozen dishes are to be used in outside catering, provision should be available for transporting them in refrigerated transport and if necessary, a subsidiary deep-freeze store should be provided for them on arrival.

The reheating of frozen cooked portions   In any catering system in which a blast-freezing tunnel has been installed to freeze pre-cooked food, previously portioned and packed in metal foil or other individual containers, it is obviously rational to install equipment that is particularly designed for the purpose of reheating the items ready to be served. The blast-freezing system is effective because it is, in design, a specially powerful form of forced convection heat exchanger arranged to extract heat. It follows that an equally appropriate system for replacing heat is the use of a force convection oven, specially for the reception of trays of frozen portions. Where such an oven is equipped with an efficient thermostat and adequate control of the air circulation system, standardized setting times for the controls can be laid down for the regeneration of the various types of dishes that need to be reheated.

Quality control

Adequate control of bacterial contamination and growth, which are hazards in any kitchen, can be achieved by a survey of the initial installation by a qualified analyst and regular checks taken on every batch of food cooked. Very large kitchens employ a full-time food technologist/bacteriologist. In smaller operations the occasional services of a microbiologist from the public health authority should be used.

Overall benefits of cook–chill/cook–freeze

To the operation:

* portions control and reduced waste
* no over-production
* central purchasing – bulk buying discounts
* full utilization of equipment
* full utilization of staff time
* overall savings in staff
* savings on equipment, space and fuel
* fewer staff with better conditions – no unsocial hours, no weekend work, no overtime
* simplified delivery to units – less frequent
* solve problem of moving hot food (EC regulations forbid the movement of hot foods unless the temperature is maintained over 65 °C (149 °F). Maintaining 65 °C is regarded as very difficult to achieve and high temperatures inevitably will be harmful to foods.)

To the customer:

* increased variety and selection
* improved quality, with standards maintained
* more nutritious foods
* services can be maintained at all times, regardless of staff absences

Advantages of cook–freeze over cook–chill

* Seasonal purchasing provides considerable savings.
* Delivery to units will be far less frequent.
* Long-term planning of production and menus becomes possible.
* Less dependent on price fluctuations.
* More suitable for vending machines incorporating microwave.

Advantages of cook–chill over cook–freeze

* Regeneration systems are simpler – infra-red and steam convection ovens are mostly used and only approximately 12 minutes is required to reheat all foods perfectly.
* Thawing time is eliminated.

- Smaller capacity storage is required: 3–4 days' supply as opposed to up to 120 days.
- Chiller storage is cheaper to install and run than freezer storage.
- Blast chillers are cheaper to install and run than blast freezers.
- Cooking techniques are unaltered (additives and revised recipes are needed for freezing).
- All foods can be chilled so the range of dishes is wider (some foods cannot be frozen). Cooked eggs, steaks and sauces such as hollandaise can be chilled (after some recipe modification where necessary).
- No system is too small to adapt to cook–chill.

Sous-vide This is a form of cook–chill: a combination of vacuum sealing in plastic pouches, cooking by steam and then rapidly cooking and chilling. The objective is to rationalize kitchen procedures without having a detrimental effect on the quality of individual dishes. Vacuum pressures are as important as the cooking temperatures with regard to weight loss and heat absorption. The highest temperature used in sous-vide cooking is 100 °C (212 °F) and 1000 millibars is the minimum amount of vacuum pressure used.

As there is no oxidation or discoloration it is ideal for conserving fruits, such as apples and pears, e.g. pears in red wine, fruits in syrup. When preparing meats in sauces the meat is pre-blanched and then added to the completed sauce.

Sous-vide is a combination of vacuum sealing, tightly controlled *en papillote* cooking and rapid chilling. Potential users are brasseries, wine bars, airlines, private hospitals and function caterers seeking to provide top quality with portion convenience.

The sous-vide process

1. Individual portions of prepared food are first placed in special plastic pouches. The food can be fish, poultry, meats, vegetables, etc. to which seasoning, a garnish, sauce, stock, wine, flavourings, vegetables, herbs and/or spices can be added.
2. The pouches of food are then placed in a vacuum-packing machine which evacuates all the air and tightly seals the pouch.
3. The pouches are next cooked by steam. This is usually in a special oven equipped with a steam control programme, which controls the injection of steam in the oven, to give steam cooking at an oven temperature below 100 °C (212 °F). Each food item has its own ideal cooking time and temperature.
4. When cooked, the pouches are rapidly cooled down to 3 °C (37 °F) – usually in an iced water chiller or an air blast chiller for larger operations.

5. The pouches are then labelled and stored in a holding refrigerator at an optimum temperature of 3 °C.

6. When required for service the pouches are regenerated in boiling water or a steam combination oven until the required temperature is reached, cut open and the food presented.

Advantages

- Long shelf-life, up to 21 days – refrigerated.
- Ability to produce meals in advance means better deployment of staff and skills.
- Vacuum-packed foods can be mixed in cold store without the risk of cross-contamination.
- Reduces labour costs at point of service.
- Beneficial cooking effects on certain foods, especially moulded items and pâtés. Reduced weight loss on meat joints.
- Full flavour and texture are retained as food cooks in its own juices.
- Economizes on ingredients (less butter, marinades, etc.).
- Makes pre-cooking a possibility for à la carte menus.
- Inexpensive regeneration.
- Allows a small operation to set up bulk production.
- Facilitates portion control and uniformity of standard.
- Has a tenderizing effect on tougher cuts of meat and matures game without dehydration.

Disadvantages

- Extra cost of vacuum pouches and vacuum-packing machine.
- Unsuitable for some meats (e.g. fillet steak) and vegetables which absorb colour.
- All portions in a batch must be identically sized to ensure even results.
- Most dishes require twice the conventional cooking time.
- Unsuitable for large joints as chilling time exceeds 90 minutes.
- Complete meals (e.g. meat and two vegetables) not feasible; meat component needs to be cooked and stored in separate bags.
- Extremely tight management and hygiene controls are imperative.
- Potentially adverse customer reaction (boil-in-the-bag syndrome).

Volume in food production

The food production process may be seen in the general model for food production as shown in Fig 3.2 (page 40). This model identifies seven stages in the general food production process. These are :

1. foods in
2. storage
3. preparation
4. cooking
5. holding
6. regeneration
7. presentation

Each of these stages has an effect on the potential volume of the operation. Also differing operations will route foods in different ways. Thus, for instance, a fast-food process will flow from foods in to store to preparation or cooking, then to holding and then to presentation. A cook–chill process will flow from foods in to store to preparation to holding or cooking, then to regeneration and then to presentation.

It is, however, difficult to determine the key process that limits the potential volume as each of the stages has a separate effect on the capacity of food able to be processed at any time, as detailed as follows (Cousins, 1994).

Foods in   The availability of food and the frequency of delivery clearly have an impact on the maximum food capacity of the operation. Greater and more frequent delivery opportunities increase the potential capacity. In addition the variety of foods being bought either in terms of food type or supplier source will also affect food capacity.

Storage   The storage space and type of storage available determine the type of food that can be bought and the quantities that can be available at a given time. Capacity can be increased by altering the nature of foods being bought, for instance from fresh to convenience, and/or by increasing the delivery frequency.

Preparation   The extent to which food has to be prepared also impacts on capacity. High preparation requirements increase the space and the layout required. This stage can be greatly affected by increasing the use of ready prepared foods and by the use of equipment for bulk preparation activities.

Cooking   The availability of cooking space and the time cooking takes can limit capacity. Again this can be affected by variations in the needs for cooking and the type of cooking required. In addition the type of equipment used for the cooking processes can be altered to increase the volume of cooking that can be done at a given time.

Holding   Food capacity is limited by the type and availability of holding space. Variations in the need for holding in a given operation can vary the potential food capacity.

Regeneration   This stage follows from holding and has similar characteristics. However, the regeneration potential can be less than the full holding potential depending on the nature of demand required at a given time.

Presentation   The food capacity at this stage is usually determined by the speed of the service process. This assumes that a critical path analysis approach has been used to ensure that the full range of foods required at a given time are available at the same time. Overall the need to meet the demands of the presentation stage is determined by the expected volume of business at a given time. Each of the previous stages through the application of careful critical path analysis approaches should be able to be planned and operated to meet the presentation demand.

Menu planning

The menu is often considered to be the prime selling tool and therefore should be written to inform and sell. The menu or bill of fare, is a means of communication, informing the customer of what the caterer has to offer. The compiling of the menu is one of the caterer's most important jobs, whether it be for establishments in the profit sector, or for those working to a budget, such as hospitals, schools or other similar institutions. The menu is a central management document that directs and controls the operation. It establishes what is going to be purchased, the cost, what staff and other resources are required and the types of service needed. The operation's décor, atmosphere, theme or logo and service revolve around the menu. In both the front and back of house, the menu determines what is to be done.

Types of menus   There are several types of menus:

- Table d'hôte – a set menu forming a complete meal at a set price. A choice of dishes may be offered at all courses; the choice and number of courses will usually be limited to two, three or four.
- À la carte – a menu with all the dishes individually priced. The customers can therefore compile their own menu. A true à la carte dish should be cooked to order and the customer should be prepared to wait for this service.
- Special party or function menus – for banquets or functions of all kinds.
- Ethnic or speciality menus – these can be table d'hôte or à la carte specializing in the food (or religion) of the country or in a specialized food itself.
- Hospital menus – these usually take the form of a menu card given to the patient the day before service so that his or her preferences can be

ticked. Both National Health Service and private hospitals cater for vegetarians and also for religious requirements. In many cases a dietitian is involved in menu compilation to ensure nothing is given to the patients that would be detrimental to their health. Usually hospital meals are of two or three courses.

- Menus for people at work – these are menus which are served to people at their place of work. Such menus vary in standard and extent from one employer to another.
- Menus for children – schools should emphasize healthy eating and a balanced diet. Those areas with children of various cultural and religious backgrounds have appropriate items available on the menu.

Cyclical menus These are menus which are compiled to cover a given period of time, i.e. 1 month, 3 months. They consist of a number of set menus for a particular establishment, e.g. industrial catering restaurant, cafeteria, canteen, directors' dining room, hospital or college refectory. At the end of each period the menus can be used again, thus overcoming the need to keep compiling new ones. The length of the cycle is determined by management policy, by the time of the year and by different foods available. These menus must be monitored carefully to take account of changes in customer requirements and any variations in weather conditions which are likely to affect demand for certain dishes. If cyclical menus are designed to remain in operation for long periods of time, then they must be carefully compiled in order that they do not have to be changed too drastically during operation.

Advantages of cyclical menus
- They save time by removing the daily or weekly task of compiling menus, although they may require slight alterations for the next period.
- When used in association with cook–freeze operations, it is possible to produce the entire number of portions of each item to last the whole cycle, having determined that the standardized recipes are correct.
- They give greater efficiency in time and labour.
- They can cut down on the number of commodities held in stock and can assist in planning storage requirements.

Disadvantages
- When used in establishments with a captive clientele, then the cycle has to be long enough so that customers do not get bored with the repetition of dishes.
- The caterer cannot easily take advantage of 'good buys' offered by suppliers on a daily or weekly basis unless such items are required for the cyclical menu.

Preplanned and predesigned menus

Advantages

- Preplanned or predesigned menus enable the caterer to ensure that good menu planning is practised.
- Before selecting dishes that he or she prefers, the caterer should consider what the customer likes and the effect of these dishes upon the meal as a whole.
- Menus which are planned and costed in advance allow banqueting managers to quote prices instantly to a customer.
- Menus can be planned taking into account the availability of kitchen and service equipment, without placing unnecessary strain upon such equipment.
- The quality of food is likely to be higher if kitchen staff are preparing dishes that they are familiar with and have prepared a number of times before.

Disadvantages

- Preplanned and predesigned menus may be too limited to appeal to a wide range of customers.
- They may reduce job satisfaction for staff who have to prepare the same menu repetitively.
- They may limit the chef's creativity and originality.

Food and restaurant styles

Over the past few years a number of terms have been adopted to signify differing types of food and establishment styles. The *Ackerman Martell Guide* identifies these as follows.

Bistro   This is normally a smaller establishment, with check tablecloths, bentwood chairs, cluttered décor, friendly informal staff. Honest, basic and robust cooking, possible coarse pâtés, thick soups, casseroles served in large portions.

Brasserie   This is a largish, styled room, often with long bar, normally serving one-plate items rather than formal meals (though some offer both). Often possible just to have a drink, or coffee, or just a small amount to eat. Traditional dishes include *charcuterie, moules marinières, steak frites*. Service generally by waiters in long aprons and black waistcoats.

Farmhouse cooking   This is usually simply cooked with generous portions of basic, home-produced fare using good, local ingredients.

Country house hotel cooking   This can vary from establishment to establishment but usually modern English style with some influence from classic or even farmhouse style.

Classic/haute cuisine   This is the classical style of cooking evolved through many centuries, best chronicled by Escoffier. Greater depth of flavour. Style does not necessarily mean the most expensive ingredients – can include simply poached and boiled dishes such as chicken, tongue and offal. Classical presentation can be served at table or plated.

Cordon bleu   This derives from the cookery school of the same name, perhaps normally associated with dinner party or private house cooking.

New/modern English/French   This draws from the classical style but with new-style saucing and the better aspects of *nouvelle* presentation. Plated in the kitchen, allowing the chef the final responsibility for presentation.

Nouvelle cuisine   At its best, a distinctive style and presentation with a lighter and more innovative approach to some standard dishes. Concentrates on subtle flavours and unusual combinations. Plated, often referred to as 'art on the plate'. Has gained an unfortunate reputation for offering inadequate portions and concentrating more on presentation than content, but at its best it can be exceptionally good.

Essential considerations prior to planning the menu

- The location of an establishment should allow easy access to both customers and suppliers as and when required. A difficult journey can be offputting no matter how good the quality of food on offer and can affect repeat business and profitability. If the establishment is in an area noted for regional speciality foods or dishes, the inclusion of a selection of these on the menu can give extra menu appeal.
- Competition in the locality – it is important to be aware of what is offered by competitors, including their prices and particularly their quality. As a result, it may be wiser to produce a menu quite different from those of nearby establishments.
- Suitability of a particular establishment to a particular area – a self-service restaurant situated in an affluent residential district, or a very expensive seafood restaurant in a run-down inner-city area may not be very successful.
- Anticipate and analyse the type of people you are planning to cater for – it may be sensible to create a menu to satisfy, for example, office workers in the city, with a fast lunch service. Also opportunities may exist for outdoor catering.
- The spending power of the customer – a most important consideration is how much the potential customer is able and willing to pay.
- Customer requirements – it is the customer not the caterer who selects his or her menu, so analysis of dish popularity is necessary and those dishes that are not popular should not stay on the menu. Customer

demand must be considered and traditional dishes and modern trends in food fashions need to be taken into account.

- Number of items and price range of menus – it is essential to determine the range of dishes and whether table d'hôte or à la carte menus are to be offered. Decisions regarding the range of prices have to be made. A table d'hôte menu may be considered with an extra charge or supplement for more expensive dishes, or more than one table d'hôte menu of different prices may be more suitable.
- Seat turnover – if space is limited, or there are many customers (and control of the time the customer occupies the seat is needed) then the menu can be adjusted to increase turnover, e.g. more self-service items, separate service for coffee.
- Space and equipment in kitchen — these will influence the composition of the menu and production of dishes. The menu writer must be aware of any shortcomings or deficiencies in equipment and may be wary of offering dishes that are difficult to produce. Also, certain items of equipment should not be overloaded by the menu requirements, e.g. salamanders, steamers, fritures (deep fat fryers).
- Amount and capability of labour – the availability and capability of both the preparation and service staff must be considered when planning a menu. Enough able and willing staff, both in the kitchen and the restaurant, are necessary to achieve customer satisfaction with any menu.
- Supplies and storage – menu planning is dependent on availability of supplies, that is, frequency of deliveries of the required amounts. Storage space and seasonal availability of foods need to be taken into account when planning menus.
- Cost factor – when an establishment is run for profit the menu is a crucial consideration; but, even when working to a budget, the menu is no less crucial. Costing is the crux of the success of compiling any menu.

Menu policy – summary

- provide a means of communication
- establish the essential and social needs of the customer
- accurately predict what the customer is likely to buy and how much he or she is going to spend
- purchase and prepare raw materials to preset standards in accordance with predictions – purchasing specifications
- skilfully portion and cost the product in order to keep within company profitability policy
- effectively control the complete operation from purchase to service on the plate

Menu copy

Items or groups of items should bear names people recognize and understand. If a name does not give the right connotation, additional descriptive copy may be necessary. Descriptions can be produced carefully, helping to promote the dish and the menu. However, the description should describe the item realistically and not mislead the customer. Interesting descriptive copy is a skill; a good menu designer is able to illuminate menu terms, specific culinary terms and in doing so is able to draw attention to them. Simplicity creates better understanding and endorses the communication process.

Some menus can be built around a general descriptive copy featuring the history of the establishment or around the local area in which the establishment is situated. Descriptive copy can alternatively be based on a speciality dish which has significant cultural importance to the area or the establishment. In so doing the description may wish to feature the person responsible for creating and preparing the dish – especially if the chef is reasonably well known and has appeared on national or local television or radio. The chef may have also had his/her recipes featured in the local press. This too may be included in the menu to create further interest.

Menu copy should be set in a style of print which is easily readable and well spaced. Mixing typeface is often done to achieve emphasis; if overdone the overall concept is likely to look a mess and therefore unattractive to the eye.

Emphasis may be easily achieved by using boxes on the menu. Also menu paper and colour of the print can carefully be contracted to make certain dishes stand out.

Some mistakes in menu copy are as follows:

- Descriptive copy is left out when it is required.
- The wrong emphasis is given.
- Emphasis is lost because print size and style are not correctly used.
- The menu lacks creativity.

Health and safety

The dual responsibility of employers and employees at work is to ensure that the premises and equipment are safe and that they are kept safe so as to prevent accidents. Employers need to assess any hazards or risks and implement procedures to deal with any accidents. All employees should receive training in accident prevention. Safety signs must be used to inform and instruct people using the premises so as to prevent accidents or what to do in the event of an accident. All potential hazards should be reported.

Safety regulations   From 1993 six new health and safety at work regulations came into force:

1.   The management of Health and Safety at Work Regulations 1992:

    (a) risk assessment

    (b) control of hazardous substances

    (c) training

2.   The workplace (Health, Safety and Welfare Regulations 1992):

    (a) floors to be of suitable construction

    (b) floors free from hazardous articles or substances

    (c) steps taken to avoid slips, trips or falls

3.   Manual Handling Operations Regulations 1992:

    (a) reducing incorrect handling of loads

    (b) preventing hazardous handling

4.   Fire precautions:

    (a) means of fire fighting

    (b) evacuation procedures

    (c) raising the alarm

5.   Provision and use of work equipment:

    (a) ensure correct usage

    (b) properly maintained

    (c) training given

6.   Health and safety (display screen equipment): To see that staff using visual display units have a suitable workplace and take regular breaks

Risk assessment   Prevention of accidents and preventing food poisoning in catering establishments are essential, therefore it is necessary to assess the situation and decide what action is to be taken. Risk assessment can be divided into four areas:

1.   Minimal risk – safe conditions with safety measures in place.

2.   Some risk – acceptable risk; however, attention must be given to ensure safety measures operate.

3.   Significant risk – where safety measures are not fully in operation, also includes foods most likely to cause food poisoning. Requires immediate attention.

4.   Dangerous risk – requires the cessation of the process and/or discontinuing of the use of the equipment in the system and the complete checking and clearance before continuation.

To operate an assessment of risks the following points should be considered:

- assess the risks
- determine preventative measures
- decide who carries out safety inspections
- frequency of inspections
- methodology of reporting back and to whom
- detail how to ensure inspections are effective
- see that on the job training in safety is related to the job

The purpose of the exercise of assessing the possibility of risks and hazards is to prevent accidents. Firstly it is necessary to monitor the situation to have regular and random checks to observe that the standards set are being complied with. It is essential that an investigation is made if any incidents or accidents occur. The investigation must aim to track down any defects in the system and proceed to remedy these at once.

Control of substances hazardous to health

Substances dangerous to health are labelled very toxic, toxic harmful, irritant or corrosive. While only a small number of such chemicals are used in catering for cleaning, it is necessary to be aware of the regulations introduced in 1989. Those persons using such substances must be made aware of their correct use, proper dilution where appropriate and to wear protective goggles, gloves and face masks. It is essential that staff are trained to take precautions and not to take risks.

Control of substances hazadous to health requires the employer to do the following:

- Assess the risk to health arising from work and what precautions are needed.
- Introduce appropriate measures to prevent or control the risk.
- Ensure that control measures are used and that equipment is properly maintained and procedures observed.
- Where necessary, monitor the exposure of the workers and carry out an appropriate form of surveillance of their health.
- Inform, instruct and train employees about the risks and the precautions to be taken.

Assessment

This is an essential requirement for all employees.

As in tackling any problem, you need to know what the problem is and the extent of it before deciding what, if anything, you need to do about it. By going through the assessment procedure step by step, you can ensure that the health of those who could be affected by the work activities is protected and that money and effort are correctly spent and not wasted. The assessment must be a systematic review of the substances present, their effect, and how they are used and handled. For example, are there any harmful fumes given off?

The food production area

The highest number of accidents occurring in catering premises are due to people falling, slipping or tripping on kitchen floors. A major reason for the high incidence of this kind of accidents is that water and grease are likely to be spilt and the combination of them is treacherous. Staff must be trained to clean floors immediately after spillages.

Another cause of people falling is the placing of articles on the floor in corridors, passage ways or between stores and tables. Persons carrying trays and containers have their vision obstructed and items on the floor may not be visible. As the fall may occur on to a hot stove and the item being carried may be hot, these falls may have serious consequences. Nothing should be left on the kitchen floor. Kitchen staff must be trained to think and work safely.

Manual handling
The incorrect handling of heavy and awkward loads causes accidents, goods lifting, products and equipment on and off trolleys, tables, service area, etc.

Fire regulations
All food production staff must have a knowledge of the fire drill. They should be trained in how to extinguish small fires and clearly understand which extinguisher is used for which fire.

Provision and use of work equipment
All equipment must be suitable for the job it is used for. All equipment must be regularly maintained and serviced. All equipment must comply to European Safety Directives.

Personal protective clothing
All kitchen staff must wear protective clothing and protective safety footwear.

Kitchen equipment
All equipment must be maintained so that it is both safe and in working order. Manufacturers' instructions should be adhered to. All new equipment, especially gas and electric, must comply with the European Safety Directives.

Each organization is required to have a health and safety committee to regularly review safety at work.

The health of an individual can also affect that individual's safety and the safety of others. For this reason many companies have a occupational health policy which aims to promote good health practices at work. This involves regular medical checks and advice on maintaining a healthy life style. In many cases such a policy has helped to reduce staff absenteeism through illness.

Food hygiene policies   These policies set down a commitment by the company, organization or operation to encourage food hygiene practices within the organization. These must be seen as laying down clear guidelines and objectives for both management, chefs and other personnel. Some of these policies have been modelled closely on health and safety lines giving a detailed set of broad objectives with guidance in relation to particular processes. Emphasis must be on clear accurate guidance to ensure kitchen staff comply and that the policy is accepted by all who work for the organization. Some establishments ask staff to sign that they understand the policy and that they mean to comply with its objectives to maintain high standards of hygiene. Failure to comply once signed may lead to disciplinary action. The success of the policy must be judged on the commitment of the workforce, therefore before formulating any document it is advisable to consult with staff. It is important that any policy is simple to understand and is practical to operate.

Hygiene committees

Food hygiene involves everyone in the production system from goods inwards to final product. In order to focus attention on the subject and to maintain a continued interest throughout the workforce it is advisable to set up a hygiene committee. Such a committee comprises those who have immediate responsibility for maintaining hygiene standards, quality control, production, service, training, etc. Staff representatives from various areas should be involved. Members should be changed from time to time to avoid complacency and to maintain interest.

Hazard analysis and critical control point (HACCP)

Developed in the USA in the mid-1970s, HACCP is widely used by food manufacturers and processors and is now being applied in the catering industry. HACCP is a process which examines each stage in the process which may appear vulnerable in terms of introducing a hazard into the food. Particular attention is then given to this stage in the process. HACCP critically examines each stage of food production through to the final product and the consumer.

Once potential hazards in the processes have been identified, whether it is within the preparation, processing, storage or service, then particular attention must be given to either eliminating or minimizing the hazard. One of the advantages of HACCP is that a multi disciplinary team is involved because it covers the wide range of activities associated with the food product. Staff must be trained in HACCP for the process to be successful, they too must have commitment.

On introducing the HACCP process into food production the following elements have to be implemented:

- A detailed flow chart needs to be drawn up showing the path of the food throughout the manufacturing or kitchen process.
- All production details need to be identified so that any special characteristics are noted that could become a cause for concern.
- Each stage in the production must be carefully examined to see if there is the possibility that a hazard could occur. The risks are then recorded as high, medium or low. Monitoring controls are then implemented.

Taking food samples and bacterial swabs also help to complement the HACCP programme.

HACCP can be adapted by all sectors of the catering industry. The process is not just confined to large operators. A simplified version of HACCP has also been introduced called Assured Safe Catering.

Examples of critical control points (CCPs)
- inspection (including temperature checks) of goods on delivery and before use
- Separate storage and handling of ingredients and the finished product
- correct temperature ranges for refrigerated and frozen goods
- cleaning procedures for equipment and utensils
- cross-contamination with other menu items in process
- personal hygiene and health standards
- proficiency in use and cleaning of equipment

How to establish HACCP
1. Select a specific menu item or group of menu items.
2. Draft a flow diagram showing how it is/they are made (see Fig. 3.3).

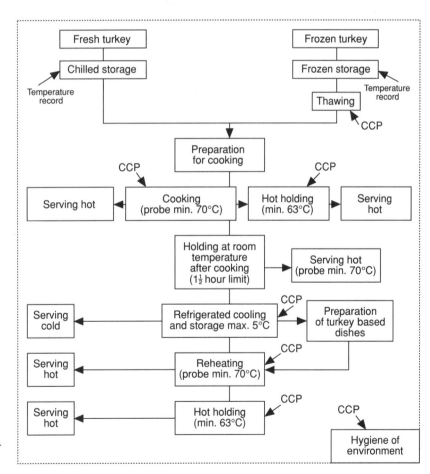

Fig. 3.3 Specimen flow diagram (*source:* HCIMA Technical Brief, November 1991)

3. Select the most relevant person who should:
   (a) amend the flow diagram if necessary;
   (b) examine each stage and identify where significant hazards could occur under both normal and occasional conditions;
   (c) list all probable causes of each hazard;
   (d) identify the CCPs at which these causes can be controlled.
4. Specify the control procedures at each CCP and change working practices as necessary.

How to maintain HACCP

- Monitor the information (e.g. temperature record charts) and take effective action when appropriate.
- If any feature of ingredients, processes or environment changes, alter the HACCP system as necessary.
- Carry out periodic checks to ensure the accuracy of any necessary instruments.
- Periodic laboratory testing of the microbiological condition of raw materials, equipment environment and product should be made wherever possible.
- Ensure adequate personnel monitoring, training and retraining.

Use of HACCP in catering

The most important aspects to be considered are:

- handling and storage procedures from delivery to service of the menu items
- holding items and temperatures
- cooling times
- personnel training

A specimen flow diagram is shown in Fig. 3.3. It is indicative only and is not applicable to turkey in all situations.

Food hygiene audits Food hygiene audits are carried out by management to scrutinize the food production operation. The audit is intended to record deficiencies and areas for improvement and to monitor performance at certain points. These may be linked to any quality assurance (including BS 5750) criteria.

The audit usually requires a suitably qualified person to carry out an in-depth inspection of the premises, plant and practices. The report is presented to management which notes observation and recommendations.

Many catering establishments do change their techniques and procedures of operation without being aware of hazards that are introduced. It is all too easy for people who are familiar with the kitchen or plant to fail to see what to outsiders are obvious problem areas emerging. Buildings may also be suffering from wear and tear and lack of repair. Equipment may also need overhauling. Often a hygiene audit is the only way of looking critically at the environment and thus picking up the problem areas or practices.

The frequency of these audits may vary, depending on the type of premises. High-volume production will justify more frequent audits. Establishments processing high-risk fresh commodities will also require more frequent audits. All in-depth inspections require properly recorded documentation, finalizing with reports which go to the appropriate people, who in turn are able to act. Otherwise their value is diminished. Reports should prioritize, to assist management in their decision-making, especially when financial implications have to be assessed and considered. It is always advisable to inform the local environmental health officer of the audits and the prioritized reports. The process of food hygiene management is shown in Fig. 3.4.

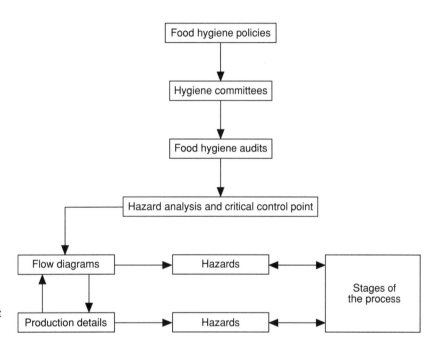

Fig. 3.4 The process of food hygiene management for food production

Quality assurance   BS 5750 lays down a standard of carrying out operations by which all materials and components are subjected to comprehensive regular checks at critical points throughout the food production process. Complying with BS 5750 is a guarantee of a quality product because it attempts to ensure that the manufacturing management system is subjected to regular independent checks and rigorous scrutiny. The accreditation certificate can be withdrawn if the company fails to adhere to the specification at any time.

Large food production companies and major catering companies are becoming accredited for BS 5750 in order to supply a guaranteed quality product which enables them to use the 'due diligence' defence under the Food Safety Act.

Purchasing and control

Once a menu is planned, a number of activities must occur to bring it into reality. One of the first and most important stages is to purchase and receive the materials needed to produce the menu items. Skilful purchasing with good receiving can do much to maximize the results of a good menu. Six important steps must occur if purchasing and receiving functions are to be successful:

1.   know the market
2.   determine purchasing needs
3.   establish and use specifications
4.   design the purchase procedures
5.   receiving
6.   evaluating the purchasing task

Since markets vary considerably, to do a good job of purchasing a buyer must know the characteristics of each market.

A market is a place in which ownership of commodity changes from one person to another. This could occur using the telephone, on a street corner, in a retail or wholesale establishment or at an auction.

It is important that a food and beverage purchaser has knowledge of the items to be purchased. For example:

- where they are grown
- seasons of production
- approximate costs
- conditions of supply and demand
- laws and regulations governing the market and the products
- marketing agents and their services
- processing
- storage requirements
- commodity and product, class and grade

Classification of markets and methods of purchasing

The primary market

Raw materials may be purchased at the source of supply, the grower, producer or manufacturer or from central markets such as Smithfield, Covent Garden, Nine Elms or Isle of Dogs in London. Some establishments or large organizations will have a buyer who will buy directly from the primary markets. Also, a number of small establishments may adopt this method for some of their needs, i.e. the chef patron may buy his fish, meat and vegetables directly from the market.

The secondary market

Goods are bought wholesale from a distributor or middleman; the catering establishment will pay wholesale prices and obtain possible discounts.

The tertiary market

The retail or cash and carry warehouse is a method suitable for smaller companies. A current pass obtained from the warehouse is required in order to gain access. This method also requires the user to have his or her own transport. Some cash and carry organizations require a VAT number before they will issue an authorized card. It is important to remember that these are added costs:

- running the vehicle and petrol used
- the person's time for going to the warehouse

Cash and carry is often an impersonal way of buying as there are no staff to discuss quality and prices.

The buyer
The buyer is the key person who makes decisions regarding quality, amounts, price, what will satisfy the customers and profit of commodities. The wisdom of the buyer's decisions will be reflected in the success or failure of the operation. The buyer must not only be knowledgeable about the products, but must have the necessary skills required in dealing with sales people, suppliers and other market agents. The buyer must be prepared for hard and often aggressive negotiations.

Buying demands integrity, maturity, bargaining skills and even disposition. Often buyers are subjected to bribes and other inducements by unscrupulous suppliers. Many suppliers will use pressure in order to get the buyer to purchase from specific sources. It is important to remember to treat the company's money as if it were your own. Use firm, friendly tactics and only socialize if it means that it will improve your buying position or benefit the company in some way. A buyer must always retain the right to be a free agent.

Buying associations have ethical codes to which members subscribe. They require a high standard of ethical relationship between buyer and seller.

A buyer must have knowledge of the internal organization of the company, especially the operational needs, and be able to obtain the product needs at a competitive price. The buyer must also be acquainted with the procedures of production and how these items are going to be used in the production operations, in order that the right item is purchased. For example, the item required may not always be of prime quality; for example, tomatoes for soups and sauces, to be cost-effective, do not need to be grade A or class I. Another example is certain types of nuts which do not have to be whole prime quality nuts for certain pastry goods or salads. Therefore, to reduce costs it is better to purchase broken nuts. A buyer must also know the storage requirements for each item and the space available, and the ability of the operation to finance special purchases in order to make good use of market conditions. For example, if there is a glut of fresh salmon at low cost, has the organization the facility to make use of the extra salmon purchases? Is there sufficient freezer space? Can the chef make use of salmon, by creating a demand on the menu? The buyer must also have a knowledge of yield testing procedures and know how to work closely with the chef and food production team to establish a specification so the right item is obtained.

Buying methods   These depend on the type of market and the kind of operation. Purchasing procedures are usually formal or informal. Both have advantages and disadvantages. Informal methods are suitable for casual buying, where the amount involved is not large and speed and simplicity are desirable. Formal contracts are best for large contracts for commodities purchased over a long period of time. Prices do not vary much during a year, once the basic price has been established. Using informal methods, prices and supply tend to fluctuate.

Informal buying

This usually involves oral negotiations, talking directly to salespeople, face to face or using the telephone. Informal methods vary according to market conditions.

The quotation and order sheet method   This uses a list of particular commodities always wanted in quantity and quality. Columns are provided to record prices from different suppliers. Prices are compared and orders given.

The blank cheque method   This is when there is an extreme shortage of a commodity or some other market condition exists where the buyer must get the commodity at any cost. This usually only operates in extreme circumstances.

The cost plus method   This is used when prices are not known or the market is unstable. Many suppliers like this arrangement, so that they do not have to add a safety factor to take care of risk, if commodities fluctuate considerably in price. They are free to buy at the most favourable price and then add on what they require to cover costs and give a profit. The amount over and above the cost paid for the item charged to the buyer is usually a standard percentage. Thus a supplier may buy fruit and vegetables and charge the buyer the price paid, plus 10 per cent.

Formal buying

This is known as competitive buying, giving suppliers written specifications and quantity needs. Negotiations are normally written. Methods are detailed as follows.

The competitive bid method The sellers are invited to submit bids through written communications. The suppliers then send prices and other information on the commodities to the buyer. Bids are opened at a specified time to determine awards. Only those sellers able to meet the established purchase conditions of the buyer will be considered in awarding bids. The invitation to bid usually contains certain conditions. These will include:

- terms of payment
- discounts
- method of delivery
- invoice requirements

The negotiated method This is used when suppliers are hesitant to bid because of time restrictions, fluctuating market conditions, or a high perishability of the product. Negotiations may occur using the telephone and later confirmed in writing. Several suppliers are usually contacted to compare prices. This method is useful in that it allows competitive bidding while giving flexibility.

The futures and contract method This is used by large organizations who have sufficient capital and staff to contract for future delivery of commodities at an established bid price. The advantage is that it ensures an adequate supply at an established price and avoids shortages and price fluctuations that affect prices.

Sometimes this system is used to establish a buying agreement for only a week or month for commodities such as meat, fresh fruits and vegetables, but arrangements can also extend to a short season. For items more stable in price such as canned goods, baked beans, tomato purée, canned potatoes, potato powder, tea and coffee, and frozen goods such as ice cream, gâteau, sausage rolls, vol-au-vents and pies, they are often placed on contract for long periods, up to one year.

The quantity under contract may vary and the amount purchased will depend on the amount used over a period. Contract and industrial caterers are able to forecast fairly accurately how much of each commodity they are likely to consume. A price is agreed along with quality and the quantity may also be set. For example, the price of baked beans may be dependent on the number of cases a buyer is guaranteeing to take over a period. Frequencies of delivery of the baked beans will also be determined. The maximum stock of baked beans held at any one time is determined by the buyer according to what was needed over a period of time. This is directly related to the operational need, how many food outlets have baked beans on the menu and the sales forecast of baked beans over a given period. When the stock diminishes to the reorder level, the buyer will contact the supplier for a new delivery. In some cases the supplier's salesperson may visit the company regularly to bring the inventory of the operations up to an established point. Whichever the case, such an arrangement is often called par stock supplying. This ensures that a safety stock level on the quantity of the items to be used between the time of reorder and delivery, be maintained. A reserve stock is essential or safety stock in case the delivery is late.

Selecting suppliers

Selecting suppliers is important in the purchasing process. Firstly, consider how a supplier will be able to meet the needs of your operation. Consider:

- price
- delivery
- quality/standards

Information on suppliers can be obtained from other purchasers. Visits to suppliers' establishments are to be encouraged. When interviewing prospective suppliers, you need to question how reliable a supplier will be under competition and how stable under varying market conditions.

Suppliers are also selected on experience. A buyer soon gets to know the reliable suppliers. New suppliers are often tried and tested, some are retained. Considerations leading to a decision to continue to do business with a supplier include:

1. If the supplier anticipates the needs of the organization. The supplier notes market conditions and informs the company buyer.
2. Suppliers regularly give product and market information.
3. Does the supplier break quantities down as and when required? Or does the buyer have to take a minimum quantity, which may be double the requirement needed?
4. The supplier should always maintain adequate stocks.
5. Evaluate credit terms and discounts available.
6. Assess delivery conditions.
7. A supplier may be able to offer a wide range of goods and services. Savings can often be made by consolidating products and services.

Many suppliers now offer fresh fruit and vegetables, part prepared fresh vegetables. For example, peeled and turned potatoes, peeled and sliced carrots, prepared fresh beans. They will also offer a full range of frozen vegetables and speciality goods.

Three types of needs

Perishable

Fresh fruit and vegetables, dairy products, meat and fish. Prices and suppliers may vary. Informal means of buying are frequently used. Perishables should be purchased to meet menu needs for a short period only.

Staple

Supplies of canned, bottled, dehydrated, frozen products. Formal or informal purchasing can be used. Because items are staple and can be easily stored, bid buying is frequently used to take advantage of quantity price purchasing.

Daily use needs

Daily use or contract items are delivered frequently on par stock basis. Stocks are kept up to the desired level and supply is automatic. Suppliers may be daily, several times a week, weekly or less often. Most items are perishable, therefore supplies must not be excessive, only sufficient to get through to the next delivery.

What quantity and quality

Determining quantity and quality of items to be purchased is important. This is based on the operational needs. The buyer must be informed by the chef or other members of the production team of the products needed. The chef and his/her team must establish the quality and they should be encouraged to inspect the goods on arrival. The buyer with this information then checks out the market and looks for the best quality and best price. Delivery arrangements and other factors will be handled by the buyer. In smaller establishments the chef may also be the buyer.

When considering the quantity needed, certain factors should be known:

- the number of people to be served in a given period
- the sales history
- portion sizes, determined from yield testing a standard portion control list drawn up by the chef and management teams

Buyers need to know production, often to be able to decide how many portions a given size may yield. He/she must also understand the various yields. Cooking shrinkage may vary, causing problems in portion control and yield.

The chef must inform the buyer of quantities. The buyer must also be aware of different packaging sizes, such as jars, bottles, cans and the yield from each package. There must be an indication of grades, styles, appearance, composition, varieties and quality factors such as:

- colour
- texture
- size
- absence of defects
- braising
- irregular shape
- maturity

Quality standards should be established by the chef and management team when the menu is planned. Menus and recipes are developed using standardized recipes which directly relate to the buying procedure and standard purchasing specifications.

The standard recipe
Standard recipes are a written formula for producing a food item of a specified quality and quantity for use in a particular establishment. It should show the precise quantities and qualities of the ingredients together with the sequence of preparation and service. It enables the establishment to have a greater control over cost and quantity.

Objective
To predetermine the following:

- the quantities and qualities of ingredients to be used stating the purchase specification
- the yield obtained from a recipe
- the food cost per person
- the nutritional value of a particular dish

And to facilitate:

- menu planning
- purchasing and internal requisitioning
- food preparation and production
- portion control

In addition, the standard recipe will assist new staff in preparation and production of standard products – which can be facilitated by photographs or drawings illustrating the finished product.

Standard purchasing specification
Definition (Lysons, 1989):

> A specification is a statement providing a description or list of the characteristics or requirements laid down for materials, components, processes or services.

Specifications have two functions:

1. They communicate to a supplier what the specifier wishes to have supplied to him in terms of goods and service.
2. They provide criteria against which the goods and services actually supplied can be compared.

The main advantages of specification buying are:

- Drawing up the specifications requires careful thought and a review of the buyer's needs. This frequently results in a simplification of the variety of products purchased and often reveals the possibility of using less expensive commodities. Both factors result in economies.

- Buying according to specifications frequently induces more suppliers to bid on an order, because all suppliers know exactly what is wanted and that their chances are as good as those of other suppliers because they are bidding on identical items. This increased competition for the business often results in lower prices.
- Specifications ensure the identical nature of items purchased from one or two sources. When the purchaser has more than one supplier of an item, this identity is essential and specification buying is a virtual necessity.
- Purchasing to specifications gives the person receiving the order an exact standard against which to measure the incoming materials and results in accurate inspection and a uniform quality of commodities.
- If specification buying is combined with quality control on the part of the supplier, it may be possible for the buyer to save money by doing a less complete inspection.
- Specification buying is a necessary step towards industry-wide standardization and standardization programmes hold the promise of substantial savings.

The principal disadvantages of buying by specifications are:

- It is not economical to prepare specifications for small-lot purchases. This rules out the possibility of specification buying for many items.
- Specification buying adds to the purchaser's responsibilities. They must be able to state precisely what they want and the supplier's obligations extend only to complying with those terms. If the product does not live up to expectations, the liability rests with the buyer.
- In specification buying the cost of inspection is greater than in purchasing by brand-name where you are guaranteed a standard through experience. Items purchased to specification must be examined, whereas branded items need little more than a casual check and count.
- There is always the danger of becoming over-defined in preparing specifications and as a consequence, paying more than necessary for items.
- There is also a danger of assuming that after specifications are established, the characteristics of the item have been permanently set. Unless specifications are periodically reviewed, there is a chance that the buyer will lose out on product improvements.

The content of a specification varies according to whether it is written for a user, designer, manufacturer or seller. A simple item may only require a brief description, whereas in the case of a complex assembly, the specification will be a comprehensive document, perhaps running to several pages. The content which may be required in a specification is listed in the *Guide to the Preparation of Specifications* issued by the BSI (PD 6112) in May 1967. These are categorized under the following headings:

- characteristics
- performance
- control of quality
- packaging and protection

Most books available suggest that when writing specifications it is convenient to write them in a standard form. An example of information is as follows.

Definition of the item   Care must be taken so that a common catering term used by the buyer means exactly the same thing to the supplier; for example, whole sirloin means with bone and striploin without the bone; washed and sliced potatoes means after they have been peeled and of a thickness of no more than the specification.

Grade or brand-name   For example, apples – grade extra class, or Granny Smiths; Lea and Perrins Worcester Sauce; where available it should state the desired variety and next acceptable substitute.

Weight, size or count   For example, pounds, kilos; A2s or A10s; lemons 120s, pineapples 12s. Counts vary from country to country, therefore desired country of origin should be quoted against the count and the substitute country with the alternative count noted.

Unit against which prices should be quoted   For example, per pound, per case, per box, per sack, each.

Special notes for the commodity   For example, for meat it could contain details of the preparation of a particular cut of meat, or details of special packaging and delivery requirements. In the near future this will be with regard to the Food Safety Act of 1990, where chilled delivery vehicles are a legal requirement.

The contents which may be required in a specification

These are taken from the *Guide to the Preparation of Specifications* issued by the BSI (PD 6112) in May 1967.

1. title of specification
2. list of contents
3. foreword including why the specification has been written and on whose authority
4. scope of the specification (If the specification is limited to certain aspects only, e.g. workmanship and dimensions, these should be stated. Attention should be drawn to excluded factors.)

5. the purpose of the equipment or material
6. definition of terminology, symbols, abbreviations and measuring systems
7. relevant authorities to be consulted
8. reference to other related documents, e.g. statutory regulations, national and international standards
9. conditions in which the item or material is to be installed, used, manufactured or stored
10. characteristics: these may be shown by:
    (a) design, samples, drawings, models, preliminary tests or investigations
    (b) properties, e.g. strength, dimensions, weight, safety, with tolerances where applicable
    (c) interchangeability (functional, dimensional)
    (d) material and their properties (including permissible variability, approved or excluded materials)
    (e) requirements for a manufacturing process, e.g. heat treatment. (This should be specified only when critical to design considerations.)
    (f) appearance, texture, finish, including colour, protection, etc.
    (g) identification marks, operating symbols on controls, weight of items, safety indications, etc.
    (h) method of marking
11. performance:
    (a) performance under specified conditions
    (b) test methods and equipment for assessing performance; where, how and by whom carried out; reference to correlation with behaviour in operation
    (c) criteria for passing tests, including accuracy and interpretations of results
    (d) acceptance standards
    (e) certification and/or reporting, i.e. reports, test schedules or certificates required
12. life
13. reliability, i.e. under stipulated conditions and tests and control procedures for assessing reliability
14. control of quality checking for compliance with specification:
    (a) method of checking compliance
    (b) production tests on raw materials, components, subassemblies and assemblies
    (c) assurance of compliance, e.g. by supplier's certificates or independent certification schemes.
    (d) inspection facilities required by the user/designer or offered to the manufacturer/supplier

(e) instructions regarding reject materials or items

(f) instructions with regard to modifications of process

(g) applicability of quality control to subcontracts, etc.

(h) acceptable conditions

15. packaging protection:

(a) specification of packaging, including any special conditions in transit

(b) condition in which the item is to be supplied, e.g. protected, lubricant free

(c) period of storage

(d) marking of packaging

16. information from the supplier to the user, e.g. instructions and advice on installation, operation and maintenance

17. after-sales service

Centralized purchasing within a company operating a number of units

There are advantages for large organizations in establishing a specialist department through which all purchasing is channelled. These include the following:

1. Economies of scale enabling the use of bargaining power and resources to the best effect. This is done thus:

(a) A consolidation of quantities can take place resulting in quantity discounts.

(b) Suppliers dealing with a central purchasing department have the incentive of comparing for the whole or substantial proportion of the requirements.

(c) Cheaper prices may result since the fixed overheads of the supplier can be spread over longer production runs; however, as food is a perishable commodity this may not have a major impact.

(d) Specialist purchasing staff can be employed for each of the major categories of purchase.

(e) Cheaper prices may be achieved by going directly to the grower and not via the market-place, e.g. buying the whole crop of one farm at a negotiated rate.

(f) Lower administrative costs apply; for example, it is cheaper to process one order for £10 000 than ten each of £1000.

(g) The use of computerization can be used to facilitate the collection, summary and analysis of data which in turn can improve purchasing efficiency.

2. Co-ordination of the activity:

(a) Uniform policies can be adopted.

(b) Uniform purchasing procedures can be followed.

(c) Standardization is achieved by the use of company specifications.

(d) Back-up services, especially stock control, can be co-ordinated.

(e) Staff training and development can be undertaken on a smaller scale with better results.

(f) Research into sources, qualities and supplier performance can be achieved.

(g) It is more convenient for the supplier to approach a central purchasing department.

3. Control of the activity:

(a) The performance of the purchasing department can be monitored by fixing objectives and comparing actual results with predetermined standards.

(b) Stock rotation is achieved and loss of wastage due to out of date stock can be minimized.

(c) Uniform pricing is achieved and assists in standard costings nationwide.

A centralized role in a company such as catering retail (family food service restaurants) can work very well, as each of the restaurants has a set menu and therefore is limited to the commodities it requires, perhaps 200 at most. In a unit which has contract catering the requirement varies from unit to unit. A directors' dining room will require fillet steak and smoked salmon, a school kitchen would never order such commodities. Therefore a centralized purchasing department would have to order many thousands of different commodities due to the diversity of the business.

Purchasing may be completely decentralized with each unit undertaking its own purchasing, although unit buyers are given some guidelines upon which to purchase. It is at this level that food specifications are most needed to give the non specialist food purchasers some technical guidelines upon which to buy.

A combination of centralization and decentralization may apply. It could be said that the function of the purchasing administration is already done centrally under the purchasing director, but no physical purchasing is done at this level. It is necessary to have central administration to ensure the achievement of company purchasing standards.

However, it is possible for non-perishable goods and commodities with an extended shelf-life, to be bought centrally and delivered to the unit on a weekly basis. This would improve the effectiveness of this area. But the perishable items, i.e. bakery goods, dairy produce, fresh meat and fish, fresh fruit and vegetables, would be purchased straight into the unit. Alternatively, there could be a system whereby the unit informs a central office, operated by purchasing specialists, of their requirements, who then place the order and organize delivery to the unit.

No matter which system is adopted, there is always a need for purchasing specifications to assist in the task. Even specialists with technical training need to know the standard which the company expects its suppliers to reach. A standard indicated in a specification lends itself to the ultimate standard which a company wants to achieve. Good specifications aimed at the right standard will ensure:

- quality products
- quality service
- acceptable prices

Commodities which can be specified:

Grown (primary)	Butcher's meat
	Fresh fish
	Fresh fruit and vegetables
	Milk and eggs
Manufactured (secondary)	Bakery goods
	Dairy products
Processed (tertiary)	Frozen foods including:
	meat, fish and fruit and vegetables
	Dried goods
	Canned goods

It can be seen that any food product can have a specification attached to it.

However, the primary specifications focus on raw materials and ensuring the quality of these commodities. Without quality at this level, a secondary or tertiary specification is useless. For example, to specify a frozen apple pie. This product would use:

- a primary specification for the apple
- a secondary specification for the pastry and a tertiary specification for the process, i.e. freezing

But no matter how good the secondary or tertiary specifications are, if the apples used in the beginning are not of a very high quality, the whole product is not of a good quality. Therefore, primary specifications are most important as they lay down the basic foundations upon which manufacturing and processing specifications can be built. The most useful specifications for use at unit level are likely to be for basic raw materials, as it is the chefs who implement the manufacture or process of the commodity. Control can be gained in this area by developing a series of standardized recipes so that the customer can be guaranteed a constant product at all time. It can, therefore, be seen that further development of primary specifications is necessary to continue the development of quality.

Problems in preparing purchasing specifications in the UK

Preparing specifications in the UK and many other countries is rather difficult, owing to a lack of government grading of many foods. However, the position of fruit and vegetable suppliers has improved recently with the grading of fruits and vegetables produced in the UK. This is also the case with the recommended classification of carcass meat by the Meat and Livestock Commission. This is explained further in the following extract from the book, *Food and Beverage Control* (Kotas and Davis, 1981):

> By comparison with the USA, it is much more difficult to prepare specifications in the UK because of an almost total lack of grading of food commodities. Many specifications in UK are therefore much more detailed, but even then do not have the guaranteed accuracy of those in the USA, which is backed by government and state legislation.

An important factor in finding suppliers interested in selling commodities to a specification prepared by a caterer is that of the purchasing power of the caterer. If a caterer is large enough, he is able to influence the supply trade quite easily. The small caterer has a problem of purchasing only what suppliers have readily available to sell, as he has only a low purchasing power. To find suppliers to prepare commodities to his specification is rare and if fortunate enough to find any interested, extremely costly. At times, the difficulty can be overcome by finding suppliers who are already producing an item for a larger concern to a similar specification and who therefore accept a compromise which partly goes towards the aim of the small caterer's specification.

The Agriculture and Horticulture Act of 1964, which gave the Minister power to prescribe grades for fruit and vegetables, to enforce labelling and size of packaging units and powers of inspection at the wholesale level, is seen as a very good aid to the caterer when preparing purchasing specifications. Since February 1973, there has been a gradual introduction of the EC quality grading for fresh fruit and vegetables on the UK market. Each product is graded at four levels:

- extra class
- class 1
- class 2
- class 3

Operational control

Food is expensive and efficient stock control levels are essential to help the profitability of the business. The main difficulties of controlling food are as follows:

- Food prices fluctuate because of inflation and falls in the demand and supply – through poor harvests, bad weather conditions, etc.

- Transport costs, which rise due to wage demands and cost of petrol.
- Fuel costs rise, which affects food companies' and producers' costs.
- Removal of food subsidies to bring the UK into line with the EC.
- Changes in the amount demanded by the customer; increased advertising increases demand. Changes in taste and fashion influence demand from one produce to another.
- Media focus on certain products which are labelled healthy and unhealthy will affect demand, e.g. butter being high in saturated fats. Sunflower margarine is high in polyunsaturates.

Each establishment should devise its own control system to suit the needs of that establishment.

Factors which affect a control system are:

- regular changes in the menu
- menus with a large number of dishes
- dishes with a large number of ingredients
- problems with assessing customer demand
- difficulties in not adhering to or operating standardized recipes
- raw materials purchased incorrectly

Factors assisting a control system:

- constant menu, e.g. McDonalds, Harvester
- standardized recipes and purchasing specifications
- menu with a limited number of dishes

Stocktaking is therefore easier and costing more accurate.

In order to carry out a control system, food stocks must be secure, refrigerators and deep-freezers should be kept locked. Portion control must be accurate. A bookkeeping system must be developed to monitor the daily operation.

The control cycle of daily operation is shown in Fig. 3.5.

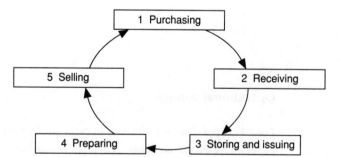

Fig. 3.5 The control cycle of daily operation

Purchasing The purchasing transaction is shown diagrammatically in Fig. 3.6. It is important to determine yields from the range of commodities in use which will determine the unit costs. Yield testing indicates the number of items or portions obtained and helps to provide the information required for producing, purchasing and specification. Yield testing should not be confused with product testing which is concerned with the physical properties of the food – texture, flavour and quality. In reality tests are frequently carried out which combine these objectives.

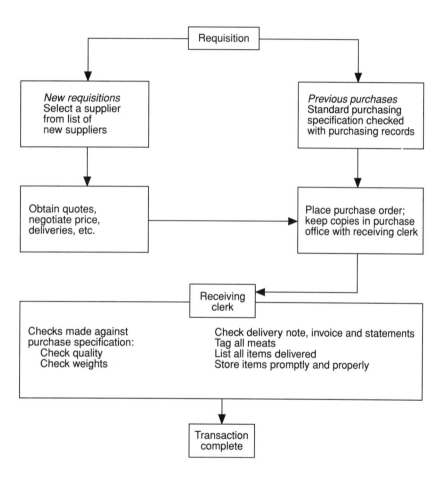

Fig. 3.6 Summary of the purchasing transaction

Unless communication lines are set up to inform buyers of production needs and to inform receiving clerks, accounting personnel and others of orders and expected arrival times, poor buying and control occur. Management will establish many requirements that must be met in control: the routeing of paperwork, payment policies, receiving procedures, checks to ascertain quality.

Requisition and inventory control must be implemented. Control begins with the calculation of the amount and the writing of the specification. Orders are usually placed through a purchase order. This states the item or items required, amount, size, weight and other pertinent information.

All purchase orders have numbers so that they can be quickly identified. Purchase orders should only be signed by an authorized person. One copy is normally held by the individual issuing it, one may go to the accounting department and another to the receiving rooms. Copies are sent to the supplier. In some cases, it may be a requirement to have the purchase order signed and returned by some individual in the supplier's company so it is known that the order will be honoured.

Regular purchase orders are for one single order to be delivered at a specified date. 'Open delivery' purchase orders establish the purchase of items over a period of time. Items needed daily or weekly are often purchased by open delivery orders.

A purchase record may be maintained. This record may indicate what was ordered and from whom, as well as any other information that may be needed to be maintained. A purchase price record usually is maintained on cards to keep information on the price paid for a particular item.

Receiving
Receiving practices vary with different organizations. General principles of control are as follows:

1. Check delivery note to see if the products delivered agree with it.
2. Inspect products/raw materials to determine if they are in agreement with the purchase order and specification.
3. Tag all meats with date of receipt, weight and other information needed to identify the delivery properly.
4. List all items received on the daily receiving report.
5. Accept the products/raw materials by signing the delivery note and returning the copy to the driver/delivery person.
6. Store or deliver to the correct place.

In large organizations, receiving is a specialized job. This job may be combined with the storeroom job. Authority and responsibility must be given to the individual receiving. This must include jurisdiction over those who help receive and store.

Invoice receiving

If the invoice accompanies the delivery with the delivery note, check the invoice against the delivery and check with the purchase order or the quotation and the order sheet, or other documents. Note any discrepancies. Check quality and quantity against documentation.

Blind check receiving

A blind receiving method may be used. For this the clerk is given a blank invoice or purchase order listing the incoming products/raw materials. The quantities, quality, weights and prices are omitted. The receiving clerk must add these in when the products/raw materials are delivered. This enforces a formal checking system and not merely a glancing job to see if the goods agree with the figures on the invoice. The receiving clerk must weigh items to record their correct weight. A count is required in addition to a quality check. Another invoice with quantities, weights, quality and prices is sent to the finance office. This is checked against the invoice of the receiving clerk and the figures verified. Blind receiving is an accurate method of checking merchandise and verifying deliveries. It does take more time and costs more since it requires the clerk to prepare a complete record of all incoming products/raw materials.

Partial blind receiving

A combination of invoice receiving and blind receiving. The receiving clerk has itemized purchase orders, delivery notes and invoices with the quantities omitted. When the goods, products and raw materials are checked, the quantity of each item is listed in the space provided. This is not as accurate as the previous method, but is faster and less costly. It is essential in both methods that the supplier's invoice does not accompany the goods, products or raw materials. If it does, the information on quantity must be omitted or made invisible by a blank area where such information would appear.

Good principles of receiving are important for control. These are:

1. Being ready and prepared for the delivery.
2. Checking the incoming goods thoroughly against the purchase order and the purchase specification. Open cases if they appear to be damaged or tampered with. Date all canned goods before storing.
3. Weigh items separately. When receiving bulk items, remove excess paper, ice, etc.
4. Weigh meats and tag them. The practice prevents disputes with the supplier about over- and underweights. Tagging also reduces the chance of spoilage or excess weight loss. It also simplifies calculation of food costs, since a good record of meat withdrawals can be obtained from the tags taken from meat as it comes from the inventory.

Meat tags should be used on all large cuts of incoming meats for the following reasons:

- To show the supplier, should there be a question of quality and quantity.
- To prevent reweighing on issuing (provided the entire unit is used).
- Provide a check on the accuracy of the receiving clerk.
- Help stock rotation.
- Speed inventory taking.

- Facilitate ordering (bottom half sent to purchasing agent when item is used).
- Check for quality – checking for quality is often neglected by the receiving clerk. It is important to see that the grade and quality of the raw materials or goods agree with those shown on the delivery note and invoice, i.e. purchase order.
- Store, items promptly and properly.

An example meat tag is shown in Fig. 3.7.

Recording incoming deliveries is as important as checking quality and quantity. The form or style of doing this may vary.

No:	_____
Date:	20/4/93
Supplier:	Meadowbank Meats
Origin:	Scottish Aberdeen Angus
Cut:	Strip loin
Weight:	15 lbs
Unit price:	4.50 per lb
Checked by:	Mr Williams, Head Storeman
No:	_____
Date:	20/4/93
Supplier:	_____
Origin:	_____
Cut:	_____
Weight:	_____
Unit price:	_____
Checked by:	_____

Fig. 3.7 Meat tag – bottom half is sent to purchasing agent when item is used

Storing and issuing Raw materials should be stored correctly under the right conditions, temperature, etc. A method of pricing the materials must be decided and one of the following should be adopted for charging the food to the various departments. The cost of items does not remain fixed over a period of time; over a period of one year a stores item may well have several prices. The establishment must decide which price to use:

- actual purchase price
- simple average weight
- weighted average price

- inflated price (price goes up after purchase)
- standard price (fixed price)

Weighted average price example (dried fruit)

$$10 \text{ lb} \times 40\text{p} = 400\text{p}$$
$$20 \text{ lb} \times 50\text{p} = 1000\text{p}$$

Total   1400p

So 1400 divided by 30 lb = 46.6p per lb weighted average price.

Preparing/production

This is an important stage of the control cycle. The cost of the food consumed depends on two factors:

1. the number of meals produced
2. the cost per meal

In order to control food costs we must be able to:

- control the number to be catered for
- control the food cost per meal in advance of production and service by using system of pre-costing, using standardized recipes, indicating portion control

Sales and volume forecasting

This requires predicting the volume of sales for a future period. In order to be of practical value the forecast must:

- predict the total number of covers (customers)
- predict the choice of menu items

Therefore, it is important to:

- keep a record of the numbers of each dish sold from a menu
- work out the average spent per customer
- calculate the proportion, expressed as a percentage, of each dish sold in relation to total sales

Forecasting is in two stages:

1. Initial forecasting – this is done once a week in respect of each day of the following week. It is based on sales histories, information related to advance bookings and current trends and when this has been completed, the predicted sales are converted into the food/ingredients requirements. Purchase orders are then prepared and sent to suppliers.
2. The final forecast – this normally takes place the day before the actual preparation and service of the food. This forecast must take into account

the latest developments, e.g. the weather and any food that needs to be used up; if necessary suppliers' orders may need to be adjusted.

Sales forecasting is not a perfect method of prediction, but does help with production planning. Sales forecasting, however, is important when used in conjunction with cyclical menu planning.

Pre-costing of dishes

This method of costing is associated with standardized recipes which gives the total cost of the dish per portion and often with a selling price.

This is a summary of the factors which will affect the profitability of the establishment:

- overcooking food resulting in portion loss
- inefficient preparation of raw materials
- poor portion control
- too much wastage, insufficient use of raw materials, left-over food not being utilized
- theft
- inaccurate ordering procedures
- inadequate checking procedures
- no reference mark to standardized recipes and yield factors
- insufficient research into suppliers
- inaccurate forecasting
- bad menu planning

Storekeeping

Keeping a properly run and efficient storeroom is essential in order to maintain the unified process of control throughout the establishment/organization. A clean, orderly food store, run efficiently, is essential in any catering establishment for the following reasons:

- Stocks of food can be kept at a suitable level, so eliminating the risk of running out of any raw material.
- All food entering and leaving the stores can be properly checked; this helps to prevent wastage.
- A check can be kept on the percentage profit of each department of the establishment.

Summary

The chapter has aimed to identify the principles, practices and applications of food production in the hotel and catering industry. It has focused on the knowledge required by a manager to effectively operate and manage a food production system. This knowledge is gained through an understanding of the basic principles of menu planning which is explicably linked to the purchasing and planning process. Inherent in this process of planning is the hygiene unit and the hygiene management concept to deliver a clean, safe and healthy product.

As with every manufacturing system, standardization is essential to maintain consistent products within the financial constraints, therefore the chapter has tried to demonstrate the importance of operations control within the catering industry.

References

Cousins J 1994 Managing capacity. In Jones P (ed) *The management of food-service operations* Cassell, London: pp. 174–87

Kotas R and Davis B 1981 *Food and Beverage Control* International Text Book Company, Glasgow: p. 60

Lysons C K 1989 *Purchasing* 2nd Edition, ME Handbooks: Business and Management, London: p. 88

4 Wine and drinks

Aim   This chapter considers the wine and drinks provision within food service operations.

Objective   This chapter will enable you to:

- outline the legal framework within which alcoholic beverages are sold
- identify factors which affect the compilation of wine and drinks lists and to consider types of lists
- consider approaches to pricing
- identify factors for the purchasing, storage and control of wine and drinks

The legal framework

In order to sell intoxicating liquor in the UK, licences are required. These licences govern the type of liquor which can be sold, the extent of the market which can be served and the times of opening (or permitted hours). There are also regulations on restrictions to young persons and on measures. These restrictions are made by the government and penalties for infringement are applied, not only to the licensee or their staff, but also to the customer.

Alcoholic beverages are sold in two main types of licensed establishment. These are known as free houses and tied houses:

- Free house – This is a licensed establishment which has no attachment to one particular supply source.
- Tied house – This is a licensed establishment which is tenanted or managed and is linked (tied) to a particular source of supply.
  Tenanted   The tenant leases the property from the brewer and is tied to that brewer for the purchase of beer and possibly other drinks.
  Managed   A manager is paid a salary to run the premises which are owned by a particular brewery.

Traditionally it is the premises which are licensed and the person who holds the licence is known as the licensee. Recently there has been the trial of a new National Licensee's Certificate and it is likely that the local licensing committees, where the trials have been taking place, will be taking the certificate into account when considering applications for new licences in the course of 1995. It also seems likely that the number of licensing committees being involved in the trial is likely to increase. This development has also been supported by a number of brewery companies, pub chains and leisure operators who have already incorporated the national licensee's certificate training into their training programmes.

Types of licence

The various types of licence available in the UK are described below.

Full on-licence

This allows the licensee to sell all types of intoxicating liquor for consumption on and off the premises. However, there are a few examples of on-licences where the type of alcohol is limited, e.g. beer only or beer and wine only.

Restricted on-licences

Restaurant licence   This applies to the sale of alcoholic liquor to persons taking main meals only.

Residential licence   This applies to the sale of alcoholic liquor to persons residing on the premises or to their private friends who are being genuinely entertained by the guests at the guests' expense.

Combined licence   This is a combined restaurant and residential licence.

Club licences

Licensed club   Normally this is a licence to run a club, which is operated by individuals or a limited company, as a commercial enterprise. The sale of alcoholic liquor is to members only.

Members' club   A licence to run a club, normally by a committee of members, as a non-profit-making organization. The members own the stock of liquor and sale is to members only.

Off-Licence

A licence authorizing the sale of intoxicating liquor for consumption off the premises only.

Note: The definitions for the licences quoted here apply to England and Wales. In Scotland, the licensing pattern is similar although there are differences in the definitions and in the permitted hours. Licensing definitions in Northern Ireland are similar to those in England and Wales.

Occasional licence

This is granted to holders of on-licences and restaurant or combined licences enabling them to sell alcoholic liquor at another place for a specified time, e.g. a licensee may be able to set up a bar for a local village hall function.

Occasional permission

This is similar to an occasional licence but may be applied for by non-licence holders, e.g. a charity may apply for occasional permission in order to sell alcoholic drink at a specific fund-raising event.

Music and dancing licences

These licences are not liquor licences but are required for public music and dancing. The licences are granted by local councils and the law varies from place to place. Licences are not required where radio, television and recorded music are used or where there are no more than two live performers, although if dancing takes place, a licence is required.

Permitted hours   Currently permitted hours are as follows for England and Wales:

Weekdays	11.00 to 23.00 hours (off-licences including)
	08.00 to 22.30 or 23.00 (Good Friday)
Sundays and	12.00 to 22.30 hours
Good Friday	(off-licences may open from 10.00 on Sundays)
Christmas Day	12.00 to 15.00 hours and 19.00 to 22.30 hours
	(the hours for off-licences are the same)
	Local Magistrates may also allow weekday
	opening from 10.00 hours.

Within these permitted hours the licensee can choose when and for how long to close the premises.

Exceptions to permitted hours

The following exceptions apply to permitted hours:

- The first 20 minutes after the end of permitted hours is for consumption only.
- The first 30 minutes after the end of permitted hours for those taking table meals is again for consumption only.
- Residents and their guests may be (but do not have to be) served at any time as long as only the resident makes the purchase.

Note: Permitted hours in Scotland are similar to those above.

Extensions to permitted hours

Special Order of Exemption   This is available for specific occasions, e.g. a wedding, dinner dance or carnival.

General Order of Exemption   This applies to an area where a particular trade or calling is going on, e.g. market day or food markets which are operating early in the morning.

Supper Hour Certificate   This allows for an additional hour at the end of permitted hours for licensed restaurants.

Extended Hours Certificate   This is an extension for establishments which already hold a supper hours certificate and provide some form of entertainment. The extension is until 1 a.m.

Special Hours Certificate   This allows for extensions of permitted hours to premises which are licensed, hold a music and dancing licence and provide substantial refreshment. The extension can be until 3 a.m. in the West End of London and until 2 a.m. elsewhere.

Young persons   It is an offence for persons under 18 to be served in a licensed bar. It is also an offence to allow persons under 18 to consume alcoholic beverages in a bar. Similarly, it is an offence for the person under 18 to attempt to purchase or to purchase or consume alcoholic beverages in a bar. The position regarding young persons is summarized in Table 4.1.

From January 1995, the holder of an on-licence may apply to the local Licensing Committee for a Children's Certificate. The Certificate allows children to enter a bar, accompanied by adults, up to 9 p.m. There is also 30

Table 4.1 Young persons and licensed premises

Age	Purchase in a bar	Consume in a bar	Enter a bar	Purchase in a restaurant	Consume in a restaurant
Under 14	No	No	No[1]	No	Yes[2]
Under 16	No	No	Yes	No	Yes[2]
Under 18	No	No	Yes	Yes[3]	Yes

1. See note on Children Certificates in text.
2. As long as the alcoholic beverage is bought by a person over 18.
3. Beer, cider and perry only.

Note: Tobacco should not be sold to persons under 16.

minutes drinking up time. A later time may be applied for different parts of the year such as the summer months.

The certificate applies to publicans and other licensees with ordinary bars from which children under 14 are currently prohibited during permitted hours. The main requirements are that there must be 'an environment in which it is suitable for persons under fourteen to be present' and that meals and soft drinks must be available at the times when children are allowed.

This change does not, however, affect the restrictions on young persons being employed in a bar. Persons under 18 years may not be employed in a bar. However, they may be employed, as now, in licensed premises as long as it is not in a bar. Persons under 18 may therefore be employed in a restaurant for instance; where the restaurant is a place set aside for the consumption of table meals and where the drink is ancilliary to the meal. Persons under 18 years may also serve alcoholic drinks as long as the drink orders are obtained from a dispense bar.

Weights and measures

Beer and cider

Unless sold in a sealed container, beer and cider may only be sold in measures of $\frac{1}{3}$ or $\frac{1}{2}$ pint or multiples of $\frac{1}{2}$ pint. This does not apply to mixtures of two or more liquids, e.g. a shandy.

Spirits

Under an EC directive, the UK has introduced metric measures based on 25 ml. For whisky, gin, vodka and rum where these are sold by the measure, they must be sold in measures of 25 ml, 35 ml or multiples thereof. A notice must be displayed in the establishment indicating the measure that is being used. This restriction does not apply to mixtures of three or more liquids, e.g. for cocktails.

Wines

Wines sold open in carafes must be sold only in measures of 25, 50 or 75 cl or 1 litre. (The imperial measures of 10 or 20 fluid ounces ceased to be legal measures on October 1st 1995.) For wine by the glass measures are 125 ml, 175 ml or multiples thereof.

Other changes

In addition to the existing licensing provision, there are reforms being considered by government.

First, changes in the grounds on which licensing justices decide on applications which includes consideration of the suitability of the licensee, the premises and the likelihood of public nuisance or threat to public safety. This might also include taking into account the number of licences already granted for a particular area.

The second is for a new category of licence which will allow the sale of alcoholic drinks in café-style premises, without a bar counter, provided that food and non-alcoholic drinks are on sale at the same time. Again, it is considered that accompanied young people should be allowed into such places.

Alcoholic strength

"There is no longer a requirement for indicating the alcoholic strength of wine and other drinks on wine and drink lists. The alcoholic content of drinks, by volume, is now almost always shown on labels. The scale used is the Organisation Internationale Métrologie Légal (OIML) scale which is directly equal to the percentage by volume of pure alcohol in a drink at 20°C. 'Low alcohol' drinks may contain up to 1.2% of alcohol, 'de-alcoholised' must have not more than 0.5% and 'alcohol free' not more than 0.05% alcohol by volume."

Other legal requirements

In addition to the licensing requirements for the sale of alcoholic beverage note must be taken of the law regarding:

- sale of goods and trades descriptions
- discrimination
- the provision of services
- price list requirements
- health and safety
- customers property and debt
- service, cover and other minimum charges

Compiling wine and drinks lists

The wine and drinks list of an establishment are primarily a selling aid. The lists identify for the customer what is on offer, the price of the item and information on things such as the measures in which the item is to be sold.

Wine and drinks lists come in a variety of different styles usually reflecting the type of establishment. In compiling wine and drinks lists for particular establishments there are a number of factors to be taken into account. These are:

- ensuring that the overall presentation and style, including the colour scheme, are in keeping with the style of operation
- ensuring that the size and shape of the list make it easy to handle and use by both by guests and staff
- taking into account the advantages which come from a flexible design in being able to make changes as vintages change and for the inclusion of special promotions
- considering the length of time that the list will be in operation and ensuring that the list will be durable for this time

- considering the design and legibility of the lists which may include illustrations or a contents page if the list is extensive
- taking into account the information that will be provided to assist the customer as well as legal requirements
- making decisions on the actual contents of the list

Types of wine and drinks lists

The wine and drink contents of a list may include:

- non-alcoholic drinks including natural spring and mineral waters, aerated waters, squashes, juices and syrups
- cocktails including non-alcoholic cocktails
- bitters as aperitifs and for mixed drinks and cocktails
- wines including still wine, sparkling wines, alcohol-free, de-alcoholized and low-alcohol wines, fortified wines and aromatized wines
- spirits
- liqueurs
- beers including draught and packaged beers and reduced alcohol beers
- cider and perry

The order of wines and drinks on a list tends to follow the order of consumption or be grouped under types of wine or drink:

1. cocktails
2. aperitifs
3. cups
4. spirits
5. wines
6. liqueurs
7. beers, minerals and squashes

Wines are often listed by area, with the white wines of one region first followed by the red wines of that region. A more modern trend is to list all the white wines available area by area followed by the red wines arranged in a similar way. This type of layout is often more useful to the customer. However, in all wine lists sparkling wines, and therefore the champagnes, are often listed before all other wines available.

Bar and cocktail lists These may range from a basic standard list offering the common everyday aperitifs, a selection of spirits with mixers, beers and soft drinks together with a limited range of cocktails, to a very comprehensive list offering a wide choice in all areas.

Restaurant wine lists These may take the following format:

- a full and very comprehensive list of wines from all countries, but emphasis on the classic areas such as Bordeaux/Burgundy plus a fine wine/prestige selection
- a middle of the road, traditional selection, e.g. some French, German, Italian together with some 'New World' wines
- a small selection for well-known or branded wines – a prestige list
- predominantly wines of one specific country

After-meal drinks lists (*digestifs*)

- These are often combined with the wine list – although are occasionally presented as a separate liqueur list.
- The list should offer a range of liqueurs together with possibly a specialist range of brandies and/or a specialist range of malt whiskies. Vintage and LBV port may also be offered here.
- A range of speciality liqueur/spirit coffees might also be included.

Banqueting wine lists
- The length is generally according to size and style of operation.
- In most instances there is a selection of popular wine names/styles on offer.
- There would be a range of prices from house wines to some fine wines to suit all customer preferences.
- In some instances the banqueting wine will draw wines from the restaurant wine list.

Room service drinks list
- There may be a mini-bar or choice from a standard bar list.
- They usually offer a limited range of wines.

Pricing of wines and drinks

Pricing tends to be based on three basic methods of pricing.

Cost plus pricing Here, the selling price of a drink is determined by the addition of specific percentage, of the cost price, to the cost of the drink in order to achieve a predetermined percentage gross profit (gross profit = sales less the cost of sales). In practice, percentages are varied to achieve standard pricing for similar groups of products, e.g. all spirits or all minerals.

Rate of return Here, the total costs of the business are determined for a given business level and from this the percentage of the cost price required to be added to the cost price is determined in order to ensure that the business will be viable.

Market orientated   Here, selling prices are determined by considering both what the customer is likely to pay as well as what others in similar operations, locally, are charging.

In practice, a combination of these methods is used. For drinks other than wine, it is usual to find that similar products will have the same prices. This makes it easier for staff to remember prices and avoids each item having a different price. In addition, the percentage of cost prices that is added will vary in order to achieve a balance of selling prices between various items. This is to ensure that the selling prices are in line with what the customer is likely to expect. Thus, lower-cost items such as minerals tend to have a higher percentage of the cost price added to them whereas higher-cost items such as spirits have a lower percentage of the cost price added.

For wines, the simple cost plus approach tends to be used as well as various formula approaches. One such formula approach is double the cost plus. This takes the cost price of the wine, doubles it and then adds a fixed amount. The difficulty with both the cost plus and formula approaches is that the more expensive wines tend therefore to have a disproportionately higher selling price on the wine list and this does not encourage the sales of these higher-priced items.

An alternative to the cost plus and formula approaches is to recognize that the gross profit cash contribution derives from the total number of sales of an item multiplied by the cash profit that the item provides. Thus, the most profitable item is the one that gives the highest total cash contribution. In this approach, the pricing of wines achieves a potential profit irrespective of the cost price of the wine. Prices in this method are determined by adding a fixed amount to the cost price. In some cases a banding system is used where the fixed amount is increased slightly the higher the cost price of the wine. With this approach, the higher-priced wines look more attractive to the customer and this encourages sales. (Also see general notes on pricing on pp. 31–3.)

Purchasing

The objective of good purchasing is to achieve the right amount of stock, at the right quality, at the right level and at the right price. In contrast to food, beverages generally have longer shelf-lives with the exception of cask and keg beers. However, all items do have a limited life although in the case of good wines this could be several decades.

Although longer shelf-lives will mean that greater stocks can be held, the cost of storage both in fuel and space costs has to be taken into account. In addition, the holding of stock ties up capital that could be used for other purposes.

For tied house premises, where the establishment is linked to a particular brewer, the sources for purchasing beverages are determined by the brewer. It is common for brewers to own or have links or associations with specific suppliers of spirits, minerals and other drinks. In these cases, the opportunities for selective purchasing are limited.

For free house premises, the establishment can determine who they wish to buy from. Some considerations are as follows.

Using one main supplier   This has the advantage of buying from one supplier rather than many which reduces administrative costs. Deliveries will be regular and will cover all items. There are also additional benefits from the support that can be had from suppliers in producing wine and drinks lists and menu covers and from discounts that are available depending on amounts purchased. On the other hand, the range of beverages may be limiting in some way, thus reducing the potential range of beverages on offer in a particular establishment. In addition, using one main supplier can make the establishment overly dependent on that source.

Using a variety of suppliers   This has the advantage for the establishment of being able to buy to achieve a particular range of beverages on offer and reduces dependency on any one particular source. It also means that advantage can be taken of special promotions or discounts at particular times and from differing sources. Potential disadvantages are that this approach increases the number of separate deliveries, increases paperwork and can lead to inconsistencies in the range of beverages on offer.

Generally, establishments use a combination of the two approaches above: on the one hand, using one main supplier but with additional purchases coming from other sources.

Depending on the particular policy of the establishment, the buying of wines needs some further consideration. Buying for laying down and service at some future time can build up a good stock of fine wines which can, when sold, produce good profits. However, the downside is the storage and initial capital costs together with the risks that could be associated with this approach.

The costs of purchasing

There are three areas of cost associated with purchasing. These are:

1.   the costs of acquisition:
   (a) preliminary costs – for example:

(i)   preparation of specifications

(ii) supplier selection

(iii) negotiation

(b) placement costs – for example:

(i)   order preparation

(ii) stationery

(iii) postage

(iv) telephone

(c) post-placement costs – for example:

(i)   progressing

(ii) receipt of goods

(iii) inspection of goods

(iv) payment of invoices

(v)   other clerical controls

2.   the holding costs:

(a) financial costs, e.g. interest on capital tied up in inventory cost of insurance

(b) losses through deterioration, pilferage

(c) storage costs – for example:

(i)   space

(ii) handling and inspection

(iii) stores lighting

(iv) heating/refrigeration

(d) clerical costs, e.g. stores records and documentation

3.   the cost of stockouts:

(a) cost of alternatives – for example:

(i)   buying at enhanced prices

(ii) using more expensive substitutes

Determining stock levels

Stock levels may be determined by using past sales data. A formula which can also be useful is:

$$M = W(T + 1) + S$$

where M is the maximum stock, W the average usage rate, T the review period, L the lead time and S the safety stock (buffer or minimum).

An example of using this formula could be:

W = 24 bottles per week

T = 4 weeks

L = 1 week

S = 1 week's usage, i.e. 24 bottles

Therefore

$$M = 24 (4 + 1) + 24$$
$$= 144 \text{ bottles}$$

Minimum stock (buffer or safety stock) may also be calculated as follows:

$$L \times W = 1 \times 24 = 24 \text{ bottles}$$

ROL (Reorder level) may also be calculated as follows:

$$(W \times L) + S = (24 \times 1) + 24$$
$$= 48 \text{ bottles}$$

Storage and cellar management

Factors and practices which determine good cellar management are:

* Good ventilation.
* High levels of cleanliness.
* Even temperatures of 13–15 °C (55–59 °F).
* Strong draughts and wide ranges of temperatures should be avoided.
* On delivery all casks should be placed immediately upon the stillions.
* Casks remaining on the floor should have the bung uppermost to withstand the pressure better.
* Spiling should take place to reduce any excess pressure in the cask.
* Tappings should be carried out 24 hours before a cask is required.
* Pipes and engines should be cleaned at regular intervals.
* Beer left in pipes after closing time should be drawn off.
* Returned beer should be filtered back into the cask from which it came.
* Care should be taken that the cellar is not overstocked.
* All spiles removed during the service should be replaced after closing time.
* All cellar equipment should be kept scrupulously clean.
* Any ullage should be returned to the brewery as soon as possible.
* All beer lines should be cleaned weekly with a diluted pipe-cleaning fluid and the cellar floor washed down weekly with a weak solution of chloride of lime (mild bleach).

Wines should be located away from excessive heat – hot water pipes, a heating plant or hot unit. Table wines should be stored on their sides in bins so that the wine remains in contact with the cork. This keeps the cork expanded and prevents air from entering the wine – a disaster which quickly turns wine to vinegar. White, sparkling and rosé wines are kept in the coolest part of the cellar and in bins nearest the ground (because warm air rises). Red wines are best stored in the upper bins. There are also special refrigerators or cooling cabinets for keeping sparkling, white and rosé wines at serving temperature.

These may be stationed in the dispense bar – a bar located between the cellar and the restaurant – to facilitate prompt service.

Spirits, liqueurs, beers, squashes, juices and mineral waters are usually stored upright in their containers, as are fortified wines. The exceptions are port-style wines which are destined for laying down.

Beverage control

Goods received book

All deliveries should be recorded in full detail in the goods received book. Each delivery entry should show, basically, the following:

- name and address of supplier
- delivery note/invoice number
- order number
- list of items delivered
- item price
- quantity
- unit
- total price
- date of delivery
- discounts if applicable

The amount and deposit cost of all containers such as kegs, casks and the number of CO_2 cylinders delivered can also be recorded in this book or in a separate returnable containers book.

Ullage, allowance, off-sales book

Each sales point should have a suitable book for recording the amount of beer wasted in cleaning the pipes, broken bottles, measures spilt, or anything that needs a credit.

Either in the same book or in a separate one, the off-sales book, must be recorded the number of bottles, whether beer or spirits, at off-sales prices and the difference in price. This difference will be allowed against the gross profit.

Transfer book

This book is used in multi-bar units to record movement of stock between bars.

Cellar stock ledger

The cellar stock ledger (see Fig. 4.1) may be used as either an extension of, or in place of, the goods received book. It shows movement of all stock into the establishment and issues out to the bars or dispensing points. All movement of stock in and out of the cellar is normally shown at cost price.

Fig. 4.1 Stock book

Name or drink	Bin No	Opening stock	Received	Total	Closing stock	Consump- tion stock	Price per unit	£

Bin cards

Bin cards (see Fig. 4.2) are used to show the physical stock of each item held in the cellar. The movement of all stock 'in and out' of the cellar is recorded on each appropriate bin card. The bin cards are also often used to show the maximum and minimum stock.

The minimum stock determines the reordering level, leaving sufficient stock in hand to carry over until the new delivery arrives. The maximum stock indicates how much to reorder and is determined by such considerations as storage space available, turnover of a particular item and to some extent by the amount of cash available within one's budget.

Stock item		Bin No.	
Date	Received	Balance	Issued

Fig. 4.2 Heading of bin card

Requisition

Each unit dispensing alcoholic beverages should use some form of requisition to draw items from the cellar. These requisitions may be controlled either by colour or serial number, and are normally in duplicate or triplicate. The copies are sent as follows:

- top copy to the cellar
- duplicate to the beverage control department
- triplicate would be used by each unit to check its goods received from the cellar

Information listed on the requisition would be:

- name of dispensing unit
- date
- list of items required
- quantity and unit of each item required
- signature of authorized person to both order and receive the goods

The purpose of the requisition is to control the movement of items from the cellar into the dispensing unit and to avoid too much stock being taken at one time, thus overstocking the bar. The level of stock held in the bar is known as par stock. The amount ordered on the requisition, each day, should bring your stock back up to par. The amount to reorder is determined simply by taking account of the following equation: opening stock plus additions (requisition) less closing stock equals consumption (the amount to reorder, each item to the nearest whole unit).

In the outlets, as all drink is checked before issue, a daily consumption sheet (see Fig. 4.3) is completed each day after the service by copying down the sales shown on the top copy of the wine checks. This can also be done from electronic till records.

At the end of the week the consumptions are totalled up, thereby showing the total sales for that period. These totals may then be transferred on to a bar stock book for costing purposes. Where drink consumed is not checked in any way then either a daily or weekly stock is taken so that the amount to be requisitioned from the cellar may be noted. This then brings the bar stock back up to its required level, which is the par stock. The daily or weekly consumption (sales) would then be costed and the cash total for sales arrived at would be related to the daily or weekly income.

Name or drink	Bin No.	Mon	Tues	Wed	Thurs	Fri	Sat	Sun	Total

Fig. 4.3 Daily consumption sheet

Goods ordered, received and issued from the cellar

When any alcoholic or non-alcoholic drinks need to be purchased for an establishment to keep up the level of stock, this is done by the cellarman. The cellarman's order should be written in duplicate on an official order form. The top copy is then sent to the supplier and the duplicate remains in the order book for control purposes when the goods are delivered. In some instances there may be three copies of the order sheet. If so they are distributed as follows:

- top copy: supplier
- duplicate copy: control and accounts department
- third copy: remains in the order book

When the goods are delivered to an establishment they should be accompanied by either a delivery note or an invoice. Whichever document it may be, the information contained thereon should be exactly the same, with one exception: invoices show the price of all goods delivered whereas delivery notes do not. The goods delivered must first of all be counted and checked against the delivery note to ensure that all the goods listed have been delivered. An extra check may be carried out by the cellarman by checking the delivery note against the copy of the order remaining in the order book. This is to ensure that the items ordered have been sent and in the correct quantities and that extra items have not been sent which were not listed on the order sheet, thereby incurring extra cost without immediately realizing it. At this stage all information concerning the goods delivered must be entered in the necessary books for control purposes.

No drinks should be issued by the cellarman unless he receives an official requisition form, correctly filled in, dated and signed by a responsible person from the department concerned. The cellarman should have a list of such signatures and ought not to issue anything unless the requisition sheet is signed by the appropriate person on the list. In order to aid the cellarman, all requisitions should be handed into him at a set time each day, when all issues will be made. In certain instances, however, depending on the organization of an establishment, it may be necessary to issue twice per day, once before opening time in the morning and again before opening time in the evening. All requisition sheets are written in duplicate. The top copy goes to the cellar for the items required to be issued, and the duplicate remains in the requisition book for the barman to check his drink on receipt from the cellar.

Determining cost of sales

The traditional approach to determining usage, or cost of sales, is to take the value of the opening stock, add to it the value of the purchases during the period and then deduct the value of the closing stock. This value is usually the cost prices. For outlets with differing gross profit mark-ups, the issues to the various outlets are also costed at selling price to ensure that the revenue is reconciled with that expected from the issues records. This is a very laborious process.

An alternative is as follows. The beverage stock of an establishment is located in two main areas, the cellar and the outlet or outlets. The outlet stock is usually set at a par level and returned to this level at a set time. This could be each day or each week. All, for control purposes, that is really important is the cost of actual sales. Therefore, only the cost of goods issued to the outlets needs to be calculated.

For the cellar, all that is really important is the physical stock. Its actual value is only required for the end-of-year accounts. If this is true then the stock control of the cellar can be as undertaken as follows.

For each stock item, a bin card or entry in the stock book is drawn up as:

- item – the name of the item
- quantity – the stock unit, this could be a dozen, six or single
- reorder level – the level of stock at which a new order is placed; this is predetermined for all items as is the quantity of the stock to be ordered
- opening stock – in unit terms
- deliveries – in unit terms
- issues to outlets – in unit terms
- closing stock – in unit terms
- current cost price

From this record for each trading period, the cost price of issues can be determined. This is the consumption as issued from the cellar to the outlets. In addition, stock levels can be first determined from the book and then physically checked against what is actually in the cellar. The advantage of this system is that only the cost of issues needs to be calculated.

For each bar or outlet, a similar system exists. There is a par stock and each day or week this is returned to the par levels. Over a period of time it will be found that the stock value of the outlet, at selling price, will be more or less constant. Thus the cost of goods issued to this outlet, at selling price, should equal the revenue.

This approach does require predetermining the stock levels, the reorder levels and ensuring that issues to the outlets are only in whole units (single, dozen, etc.).

Summary

This chapter has considered the complexity of the legal framework within which beverages are sold and the factors which affect the compilation of wine and drinks lists. In addition, it has been suggested that pricing systems need to move away from the traditional cost plus methods, especially for wine, and that stock control systems need some careful thought.

5 Food and beverage areas and equipment

Aim   This chapter aims to outline the broad and some detailed considerations in the planning, design and equipping of food service operations.

Objective   The objective of this chapter is to enable you to:

- identify general considerations in the planning, design and equipping of food and beverage service and food production areas
- appreciate how the choice of design and equipment contributes to the customer and operational needs
- detail some of the aspects of equipment availability

General considerations

The planning and equipping of food service areas are subject to a number of considerations. These fall into five broad categories.

The market needs   The needs of the market or rather the need of the establishment to provide services to meet the determined market needs may be ascertained by working through the first three stages of the catering cycle (see pp. 1–2). These are:

1. Consideration of the potential market and the needs of the consumer.
2. The determination of policies and the business objectives, including the determination of the scope of the market needs that the operation is intended to serve.
3. The interpretation of demand which identifies the type, range and scale of the services to be provided.

Following the consideration of the first three elements, stage four of the catering cycle is the planning and design of facilities required for the food and beverage operation and the plant and equipment required.

Operational needs

Included in the consideration of the planning and design of facilities is the determination of the various operational methods that will or are to be used. This includes:

- storage methods
- production systems and methods
- service system and methods
- dining arrangements
- clearing methods
- control methods
- dishwashing methods

The consideration of these operational aspects also needs to take into account the customer usage of food and beverage service areas. This will include issues such as access to the premises and facilities such as toilets. It should also include the needs of the disabled and of children.

Space allocation and requirements

Taking into account the various considerations outlined above, Fig. 5.1 gives a rough guide to the space allocation required.

Meals	Square metres per meal served/hour		
	Up to 200	200–500	500+
Cafeteria	0.45 to 0.70	0.35 to 0.45	0.25 to 0.35
Hotels	0.35 to 1.60	0.35 to 0.70	0.35 to 0.45
Restaurants	0.35 to 0.90	0.35 to 0.45	0.30 to 0.35

Fast-food outlets

The average overall size of most fast-food outlets is currently around 1000–1500 square metres.

Restaurant and hotel dining areas

(NB Space allocation includes sideboards, aisles, etc.)

Style	Space per cover
Traditional restaurant	1 square metre
Banqueting	0.9 square metre
High-class restaurants	2 square metres

(N.B. For safety reasons all aisles should be 1 metre wide)

Production areas	
Up to 100 covers	0.5 square metre
100–1000	0.3–0.4 square metre
1000 or more	0.25 square metre

Fig. 5.1 Space allocation (chart courtesy of Croner's Catering)

Finance availability   The main financial objectives of the operations will have been considered under stage two of the catering cycle (determination of policy). Under this stage the finance available will also have been determined. Consideration will also have to be given to:

- the cost of the space to be used
- the purchasing policies, e.g. buying equipment, leasing equipment, lease/rental, new or used
- the expected life of the operation in terms of the product life cycle and therefore the expected life of the equipment

Hygiene, health and safety   The design of catering facilities must at all stages reflect the need for safe and hygienic practices.

Legislation concerning food preparation areas is not comprehensive and includes:

- The Food Hygiene Act 1970
- The Office, Shops and Railway Premises Act 1963
- The Health and Safety at Work Act 1974
- The Public Health Act 1936
- The Food Safety Act 1990

The Department of Health issues guidelines, *Cook Chill and Cook Freeze Systems* (1989) and *Health Service Catering Hygiene* (1987). The Electricity Council publishes lists of equipment approved for safety updated biannually.

The early involvement of the local environmental health officer (EHO) will reduce the risk of costly later amendments bearing in mind the legal powers of the EHO to close catering premises considered unfit for food production. The limited legislation covering food preparation areas means that very much is left to local interpretation and consultation with the EHO is strongly advised. Similarly the local fire officer should be consulted prior to any significant alterations or changes of use.

Food and beverage service areas

Food and beverage service areas fall into two categories, those for guest and staff usage and those for staff usage only. Staff and guest usage areas included consumption areas such as dining areas, service areas such as in cafeterias, bars and the associated services. Staff areas include the still-room, wash-up, storage and cellar areas.

The general considerations for staff usage areas are:

- appropriate siting and logical layout of equipment
- ease of delivery access

- ease of service
- ensuring hygiene, health and safety requirements are met
- ease of cleaning
- sufficient storage space for service equipment and food items
- security

The general considerations to staff and guest usage areas include first the general considerations for staff-only areas as above and in addition take into account the meal experience factor of atmosphere (see pp. 8–9). This includes consideration of:

- décor and lighting
- heating and ventilation
- noise
- the size and shape of the areas

Décor and lighting   The general considerations on décor are:

- appropriateness to the type and style of the operation
- sufficient flexibility especially where the space has multi-usage e.g function rooms
- functional reliability
- ease of maintenance including refurbishment
- industrial rather than domestic quality
- ease of cleaning and general housekeeping needs

For lighting and colour modern designs tend towards a versatile system of lighting by which a food and beverage service area may have bright lighting at lunchtime and a more diffused form of lighting in the evening. It is also an advantage to be able to change the colour of the lights for special functions, cabarets, etc. There are two main kinds of interior illumination – incandescent and fluorescent.

Incandescent lighting is warmer in colour but less efficient to operate than fluorescent bulbs of the same wattage. It can be easily directed to specific spots such as a particular table or painting, however its warmth appeal can cause a colour problem. It may make surroundings cheerful and inviting, but the yellowish hue of its bulbs, especially when dimmed, makes meats and lettuce appear muddy in colour. Warmer bulbs such as pink light make red meats look natural but salads unappetizing.

The main virtue of fluorescent lighting is its lower operating cost, but it is often criticized for giving a dull and lifeless illumination. Food may be made to look appealing by using blue-white light from fluorescent fixtures, but the blue-white glow may also detract from a warm atmosphere.

It is therefore felt that a balance is needed for both warmth and good food appearance. Many experts recommend a lighting system made up of 70 per cent cool or blue-white fluorescent bulbs and 30 per cent incandescent. This will give mood and a pleasant and natural appearance for food.

The average food and beverage service area needs to select the correct mix of décor and functional lighting. It is only the fast-food areas for instance that may successfully eliminate décor or mood lighting altogether. Brighter lights subconsciously tell the guests to eat more quickly and leave.

The colour scheme should assist in reflecting the character of the operation. A well-designed colour scheme can easily be spoilt by a badly planned lighting system and therefore the two aspects should be considered together at the design stage.

Heating and ventilation

There are two dimensions here. First, the maintenance of a reasonable temperature and second, the ventilation of the areas.

The temperature of food and beverage service areas will change depending on the volume of customers and how long they stay in an area. For every ten people this is equivalent to a 1 kW fire being turned on. Temperature control will therefore need to take this into account especially where customers are in dining areas for a long period such as in function operations. Temperature also has an actual and a perceived reality. Customers will have preferred locations depending on their perceptions of the heating: asking to sit by windows, for example, as this is considered a cooler part of the room, or not by doors because of suspected draughts, or not near buffets because of the heat or cold. In all these examples the actual temperature may be the same as other areas of the room.

In areas where food and beverages are served there are inevitable smells which come from these areas. It is a truism that a single food smell is generally liked, for example fresh coffee or freshly baked bread, but that a combination of food smells is usually unpleasant. In general food smells are best avoided and the ventilation systems should be able to take account of this requirement. The other aspects to take account of here are the smells that result from smoking or more specifically the drifting of smoke.

Noise

Because of equipment movement and customer and staff conversation, food and beverage service areas can be noisy. The customer expectation is that generally the higher the service level and price then the lower the noise level that will be tolerated. This is also affected by the time of day; breakfast can be more acceptably noisy than dinner. Care needs to be taken in the design and selection of materials and equipment in order to contain noise at appropriate and acceptable levels.

The other issue associated with noise is the use of background music systems. This is an area of great controversy with very clear views being expressed as to why background music systems can aid or hinder operations. In general it depends on the particular style of operations and the image that the operation is trying to project. If background systems are to be used then it is worth investing in high-quality equipment. Cheap and badly regulated equipment is distressful and fatiguing for customers.

The size and shape of the areas

Not only do the size and shape of the room affect the customers' enjoyment of the meal but also in table service areas the location of the tables becomes important.

Some issues to consider are:

- the location of tables in a food service area especially taking into account the single diner and couples
- access for those with disabilities
- ease of work flow
- evenness of temperature and ventilation
- access to exits and toilets

Food and beverage service equipment

The general points to be considered when purchasing equipment for a food and beverage service area are:

- flexibility of use
- type of service being offered
- type of customer
- design
- colour
- durability
- ease of maintenance
- stackability
- costs and funds available
- availability in the future – replacements
- storage
- rate of breakage, e.g. for china
- shape
- psychological effect on guests
- delivery time

Furniture

Furniture must be chosen according to the needs of the establishment. The type of operation being run determines the specific needs as far as the dining arrangements are concerned. A summary of possible dining arrangements is given in Table 5.1.

Very often by using different materials, designs and finishes and by careful arrangement one can change the atmosphere and appearance of the food service area to suit different occasions.

Wood is the most commonly used material in dining-room furniture. There are various types of wood and wood-grain finishes, each suitable to blend with a particular décor. Wood is strong and rigid and resists wear and stains. It is found as the principal material in chairs and tables in use in all food and beverage service areas with the exception of canteens, some staff dining-rooms and cafeterias.

Although wood predominates, more metals, mainly aluminium and aluminium-plated steel or brass, are gradually being introduced into dining-room furniture. Aluminium is lightweight and hard-wearing, has a variety of finishes, is easily cleaned and the costs are reasonable. Nowadays furniture includes a wooden-topped table with a metal base, or a chair with a light-weight metal frame and a plastic finish for the seat and back.

Formica and plastic-coated table tops may be found in many cafeterias or staff dining-rooms. These are easily cleaned, hard-wearing and eliminate the use of linen. The table top comes in a variety of colours and designs suitable for all situations. If desired, place-mats may take the place of linen.

Plastic and fibreglass are now being used extensively to produce dining-room chairs. These materials are easily moulded into a single-piece seat and

Table 5.1 Dining arrangements

Type	Description of furniture
Loose random	Free-standing furniture positioned in no discernible pattern within a given area
Loose module	Free-standing furniture positioned with a given area to a predetermined pattern with or without the use of dividers to create smaller areas within a module
Booth	Fixed seating, usually high-backed, used to create secluded seating
High density	Furniture with minimum dimensions and usually fixed in nature positioned within a given area to create maximum seating capacity
Module	Seating incorporates table and chairs constructed as one and may be fixed.
In situ	Customers served in areas not designed for service, e.g. aircraft and hospital beds
Bar and lounge areas	Customers served in areas not conventionally designed for eating

back to fit the body contours, the legs usually being made of metal. The advantages are that these are durable, easily cleaned, lightweight, may be stacked, are available in a larger range of colours and designs and are relatively inexpensive. They are more frequently found in bars, lounges and staff dining-rooms.

Consideration also needs to be given to the needs of children and the manœuvrability and stacking capability of seating especially for function operations.

With seating requirements generally there is a relationship between comfort and the time the customer will tend to spend in the seat. Thus less comfortable but adequately functional seating tends to be used in fast service operations and in higher-level service areas more comfortable seating is provided.

It is also true because of differences in physiology, women tend to sit up straighter for longer than men. Therefore chairs with arms are more useful in operations meeting the needs of a male-dominated clientele.

Trays   Trays are used throughout food service operations. Their use ranges from carrying equipment and food to service on a tray as in hospital, airline and room service operations.

Additional considerations in the purchase of trays include:

- lightness and strength – trays should be able to be carried when fully loaded and not become misshapen when weight is placed upon them
- stackability
- heat resistance
- ease of cleaning
- resistance to slippage
- resistant to damage from spilt items or damp

Tables   Tables generally come in three shapes: round, square and rectangular. An establishment may have a mixture of shapes to give variety, or tables of all one shape according to the shape of the room and the style of service being offered. These tables will seat two or four people and two tables may be pushed together to seat larger parties, luncheons, dinners, weddings, etc. By using extensions a variety of shapes may be obtained allowing full use of the room and getting the maximum number of covers in the minimum space.

Sizes

Square
- 76 cm (2 ft 6 in) square to seat two people
- 1 m (3 ft) square to seat four people

Round
- 1 m (3 ft) in diameter to seat four people
- 1.52 m (5 ft) in diameter to seat eight people

Rectangular
- 137 cm × 76 cm (4 ft 6 in × 2 ft 6 in) to seat four people to which extensions would be added for larger parties

Chairs
Chairs come in an enormous range of designs, materials and colours to suit all situations and occasions. Because of the wide range of styles, the chairs vary in height and width, but as a guide, a chair seat is 46 cm (18 in) from the ground, the height from the ground to the top of the back is 1 m (39 in) and the depth from the front edge of the seat to the back of the chair is 46 cm (18 in).

Additional purchasing considerations are the size, height, shape and the variety of seating required – banquette, armchairs, straight-backed padded chairs, giving the guest a choice.

Sideboards
The style and design of a sideboard vary from establishment to establishment. They are dependent upon:

- the style of service and the menu offered
- the number of waiters working from one sideboard or work station
- the number of tables to be served from one sideboard
- the amount of equipment it is expected to hold

The majority of commercially available sideboards are insufficient in strength of construction, storage capability and worktop provision. It is more usual for operations to design and build their own sideboards or work stations, often incorporating them as part of the design of the dining area.

Linen
There are many qualities of linen in present-day use, from the finest Irish linen and cotton to synthetic materials such as nylon and viscose. The type of linen use would depend on the class of establishment, type of clientele and cost involved and the style of menu and service to be offered. The main items of linen normally to be found are as follows.

Tablecloths
- 137 × 137 cm (54 × 54 in) to fit a table 76 cm (2 ft 6 in) square or a round table 1 m (3 ft) in diameter
- 183 × 183 cm (72 × 72 in) to fit a table 1 m (3 ft) square

- 183×244 cm (72×96 in) to fit rectangular-shaped tables
- 183×137 cm (72×54 in) to fit rectangular-shaped tables

Slipcloths
- 1×1 m (36×36 in) used to cover a 'grubby' tablecloth

Serviettes
- 46–50 cm (18–20 in) square if linen
- 36–42 cm (14–17 in) square if paper

Buffet cloths
- 2×4 m (6×12 ft) – this is a minimum size; where there are longer tables there may be longer cloths.
- Trolley cloths and sideboard cloths. These are usually made from tablecloths well worn and not suitable for use on tables, mended by the housekeeping department and folded to fit a sideboard or trolley.
- Waiter's cloth or service cloth. These are used by every waiter as protection against heat and to keep uniforms clean.
- Tea and glass cloths.

China   When purchasing china factors to consider are:

- Every item of earthenware should have a complete cover of glaze to ensure a reasonable length of life.
- China should have a rolled edge which will give added reinforcement at the edge.
- The pattern should be under rather than on top of the glaze. However, this demands additional glaze and firing. Patterns on top of the glaze will wear and discolour very quickly. Therefore, china with the pattern under the glaze is more expensive but its life will be longer.

Some manufacturers stamp the date, month and year on the base of the item. From this the life of the china, under normal usage, can be determined more accurately.

Very often earthenware produced for catering purposes is given a trade name by the manufacturer to indicate its strength. Some examples of these are:

- vitreous
- vitrock
- vitrex
- vitresso
- ironstone
- vitrified

Of these, vitrified ware is recognized to be the strongest, but this does not always mean that every caterer buys vitrified hotelware as other factors apart from strength and economy are often taken into account.

Sizes

There is a wide range of items available and their exact sizes vary according to the manufacturer and the design produced. As a guide, the sizes are as follows:

Sideplate	15 cm (6 in) diameter
Sweet plate	18 cm (7 in) diameter
Fish plate	20 cm (8 in) diameter
Soup plate	20 cm (8 in) diameter
Joint plate	25 cm (10 in) diameter
Cereal/sweet plate	13 cm (5 in) diameter
Breakfast cup and saucer	23–28 cl (8–10 fl oz)
Teacup and saucer	18.93 cl ($6\frac{2}{3}$ fl oz)
Coffee cup and saucer (*demi-tasse*)	9.47 cl ($3\frac{1}{3}$ fl oz)
Teapot	28.4 cl ($\frac{1}{2}$ pt), 56.8 cl (1 pt)
	85.2 cl ($1\frac{1}{2}$ pt), 113.6 cl (2 pt)

Other items of china required may include:

Salad crescent	Sugar basin
Hot water jugs	Butter dishes
Milk jugs	Ashtrays
Cream jugs	Egg cups
Coffee pots	Soup bowl/cup
Hot milk jugs	Platter (oval plate)
Consommé cup and saucer	

Tableware   Tableware is a term which includes:

- flatware: all forms of spoon and fork
- cutlery: knives and other cutting implements
- hollow-ware: any item made from silver, apart from flatware and cutlery, e.g. teapots, milk jugs, sugar basins, oval flats

The majority of food service areas use either plated silverware or stainless steel.

For silver the manufacturer will often quote 20-, 25-, or 30-year plate. This denotes the length of life a manufacturer may claim for the plate subject to fair or normal usage. The length of life of silver also depends upon the weight of silver deposited. There are three standard grades of silverplate – full standard plate, triple plate and quadruple plate.

British Standard BS 5577 was introduced in 1978. In silverplated tableware two grades are specified:

1. standard — for general use
2. restaurant – thicker grade for restaurant use and marked with an R

The minimum thickness of silver plating quoted should give a life of at least 20 years, depending on usage.

Plain cutlery and flatware are more popular than patterned for the simple reason that they are cheaper and easier to keep clean.

Stainless steel flatware and cutlery are available in a variety of grades. The higher-priced designs usually have incorporated in them alloys of chromium (which makes the metal stainless) and nickel (which gives a fine grain and lustre). Good British flatware and cutlery are made of 18/8 stainless steel. This is 18 per cent chromium and 8 per cent nickel. A higher grade is 18/10.

Stainless steel is finished by different degrees of polishing:

*   high polish finish
*   dull polish finish
*   a light-grey matt, non-reflective finish

Glassware   Glass also contributes to the appearance of the table and the overall attraction of the room. There are many standard patterns available to the caterer (see Table 5.2). Most manufacturers now supply hotel glassware in standard sizes for convenience of ordering, availability and quick delivery.

Table 5.2

Glass	Size
Wine goblets	14.20, 18.93, 22.72 cl (5,6⅔, 8 fl oz)
German/alsace	18, 23 cl (6, 8 fl oz)
Flute	18, 23 cl (6, 8 fl oz)
Saucer champagne	18, 23 cl (6, 8 fl oz)
Cocktail glasses	4, 7 cl (2, 3 fl oz)
Sherry, port	4.735 cl
Highball	23, 28 cl (9, 10 fl oz)
Worthington	28, 34 cl (10, 12 fl oz)
Lager glass	28, 34 cl (10, 12 fl oz)
Brandy balloon	23, 28 cl, (9, 10 fl oz)
Liqueur glass	2.367 cl
Tumbler	28.40 cl (½ pint)
Beer	25, 50 cl (½, 1 pint)

Except in certain speciality restaurants or high-class establishments, where either coloured glassware or cut glassware may be used, hotel glassware is usually plain.

A good wine glass should be plain and clear so the colour and brilliance of a wine can be clearly seen; it should have a stem for holding the wine glass so that the heat of one's hand does not affect the wine on tasting; there should be a slight incurving lip to help hold the aroma and it should be large enough to hold the particular wine being tasted.

Disposables   The choice of which disposable to use may be determined by:

1.   necessity because of situations such as:
     (a)   outdoor catering
     (b)   automatic vending
     (c)   fast food
2.   cost considerations such as:
     (a)   cost of laundry
     (b)   savings on wash-up

Types of disposable

The main varieties of disposable available are used broadly speaking in the following areas:

* storage and cooking purposes
* service of food and beverages, e.g. plates, knives, forks, cups
* décor – napkins, tablecloths, slipcloths, banquet roll, place-mats
* hygiene – wipes
* clothing, e.g. aprons, chef's hats, gloves
* packaging – for marketing and presentation purposes

A considerable advance in the range of disposable available has been the introduction of disposables whose approximation to china and tableware is very close. For instance, they may have a high quality, overall finish and a smooth hard white surface. The plates themselves are strong and rigid with no tendency to bend or buckle, and a plasticizing ingredient ensures that they are grease and moisture proof, even against hot fat and gravy. Oval luncheon plate, snack trays and compartment plates are all available to the caterer.

Advantages of disposables

* Equipment and labour: disposables reduce the need for washing-up equipment, staff and materials.
* Hygiene: usage improves the standard of hygiene in an establishment.
* Time: disposables may speed up service, e.g. for fast food.
* Properties: they have good heat retention and insulation properties.

- Marketing: disposables can be used as a promotional aid.
- Capital: usage reduces the amount of capital investment.
- Carriage: they are easily transported.
- Cost: disposables are cheaper than hiring conventional equipment.

Disadvantages of disposables

- Acceptability: customer acceptability may be poor.
- Cost: disposables can be more expensive than some conventional equipment.
- Storage: back-up quantities are required.
- Supply: there is heavy reliance on supply and delivery time.

Bar areas

There are certain essentials necessary in the planning of bars. These are detailed as follows.

Area The bar staff must be given sufficient area of space in which to work and move about. There should be a minimum of 1 m from the back of the bar counter to the storage shelves and display cabinets at the rear of the bar.

Layout Careful consideration must be given, in the initial planning, to the layout. Everything should be easily to hand so that the bar staff do not have to move about more than necessary.

Plumbing and power It is essential to have hot and cold running water for glass washing. Power is necessary to provide the effective working of cooling trays, refrigerators and ice-making machines.

Storage Adequate storage should be provided, in the form or shelves, cupboard and racks, for all the stock required and equipment listed.

Safety and hygiene Great care must be observed so that the materials used in the make-up of the bar are hygienic and safe. Flooring must be non-slip. The bar top should be of a material suited to the general décor that is hard-wearing, easily wiped down and has no sharp edges. The bar top is usually of average working height – of at least 1 m (3 ft) and a width of 0.6 m (20 in).

For the purpose of the Food Hygiene Regulations, drink is food. However, special exemptions are given to some of the provisions provided that only drink (i.e. beers, spirits, liqueurs and such like) is dispensed.

Some aspects of the provisions should be given particular attention. These are:

- suitable overclothing
- possible contamination through smoking when handling food and drink
- inadequate glass-washing facilities together with the important process of glass drying
- use of 'spillage' and possibility of contamination
- correct use of materials in bar design to facilitate easy cleaning

Automatic vending

In the broadest sense, automatic vending may be defined as 'selling by automation'. It is a form of automatic retailing using one of the following:

- coin
- token
- banknote
- moneycard

The types of service available may be broken down into two areas, namely service and facilities and consumables (Table 5.3).

Within a catering framework 'automatic vending' refers to the supply of a wide range of beverages, both hot and cold, through coin/token-operated machines.

Table 5.3

Service and facilities	Consumables
TV time	Hot and cold beverages
Gas	Meals
Water	Confectionery
Electricity	Tobacco
Shoe cleaning	Alcoholic drinks
Car parking	
Toilets	
Baggage store	

Types of machine

Merchandiser

This sells its product as seen visually by the customer, e.g. confectionary machines.

Beverage vendor

This mixes the ingredients in individual cups to which water is added.

In-cup system

The ingredients are already in individual cups to which water is added.

Micro-vend system

This provides a range of hot foods from which the customer may make a selection.

Catering services

The catering services provided may come in the form of:

- hot beverages: by use of powdered ingredients
- cold beverages: by use of post-mix syrup and water (carbonated or non-carbonated)
- hot meals: by internal heating or with the use of microwaves and time cards/tokens
- meals and snacks: by means of refrigeration

The numbers and types of machines required will depend on their location, the type and number of people they are providing a service for, the cost factor and the variety of food and beverage items required.

The machines required may be installed either individually or in small groups, to supplement the conventional catering establishment or to cover a small-scale demand that does not warrant the expense of employing the extra labour and plant. The opposite to this would be the installation of a complete vending service where demand is highly volatile, space is limited and the use of staffed operations would be uneconomical.

Purchasing considerations

General factors which should be considered prior to purchasing and in relation to vending equipment may be summarized as follows:

- Cup sales: may be one to two drinks per person per day when charged but could double if offered free.
- Ingredient capacity: related to required periods of restocking.
- Number of selectors (items) available: this will often relate to the demand (anticipated number of customers).
- Hygiene: ease of cleaning.
- Extraction efficiency: for heat/steam systems.
- Restocking: ease of filling.

- Maintenance: regular servicing contract.
- Physical dimensions/acceptability: will the machine fit into the environment and blend in with the décor?
- Siting: as close as is feasible to those using the machine – that is, either on the work floor or in a food service area so as to maximize use.
- Weight (floor loading): ease of moving for cleaning and siting purposes.
- Availability: of power and plumbing.
- Capital available: should the machine be leased, purchased or taken on a contract basis?
- Training: can staff be trained easily to replenish, clean and maintain machines?
- Policy: there must be clear guidelines linked to failure of a machine and insurance cover.

Food production areas

Factors which influence kitchen planning and design are:

- the size and extent of the menu and the market it serves
- services – gas, electricity and water
- labour, level of skills of people
- amount of capital expenditure, costs
- use of prepared convenience foods
- types of equipment available
- hygiene and the Food Safety Act of 1990/91
- design and décor
- multi-usage requirements

Design of the kitchen   The size and space of the kitchen should enable the staff to be able to work safely, efficiently, speedily and in comfort. The aim when planning a kitchen is for food to be prepared and served without waste of both time and effort. Therefore, layout design must consider working methods which improve productivity and utilize equipment to reduce labour. The main considerations are:

- to design an efficient work flow
- provide adequate work space
- create appropriate sections
- . ensure access to ancillary areas
- determine number, type and size of equipment
- consider ease of supervision

Kitchens must be designed so that they can be easily managed. The management must have easy access to the areas under their control and have good visibility in the areas which have to be supervised.

Workflow	Food preparation rooms should be planned to allow a 'work flow' whereby food is processed through the premises from the point of delivery to the point of sale or service with the minimum of obstruction. The various processes should be separated as far as possible and food intended for sales should not cross paths with waste food or refuse. Staff time is valuable and a design which reduces wasteful journeys is both efficient and cost-effective. The overall sequence of receiving, storing, preparing, holding, serving and clearing needs to be achieved by:

- minimum movement
- minimal backtracking
- maximum use of space
- maximum use of equipment with minimum expenditure of time and effort

Work space	Approximately 4.2 sq m (45 sq ft) is required per person; too little space can cause staff to work in close proximity to stoves, steamers, cutting blades, mixers, etc. which creates the potential for accidents. Aisle space of approximately 1.37 m ($4\frac{1}{2}$ ft) is desirable as aisles must be adequate to enable staff to move safely. The working area must also be suitably lit and ventilated with extractor fans to remove heat, fumes and smells.

Working sections	The size and style of the menu and the ability of the staff will determine the number of sections and layout that are necessary. A straight line layout would be suitable for a snack bar while an island layout would be more suitable for a hotel restaurant.

Access to ancillary areas	A good receiving area needs to be designed for bringing in supplies easily, with nearby storage facilities suitably sited for distribution of foods to preparation and production areas.
	Hygienic considerations must be planned so that kitchen equipment is cleaned and all used equipment from the dining area is cleared, cleaned and stored. Still-room facilities may also be required.

Preparation surfaces	The choice of surfaces on which food is to be prepared is vitally important. Failure to ensure a suitable material may provide a dangerous breeding ground for bacteria. Stainless steel tables are the best, as they do not rust and their welded seams eliminate unwanted cracks and open joints. Sealed tubular legs are preferable to angular ones because again they eliminate corners in which dirt collects. Tubular legs have often been found to provide a harbourage for pests.

Preparation surfaces should be:

- jointless
- durable
- impervious
- of the correct height
- firm based

Surfaces must withstand repeated cleaning at the required temperature without premature deterioration through pitting and corrosion.

General considerations are:

- Water absorbency: softwoods draw fluids into them and with the fluids bacteria are also drawn in.
- Resistance to stains, cleaning chemicals, heat and food acids.
- Toxicity: the cutting board must not give off toxic substances.
- Durability: the cutting board must withstand wear and tear.
- All cutting boards must not split or warp.

The argument for wood against plastic

Wooden cutting boards made of hardwood if cleaned and sterilized are perfectly acceptable in catering premises.

Appearance can be deceptive. Dean Cliver and Afese Ak (as reported in *The Economist*, 1992), two researchers at the University of Wisconsin, Madison, set out ways of decontaminating wooden kitchen surfaces and ended up finding that such surfaces are pretty good at decontaminating themselves. When working with wood from nine different species of tree and four sorts of plastic, the results were always the same. They spread salmonella, listeria and *Escherichia coli* over the various samples and left them there for 3 minutes. The level of bacteria on the plastic remained the same, while the level on the wood plummeted often by as much as 99.9 per cent. Left overnight at room temperature the bacteria on the plastic actually multiplied, while the wooden surfaces cleaned themselves so thoroughly that nothing could be recorded from them.

Plants have spent millions of years fighting off bacteria. Trees live longer than plants and animals. Even when the tree is dead, its wood can remain for decades, resisting the attacks of micro-organisms.

The argument in favour of wood is based on the porous structure of the wood which was previously thought to be a disadvantage in soaking up the fluid with the bacteria in it. Once inside, the bacteria stick to the wood's fibres and they are 'strangled' by one of the many noxious antimicrobial chemicals with which living trees protect themselves.

Colour coding To avoid cross-contamination, it is important that the same equipment is not used for handling raw and high-risk products without being disinfected. To prevent the inadvertent use of equipment for raw and high-risk foods, it is recommended that, where possible, different colours and shapes are used to identify products or raw materials used. For example:

- red – raw meat
- blue – raw fish
- brown – cooked meats
- green – vegetables
- white – general purpose
- yellow – sandwiches

Fixing and siting of equipment

Where practicable, equipment should be mobile to facilitate its removal for cleaning, ideally castor-mounted with brakes on all the wheels.

Pipework and equipment directly above open food should not expose the food to any risk of contamination from dirty condensation, rust or flaking paint.

Gas and electrical supply pipes should be flexible and capable of being disconnected. In the case of gas supply the coupling to the mains must incorporate a self-sealing valve and a shut-off cock immediately upstream of the fitting. The flexible tube must conform to the Gas Board specifications and the appliances must be secured to a fixed point by a strong detached wire or chain, shorter in length than the tube to avoid accidental stretching.

Machinery must be mounted on covered raised platforms of concrete to facilitate cleaning. The bases and lower parts of machines, including motors and gears, may be difficult to clean and consequently collect dust and spillages which make ideal breeding sites for pests. In such circumstances the bases should be completely sealed. Skirting or cover plates tend to trap dust.

Stationary equipment

For planning purposes stationary equipment must be:

- 500 mm from the walls
- 250 mm clearance between the floor and underside of the equipment

to allow for the cleaning of wall and floor surfaces. Alternatively, the machines should be fixed firmly to the floor without a gap. However, the design must avoid narrow areas or angles in contact with the floor.

Electrical equipment, such as motors and switches, do pose problems for cleaning. Such equipment must always be earthed and capable of removal without tools prior to cleaning the main equipment. Ideally motors should be sited outside food rooms, to reduce cleaning problems. Any trailing wires and cables must be avoided.

When pipework is installed, consideration must be given to future cleaning. There must be sufficient space left between the pipes and the floor or the wall to allow access for easy cleaning. Pipes may also be built into the walls. When pipes are lagged an impervious cleansable finish is required.

Guards on machinery which are required under health and safety legislation, should be capable of being thoroughly cleaned and where necessary removed quickly and easily without the use of special tools.

Newly built premises should comply fully with the requirements of the appropriate hygiene and safety legislation. Plans should be discussed with the enforcement officers as it is much easier and cheaper to provide satisfactory finishes and facilities.

The use of satisfactory building materials and a well-planned layout is essential to achieve high standards of hygiene. The size of the premises must be adequate to allow efficient operation and the site must be large enough to accommodate possible future expansion, if this is a management objective.

Building fabric   Considerations for design are as follows.

Ceilings

The choice of materials for ceilings presents problems because kitchen ceilings are exposed to extreme temperature, fumes and steam and are not readily accessible for cleaning. All surfaces including ceilings must be capable of being thoroughly cleaned and have smooth continuous surfaces. Ceilings may be suspended or solid, as detailed below.

Suspended
- Suspended ceilings cover horizontal pipework and services are concealed.
- Access should be built for inspection of pest control and to allow for maintenance.
- Structural walkways are often necessary and should always be provided in large premises.
- These can be of various materials but they are normally made of metal lattice, incorporating cleansable panels. Aluminium backed and faced fibreboard.
- Flush fitting ventilation grills should also be provided.

Solid
- These give less scope for hygienic finish.
- These should be well insulated to avoid condensation and mould growth.

Ceilings should be:
- smooth
- fire-resistant

- light in colour
- covering wall joints
- easy to clean

The ceiling height must provide a satisfactory working condition and allow for the installation of equipment. A ceiling height of 3–3.6 m (10–12 ft) will not only ensure that the ceiling is accessible for cleaning but will also mean that extremes of temperatures are unlikely to arise.

Walls

Walls must as a general rule be:

- smooth
- impervious
- non-flaking
- light of colour
- capable of being thoroughly cleaned and if necessary disinfected
- solid (as those with cavities may harbour pests)
- free of crevices and ledges which cause cleaning problems

False panelling should not be used.

Wall surfaces

- resin-bonded fibre glass
- ceramic faced blocks
- glazed tiles (with water-resistant grouting)
- stainless steel
- plastic sheeting
- polypropylene

Depending on the operation, surfaces adjacent to walls surface may need to be resistant to:

- spillages
- chemicals
- grease
- heat
- impact

Stainless steel splash-backs for sinks and working surfaces are advisable. Use wall and floor stops to prevent damage to wall surfaces. Wall corners are usually made of non-corrosive metals or PVC. Also stainless steel is now used. Crash rails are also placed along walls where there is a high volume of traffic to avoid trolleys damaging wall surfaces.

Pipework and ducting should be bracketed at least 150 mm from walls to facilitate cleaning. All lagging on pipes must be smooth and impervious.

Pipes passing through external walls must be effectively sealed to prevent the ingress of pests.

Doors, windows, stairs and platforms

Doors, windows, stairs and platforms must be designed to prevent the accumulation of dirt and to facilitate easy cleaning. These areas do allow the entry of insects, dirt, dust and contamination.

- Windows should be in north-facing walls to reduce glare and solar heat gains. Solar film on windows will assist in counteracting heat.
- Cleansable fly screens must be fitted to opening windows.
- Windows must be constructed from an uncomplicated design to facilitate cleaning.
- Internal window sills should be sloped to prevent their use as shelves.
- The design of frames and windows and doors should avoid acute angles. Right-angled joints between frames and walls should be beaded and filled to form smooth continuous surfaces.
- All woodwork should be well seasoned, properly knotted, stopped, primed and given three coats of polyurethane paint.

Doors

These must be:

- smooth
- made of non-absorbent surfaces
- capable of being thoroughly cleaned
- tight-fitting
- self-closing
- fitted with finger plates if necessary

External doorways should:

- be proofed against entry of insects
- have metal kick-plates to prevent gnawing of rodents

Doorways

These must be large enough to allow for the movement of mobile equipment and possible replacement of fixed equipment.

Swing doors which open both ways should be fitted with sight panels.

Stairs, ladders and platforms must be capable of being thoroughly cleaned and should not expose food to risk of contamination.

Floor

The basic rule is that floors should be smooth, impervious and capable of being readily cleaned. When selecting a floor covering, the following criteria should be considered:

- the volume and nature of traffic
- whether the area is wet or dry
- how the area will be cleaned
- what chemical resistance is necessary
- whether production will need to be curtailed to effect repairs to the floor
- the type of subfloor

The manager/owner of the establishment must assess the cost-effectiveness of a finish. The following must be considered:

- initial cost
- durability
- performance
- safety

Floors should be:

- durable
- non-absorbent
- anti-slip
- without crevices
- capable of being effectively cleaned
- resistant to acids, grease and salts
- sloping to allow liquids to drain to trapped gulleys (a slope of 1 in 60 is the minimum recommendation).

The angle between walls and floors should be level.

Types of floor coverings
- epoxy resin
- granolithic
- welded anti-slip vinyl sheet
- anti-slip ceramic or quarry tiles

Screed systems   A magnesium oxychloride formulation is incombustible and will not support bacterial growth or allow surface contamination by grease.

Resins are available as coatings – a thin-layer screed put on to a heavy-duty screed. A thin-layer screed is 4–10 mm. A heavy-duty screed is used as an underlay and as a finished floor surface. These range in depth from 10 to 35 mm.

Resins which are typically used for flooring are:

- epoxies
- acrylics
- polyurethanes

Epoxy resins have the widest applications as they have excellent binding properties and good general resistance to floor damage, acids, alkalines, etc. They can also be solvent-free meaning that there is a minimal risk of tainting nearby materials.

Water supplies

Cold water supplies used for washing in addition to food should be mains supplied and should not be fed via an intermediate trunk, unless chlorinated.

The soteriological (life-supporting) and chemical quality of the water must be checked at frequent intervals to ensure that the water will not contaminate the product. Water companies are legally required to check the mains water continuously.

Hot water

This should be supplied to every sink with a discharge temperature of 60 °C.

In hard water areas, hot water supplies should be softened, otherwise scale build-up will cause cleaning and operations problems and add significantly to detergent usage.

Drainage

Drainage in any catering establishment must be efficient with smooth clear drainage which is continuously cleaned in good order and repair. The drainage system must be adequate to remove peak loads quickly without flooding. Sufficient drains should be installed to facilitate effective cleaning of rooms by pressure jet cleaners or by other means of cleaning.

It is advisable to use shallow, glazed half-round floor channels for uncovered drainage providing they do not expose a risk to health and safety. If covers have to be used they should be made of non-corrosive material, continuous, strong and easily removed for cleaning.

Grease traps

These should be fitted outside of food areas so as to avoid possible contamination of food and food surfaces during cleaning. All inspection chambers should also be placed outside of food rooms.

Manholes

These should be double sealed, bedded in silicon grease and screwed down with brass screws.

Drainage systems

They must have sufficient access points to allow rodding in the event of blockages.

Potato peelers and dishwashers

If connected directly to the drainage system, they should be trapped to avoid waste pipes acting as vents for sewers.

Water pipes

These should preferably be made of plastic, screw or push-fit connections to enable easy dismantling to ease blockages.

Guide to the care of drains

- Drains should be cleaned and degreased regularly.
- Construction should inhibit the harbourage and movement of vermin.
- Defective drains may result in effluent foul odours and rodents entering into food rooms.
- All external rainwater fall pipes should be fitted with balloon guards to deter rodents.
- Circumference guards should be fitted around vertical drainpipes fastening them to walls, to prevent the rodents climbing up them.

Ventilation   Ventilation is a process which provides an effective supply of clean fresh air generally from the outside. It is basically dependent upon the movement or circulation of air at a sufficient rate, to ensure that moist, stale air is removed at regular intervals.

Adequate ventilation is essential in any food establishment in order to create a comfortable working environment. In doing so ventilation must prevent:

- excessive heat
- condensation
- dust
- steam
- odours
- contaminated air

Good ventilation will assist in:

- reducing grease
- reducing staining of ceilings

A kitchen will require approximately 10–20 changes per hour, depending on the production needs of the kitchen. Many busy kitchens with high-volume production require 30 changes per hour. Those with specialist equipment such as tandoori ovens, require 60 changes per hour.

Ventilation can be achieved either naturally or artificially. Natural ventilation is supplied through windows and doors. Open windows cause problems as they allow the entry of dust and insects and in some cases birds. Because of this, windows should be covered by perforated gauze; this does prevent additional cleaning problems. Although a kitchen may have sufficient windows, they may not be positioned to give the most effective circulation when open. Constant opening and closing by food handlers cause hazards as hands become contaminated. Nearly all kitchens, therefore, require mechanical ventilation especially those in a basement or enclosed within a building.

Expert advice is needed in deciding which type of ventilation is best suited for the premises. Initial costs for ventilation are normally high, this cost depreciates over 15–20 years.

The simplest system is an electric extractor fan fitted into an external wall or window operated by either a cord or switch. The positioning of the fan is of prime importance; it should be placed so that it picks up the majority of fumes from the kitchen. Externally it should not discharge at the face level of passers-by or where it might carry to other rooms.

Apart from creating a circulation and renewal of the total air within a kitchen, particular attention must be given to the sources of heat, fumes or steam. Equipment such as stoves, boilers, steamers, fryers and bratt pans, release large volumes of heat and fumes into the atmosphere. Special provision must be built in to control these effluvia. The simplest way is to have a hood above the equipment to collect the fumes via a duct, which leads to the outside. The ducting should have a fan which creates an air current away from the source and a filter arrangement to arrest the majority of heavy materials, such as grease particles. The fan is normally situated well away from the source of heat to prevent damage to the motor. The filter is nearer the source, in order to absorb as much grease and dirt as possible to prevent any build-up in the ducting.

Permission for ducting outside the building must be granted by the local planning office and the EHO.

Cooking smells can be a nuisance in some establishments but actively encouraged in others. If the smells have to be removed, the best way is to install an activated carbon filter. These still need residual deposits of grease, dust, etc. to be removed. Some odours can be dealt with by installing an oxidizer. The effectiveness of oxidizers depends on the type and extent of the odour.

Modern buildings are often equipped with air conditioning which provides a balanced system of purified air in each part of the building and a separated ducted extraction of stale air.

As ventilation is a specialist subject always consult a ventilation engineer.

Hygiene of ventilation and water systems

Clean air and safe water are vital for a pleasant working environment and hygienic food production.

Risk of infection can be due to failure to carry out routine maintenance and cleaning of ductwork, pipes and cooling towers. This leads to what is commonly known as the sick building syndrome. Symptoms are as follows:

* dry throat
* sore eyes
* dry nose

- drowsiness
- humidifier fever (caused by poor ventilation and humidity)
- raised temperature
- respiratory problems
- headaches

Lighting   Premises should take full advantage of natural lighting through large, well-placed windows. In addition efficient, artificial lighting is always required in food production areas for the following reasons:

- to enable staff to work in an agreeable working environment
- to facilitate cleaning
- to prevent accidents
- to prevent eye strain
- to discourage insects and rodents as these normally shun well-lit areas

Adequate lighting is also essential in passageways, storerooms, stairs and in areas outside the building where staff need to go, such as refuse areas and delivery bays. Wall and ceiling finishes should be chosen to enhance available light by using light-reflecting colours.

The number and capacity of lights required in any establishment will depend on the size of the area to be illuminated. From a working point of view a number of independent lights, positioned over those areas where staff work, are preferable to fewer larger wattage lights, which need positioning fairly high to spread the light and which may well lose intensity and cause shadows in the process.

Fluorescent lights give a more efficient light than traditional bulbs. Both tubes and shades can be selected to give the most agreeable light, without glare, to those working on the premises. Tubes also have a longer life and are cheaper to run than tungsten filament bulbs.

All light fittings should be of simple design and preferably flush with the ceiling or wall to assist in cleaning. Press button or recessed switches should be avoided as they encourage the build-up of food deposits.

Electrical fittings situated near sinks, cooking ranges and refrigerators should be sealed to keep out moisture and should be made of rubber, plastic or rustproof metal. Wiring should be laid in conduit and, where possible, chased into the wall to avoid unnecessary dust traps.

In large kitchens it may be preferable to have individual or groups of lights, operated by separate switches. This gives greater flexibility and reduction in electricity, and also eliminates the need to have a larger cluster of switches which may become difficult to clean.

Refuse storage   Refuse containers must be situated outside the building preferably in a covered but not totally enclosed area.

Refuse can be divided into two types:

1.   dry waste – paper, cardboard boxes
2.   Wet waste – food and kitchen debris

The best type of container for wet waste is either metal or plastic bins with a tight-fitting lid which keeps out flies and insects.

The storage and disposal of waste

1.   Refuse must not be allowed to accumulate in food rooms and should not be left overnight.
2.   Waste may be stored in strong polythene bags and removed at the end of the working day. The stands for the bags must be maintained in a clean condition.
3.   Staff must be trained to:
      (a)   clean as they go
      (b)   replace lids
      (c)   wash their hands after receptacles are used
      (d)   not overfill sinks
      (e)   to tie full sacks to prevent problems from insects
      (f)   prevent refuse collectors from entering food rooms or dining areas
      (g)   keep waste food separate from paper and cardboard
4.   Where possible food waste should be stored under refrigeration.
5.   Food waste should be removed from food premises daily.
6.   The number and type of receptacles used will depend on:
      (a)   the type and quantity of waste
      (b)   the frequency of collections
      (c)   the access available for the refuse vehicle
7.   Dustbins should be stored clear of the ground on tubular steel racks to facilitate cleaning and removal of spillages.
8.   All receptacles should be capable of being cleaned and have tight-fitting lids to prevent insects, birds and rodents gaining access.
9.   The refuse area must be well drained, and have an impervious surface which is capable of being cleaned.
10.   Standpipes, hoses and high-pressure sprays should be provided for cleaning purposes.
11.   The receptacles and refuse area must be thoroughly cleaned after emptying.
12.   Refuse areas must not be too far from the food rooms so they discourage their use, nor should they be too close and encourage flies entering the food rooms.

Refuse compaction

•   A well-run compaction system improves hygiene.
•   Cleaning of refuse areas is also easier and spillages are reduced.

- The capital cost of refuse compactors must be compared against collection charges, cleaning and pest control.

Sanitary disposal

- The law requires that suitable hygiene provision is made for the disposal of sanitary dressing, where an establishment employs ten women or more.
- Customer welfare must be considered when selecting a method of disposal.
- A regular contract service is now available, which uses specially designed containers placed in WC cubicles to afford privacy. These are regularly collected and replaced by fresh, sterilized containers. The contractor is responsible for the safe disposal of the contents away from the customer's premises.
- Contractors should be asked to undertake a survey to establish the optimum number of sanitary towel dispensers, rate of replenishment and the number and siting of disposal units.

Accommodation for staff

Good clean accommodation for staff is essential, if they are to be encouraged to work cleanly and hygienically. If clean conditions are provided and kept clean for staff they will be encouraged to take ownership of the working practices necessary to provide an ideal hygienic working environment. This is a necessary step in total quality management.

The accommodation must be readily accessible to staff and while in smaller premises where only one or two are employed, a single lavatory may suffice, in larger premises involving numbers of employees, it will be necessary to have separate accommodation for each sex, which should be situated at each floor level.

Adequate accommodation must be provided for outdoor and other clothing and footwear not worn by the staff during working hours. These articles of clothing must not be stored in a food room and therefore, must be stored in separate lockers allocated to each member of staff.

It is advisable that a separate room be designated as a cloakroom so that clothes can be stored conveniently. Adequate washing facilities should be provided in the cloakroom, to encourage staff to wash their hands frequently and to reinforce personal hygiene.

Sanitary conveniences

Sanitary accommodation must be clean, well lit and in efficient working order. The walls, floors and ceilings must be smooth impervious surfaces capable to being easily cleaned.

All water closets and urinals must:

- Be separately ventilated to the exterior or if artificially ventilated then they should be provided at six changes per hour.
- Be entered from an intervening space, separately ventilated to the external air – they must not be entered direct from a food room or work room.
- Have foot- or knee-operated devices if possible, or light-sensitive devices.
- Have doors to intervening space; doors to sanitary accommodation should be self-closing.
- Have notices posted telling users to wash their hands in the appropriate languages, according to the profile of the employees – always in English but often supplementary languages are requested.
- Have one wash hand basin for each WC or three urinals.

Cleaning and disinfecting facilities

Within the kitchen design there must be the following:

- Adequate facilities for cleaning and disinfection of utensils and equipment must be provided.
- They should be constructed of corrosion-resistant materials such as stainless steel which is capable of being thoroughly cleaned.
- Sinks must have adequate supplies of hot and cold water.
- Taps should be wall mounted with no direct connections to sinks for easy cleaning.
- Waste pipes should be of plastic push-fit ware.
- The sink should be free-standing so that it can be removed easily after unscrewing the trap joint and easing free the waste pipe.
- Sterilizing sinks, the rinse of dishwashing and tray cleaning machines should operate at 82 °C for sterilization purposes.

Washing facilities

The kitchen and food premises must have adequate facilities for hand washing and drying in all areas of the kitchen where food processing, preparation and handling are carried out:

- Wash hand basins must be located in such a way that they are easily accessible and encourage hand washing. They should never be obstructed.
- They must always be kept clean and maintained in a good condition.
- A minimum of two wash hand basins should be fitted in premises where both raw and high-risk foods are handled.
- Washing facilities provided in food rooms should be additional to those in conjunction with sanitary conditions.
- All basins and troughs should be preferably made of stainless steel and connected to drains by properly trapped waste pipes.

Food production equipment

The type, amount and size of equipment will depend on the type of menu being provided. Not only should the equipment be suitably situated but the working height is very important to enable the equipment to be used without causing excess fatigue. Kitchen equipment manufacturers and gas and electricity suppliers can provide details of equipment relating to output and size.

The various preparation processes require different types for consideration depending on what food is involved. A vegetable preparation area means that water from the sinks and dirt from the vegetables are going to accumulate and therefore adequate facilities for drainage should be provided. Pastry preparation alternatively entails mainly dry processes.

Whatever the processes, there are certain basic rules that can be applied which not only make for easier working conditions but which help to ensure that the food hygiene regulations are complied with.

Kitchens can be divided into sections, based on the production process:

Dry areas	Stores, storage
Wet areas	Fish preparation, vegetable preparation, butchery, cold preparation
Hot wet areas *Equipment*	Boiling, poaching, steaming Atmospheric steamers, pressure steamers, combination oven, bratt pans, steam-jacketed boilers
Hot dry areas *Equipment*	Frying, roasting, grilling Cool zone fryers, pressure fryers, bratt pans, roasting ovens, charcoal grills, salamanders, induction cookers, halogen cookers, microwave, cook and hold ovens
Dirty areas *Equipment*	Refuse, pot wash areas, plate wash Compactors, refuse storage units, pot wash machines, dishwashers, glass washers

Consideration must be given to the management policy on buying raw materials. Choice will determine kitchen plans on handling raw materials.

Prepared food will require different types of equipment and labour requirements compared with part-prepared food or raw state ingredients. Prepared food examples:

- sous-vide products
- cook–chill
- cook–freeze
- prepared sweets

Part prepared:

- peeled and cut vegetables
- convenience sauces and soups
- portioned fish/meat

Raw state:

- unprepared vegetables
- meat which requires butchering
- fish requiring filleting and portioning

The choice of layout A selection of equipment will be made after detailed consideration of:

- The functions that will be carried out within the cooking area of the kitchen.
- The amount of equipment which will depend upon the complexity of the menus offered.
- The quantity of meals served.
- The policy of management in use of materials from the traditional kitchen organization using only fresh vegetables and totally unprepared items, to the use of prepared foods, chilled items, frozen foods, where the kitchen consists of a regeneration unit only.

Given, however, that a certain amount of equipment is required, the planner has the choice of a number of possible layouts, within the constraints of the building shape and size and the location of services. The most common are the island groupings, wall siting and the use of an L- or U-shaped layout and variations upon these basic themes.

Equipment design There is no UK standard for equipment design. The EHOs, the Food Manufacturers' Foundation and the Process Plant Association have drafted the following six principles of design:

1. All surfaces in contact with food should be inert and the food and constituents from their surfaces must not migrate into the food or be absorbed by the food in quantities that could endanger health.
2. All surfaces in contact with food should be smooth and non-porous so that particles of food, bacteria or insect eggs are not caught in microscopic cracks, thus becoming a potential source of contamination.
3. Equipment should be so designed that all surfaces in contact with food can be properly cleaned.
4. The design must allow for the easy dismantling of the relevant parts for manual cleaning.
5. Equipment should be so designed to protect the contents from external

contamination including accidental ingress of foreign matter, for example bolts, nuts, washers and gaskets.

6.   The exterior of non-product contact surfaces should be arranged to prevent harbouring of soils, bacteria or pests in and on the equipment.

Construction materials must be: non-toxic, non-flaking, corrosion-resistant, durable, resistant to heat and resistant to acids. Food contact surfaces should be:

- easy to clean
- smooth and continuous surfaces without breaks, cracks, open seams, chips or pitting. It is extremely difficult to clean internal corners and crevices.

Unless designed for cleaning in place, all food contact surfaces must be accessible for cleaning and inspection by easy methods of dismantling.

Equipment containing bearings and gears which require unsafe lubricants should be designed and constructed so that the lubricant used cannot leak or drip or be forced into the food or on to food contact surfaces. Only safe lubricants should be used on equipment designed to receive lubrication of bearings and gears in or within food contact surfaces.

Food contact surfaces need regular disinfection therefore care must be taken in selecting materials used for these surfaces. Stainless steel is recommended (the best available is 18/8 stainless steel: 18 per cent chromium, 8 per cent nickel).

Small items of equipment, for example knife handles and brushes, should be made of cleanable materials. Care must be taken in dealing with equipment made of copper, zinc or cadmium. These metals are absorbed by acid food and may cause metallic food poisoning.

Design and construction of equipment

Equipment must be so designed, constructed and finished that it can be easily cleaned and disinfected, safely, thoroughly and rapidly, without the need for skilled fitters or specialized tools.

Equipment such as gravity feed slicers, mixers, processors, etc. which do require dismantling for cleaning must be easy to take apart and reassemble. All edges must be smooth and rounded. Rough and sharp edges constitute a serious hazard to cleaners. If equipment is difficult to dismantle because of poor design and may result in a danger to operatives, it will mean that those responsible for cleaning will be reluctant to clean it. This results in a lowering of hygiene standards and possible health risks.

The buyer of the equipment should also observe that all joints and welds are smooth, and that nuts, bolts and screw heads are absent from food contact surfaces. All hinges should be capable of being taken apart for cleaning. No crevices in fitting panels, open joints and rough seams should be present in the equipment, if any of these are, they have a tendency to become filled with accumulations of food, grease and dirt which in turn will support bacterial growth and may then provide a food source for pest infestation.

Summary

This chapter has considered the broad and some detailed considerations in the planning, design and equipping of food service operations. The broad considerations take into account the market needs, the operational needs, the space allocation requirements, finance availability and hygiene health and safety matters. The detailed considerations have demonstrated how the choice of design and equipment needs to make a contribution both to the customer needs in terms of the whole meal experience and the operational needs of being able to provide customer services.

Reference

Looks Could Kill *The Economist* 13th February 1992

6 Food and beverage service

Aim This chapter considers various aspects in the management of food and beverage service.

Objective The objective of this chapter is to enable you to:

- develop your understanding of the service processes
- consider how operational choices in food and beverage service can affect resource productivity
- increase your awareness of food and beverage service management issues
- develop approaches to the management of the volume of demand.

Introduction

Within food and beverage operations there are two main systems operating and being managed. These are the food production process and the food service process. These can be seen as two distinct systems (Cousins, 1988). Food production has been considered in Chapter 3. This chapter considers the management of food and beverage service.

One of the key differences between the management of food and production and the management of food and beverage service is that as the volume of business increases, it requires fundamental alterations in the food production process, whereas the service process may simply be multiplied (Cousins, 1988). As the volume of food production increases, the way in which the production is organized has to change. This change can be either where the process is separated into various parts of the menu required, which is the basis of the 'partie' system, or where the production system is based on the type of processes being used. For food service, as the volume increases additional service is provided through, for instance, increasing the number of stations in a restaurant. This is much the same as the opening of additional checkouts in a supermarket or increasing the number of tellers available in a bank as the level of demand increases.

While in food service there is the possibility of changing the service methods, such changes are usually driven by needs to improve resource efficiency rather than by the need to provide for high volumes of business. An example is breakfast service. This can be provided through conventional table service at any volume of business but the need to reduce costs, especially staff costs, is the main reason behind moving to a buffet system.

Food and beverage service

Food and beverage service has traditionally been seen as a delivery system. However, the food service process actually consists of two processes which are being managed albeit at the same time (Cousins, 1988). These are:

1. the operational sequence – which is primarily concerned with delivery
2. the customer process – which is primarily concerned with managing the customer experience

Separating the service process into two separate systems in this way provides for a better understanding of the process as well as some indication of potential options in the organization of the delivery system.

The operational sequence

The operational sequence consists of seven stages (Lillicrap and Cousins, 1994). These are:

1. preparation for service
2. taking orders
3. the service of food and drink
4. billing
5. clearing
6. dishwashing
7. clearing following service

Within these seven elements, there are a variety of alternative ways of achieving the service. The service sequence is essentially the bridge between the production system and the customer experience or process. The choices on how the service sequence is designed, planned and controlled are made taking into account a number of organizational variables. These are:

- customer demand and needs
- the type and style of the food and beverage operation
- the nature of the customers (non-captive, captive or semi-captive)
- price to be charged
- production process
- volume of demand

- volume of throughput
- space available
- availability of staff
- opening hours
- booking requirements
- payment requirements
- legal requirements

The food service process

If food and beverage service is viewed as primarily a delivery process, then the customer can often be seen as a passive recipient of the service. As a result, systems and procedures tend only to be designed from the delivery perspective. However, as has been indicated in Chapter 1 (pp. 13–15), service standards cannot be drawn if they do not take account of both the infrastructure supporting the standards as well as the ability to implement standards within the interactive phase.

If the whole issue of quality is to be taken seriously, then the customers' involvement in the process must be considered. Customers are not passive but provide the impetus for the operations in the first place. In addition, the customer taking part in the service delivery is required to undertake or observe certain requirements. It must therefore make sense to ensure that the customer process is also considered and managed.

In food and beverage operations, fifteen separate service methods can be identified if the delivery system, or service sequence approach, is taken. However, this number is reduced when the analysis is taken from the customer process perspective. Four basic processes can be identified based on what the customer has to be involved in. These are:

A   service at a laid cover
B   part service at a laid cover and part self-service
C   self-service
D   service at a single point (ordering, receipt of order and payment)

In all these service processes, the customer comes to where the food and beverage service is offered and the service is provided in areas primarily designed for the purpose. There is, therefore, a need for a fifth process where the customer receives the service in another location and where the area is not primarily designed for the purpose. This can be called.

E   specialized service or service *in situ*

A summary of the five customer processes is shown in Table 6.1.

Table 6.1 Simple categorization of the customer process

Service method	Food and beverage service area	Ordering/ selection	Service	Dining/ consumption	Clearing
A Table service	Customer enters area and is seated	From menu	By staff to customer	At laid cover	By staff
B Assisted service	Customer enters area and is usually seated	From menu, buffet or passed trays	Combination of both staff and customer	Usually at laid cover	By staff
C Self-service	Customer enters	Customer selects own tray	Customer carries	Dining area or take away	Various
D Single-point service	Customer enters	Ordered at single point	Customer carries	Dining area or take away	Various
E Specialized or *in situ*	*In situ*	From menu or predetermined	Brought to customer	Where served	By staff or customer

Within this categorization, all food and beverage service methods can be shown as follows:

Group A: Table service

Service to customers at a laid cover:

1. waiter:
    - (a) silver/English
    - (b) family
    - (c) plate/American
    - (d) butler/French
    - (e) Russian
    - (f) guéridon
2. bar counter

Group B: Assisted service

Combination of table service and self-service:

3. assisted service

Group C: Self-service

Self-service of customers:

4. cafeteria:
    - (a) counter
    - (b) free flow
    - (c) echelon
    - (d) supermarket

(*Note*: some 'call order' production may be included in cafeterias.)

Group D: Single-point service
Service of customers at a single point – consumed on premises or taken away:

5. take away
6. vending
7. kiosks
8. food court
9. bar

Group E: Specialized (or *in situ*)
Service to customers in areas not primarily designed for service:

10. tray
11. trolley
12. home delivery
13. lounge
14. room
15. drive-in

Note: Banquet/function is a term used to describe catering for specific numbers of people at specific times in a variety of dining layouts. Service methods also vary. In these cases banquet/function catering refers to the organization of service rather than a specific service method.

With the exception of group E, the customer process in all other groups is similar within the service methods found in each group. Additionally the skills, knowledge, tasks and duties required are similar within each group with group A being the most complex and group D less complex. Group E has a special set of requirements, some of which are different from those found in the other groups. Taking the service sequence, it is possible to identify the commonality of tasks and duties and therefore organizational needs as well as staff development needs, within each service method group (Table 6.2).

The customer process

Viewing food and beverage service from the customer process approach on the one hand ensures a customer service based perspective but also allows the management to consider alternatives. It is possible, for instance, to alter the delivery of service without essentially changing the customer process, by moving between service methods within each group. Thus, the change from full silver service to a plate service delivery system does not essentially alter the customer process. It will, however, have effects on the way the service sequence is organized and possibly the production system. On the other hand, changing between service method groups substantially changes the customer process. If, for instance, the service method changes from one in group A to one in group C, the effects on the requirements placed on the customer are very different as indicated in Table 6.1.

Customer service versus resource productivity

On the one hand a food and beverage operation is designed to provide customer services and on the other the achievement of profit is largely determined by the efficiency of the use of resources. Customer service can be defined, as in Chapter 1, p. 14, as being a combination of five characteristics. These were presented in the model together with the resources being managed as shown in Fig. 6.1.

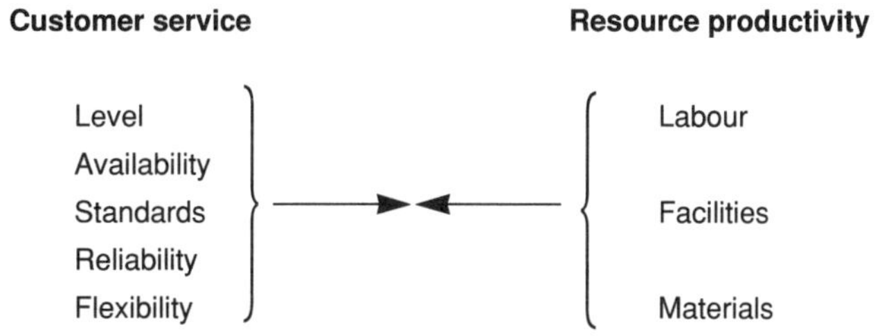

Fig. 6.1 Customer service versus resource productivity

In determining the customer service specification for a particular operation, it is necessary to consider the effect that the achievement of the service specification will have on the productivity of the resources.

The effects of variation in the five customer service characteristics and the resource utilization can be considered as follows (Cousins, 1994):

1. Service level: As the service level increases, the labour costs will increase as the number of staff required will increase as well as the level of staff professionalism. Meal-times will also become longer and therefore the potential capacity of the operation will reduce. In addition in higher levels of service, the equipment used tends to be of higher quality and the amount of equipment needed increases.

2. Availability of service: Increasing the availability of the service will potentially increase labour and material costs and will reduce the efficiency of the facilities used. In these cases it is necessary to endeavour to match the labour and materials being used to the expected volume of business which will vary over a given period.

3. Level of standards: Increasing the level of standards in the food and beverage operation will increase the cost of materials as better grade materials are used and will increase the cost of labour as the level of staffing and the staffing professionalism will need to be higher. In addition, the provision of the facilities will also have a higher cost again because of the higher grade of finishes being used.

4. Reliability of the service: In order to ensure a high reliability in the provision of the service, again the labour and material costs will increase as in order to protect the reliability of the product it will be necessary to have a higher proportion of equipment, labour and materials available.

Table 6.2

Tasks/duties	Group A Table service	Group B Assisted service	Group C Self-service	Group D Single-point service	Group E Specialized service
Preparation for service					
Taking bookings	x	x			x
Preparation of menus	x	x	x	x	x
Menu briefings	x	x	x	x	x
Layout of room	x	x	x	x	x
Handling linen	x	x			x
Handling paper items	x	x	x	x	x
Cleaning and polishing of cutlery/tableware	x	x	x	x	x
Cleaning and polishing of glassware	x	x	x	x	x
Cleaning and polishing of crockery	x	x	x	x	x
Handling disposables	x	x	x	x	x
Handling and laying of cruets, ashtrays, table nos, butter dishes	x	x	x		x
Preparation of accompaniments	x	x	x	x	x
Preparation of non-alcoholic beverages	x	x	x	x	x
Preparation of work stations (sideboards)	x	x			
Preparation of display buffet	x				
Lay-up of tables	x	x			x
Housekeeping duties	x	x	x	x	x
Preparation of trolleys	x	x			x
Preparation of check/order pads	x	x			x
Preparation of counters for counter service			x	x	
Preparation of customer buffets	x	x			
Preparation for tray service					x
Preparation for vending service				x	
Preparation of:					
Open bar	x	x		x	
Dispense bar	x	x			x
Buffet bar					x
Counter bar			x		
Preparation for restricted bar service			x	x	x
Preparation for full service	x	x			x

Tasks/duties	Group A Table service	Group B Assisted service	Group C Self-service	Group D Single-point service	Group E Specialized service
Taking orders					
Taking orders for table service	x	x			
Taking orders for single-point service				x	
Taking orders for counter service		x	x		
Taking orders for room and lounge service					x
Service of food and beverages					
Service of food:					
High level	x		x		
Medium level		x			x
Low level			x	x	x
Service of beverages:					
High level	x	x			x
Medium level				x	x
Low level			x	x	x
Billing/Cashiering					
Making up bills	x	x			x
Totalling customer selection at till			x		
Charging with service				x	
Handling cash	x	x	x	x	x
Handling other forms of payment	x	x	x	x	x
Cashiering duties	x	x	x		x
Cash transactions in single-point service				x	
Preparing analysis sheets	x	x	x	x	x
Food and beverage control	x	x	x	x	x
Clearing					
Clearing from tables:					
By hand	x	x			x
Using trays	x	x	x	x	x
Using trolleys			x	x	x
Clearing other consumption areas			x	x	x
Clearing following service					
Clearing table service areas	x	x			
Clearing other areas			x	x	x
Clearing counters			x	x	
Clearing trolleys	x	x			x
Clearing display buffets	x		x		x
Clearing customer buffets		x	x		x

5.   Flexibility of the service: Moving away from a limited standard range of product and service will increase material and labour costs and will reduce the efficiency of the facilities being used.

In all cases, the opposite of the examples given above will potentially increase the efficiency of the resources being used. The development of the customer service specification should take account of the five characteristics above and will therefore predetermine the level of resource utilization and therefore the level of efficiency possible. In summary, the higher the level of customer service, then the greater the potential for lower efficiency in the resource utilization. However, it is possible through changes in the service process to effect greater efficiency without fundamentally altering the customer process; moving from full silver service to plate service, for example.

Managing the service sequence

In developing the customer service specification, the capability of the operation needs to be considered. Similarly, once the customer service specification has been determined, then the service sequence can be designed or redesigned and managed in order to ensure that the customer service specification is achieved. Aspects of the managing the service sequence are considered below.

Preparation for service   Within the service areas, there are a variety of tasks and duties which need to be carried out (see pp. 144–5) in order to ensure that adequate preparation has been made for the expected volume of business and the type of service which is to be provided. This should also include the briefing of staff to ensure that they have adequate knowledge of the product.

One of the preparatory tasks is the taking of bookings. Systems need to be developed to ensure that bookings are taken in a way that ensures the efficiency of the operation. This includes consideration of overbooking systems in operations where bookings are taken. There are, however, risks with this approach. It is also necessary to take into account the law on contract.

A contract is made when one party agrees to the terms of an offer made by another party. In food and beverage service, there are essentially two types of customer: those who pre-book and those who do not (often called chance or casual customers).

For those who pre-book, the offer is made by them, e.g. a requirement for a table of four at 1 p.m. If the restaurant suggests an alternative, e.g. 'We do not have a table at 1 p.m., but we have one at 1.30 p.m.', then the offer is made by the restaurant.

There is a requirement for a price list to be shown (see p. 12). In operations where the customer may not have or is not required to pre-book (e.g. fast-food operations) it is likely to be considered, in law, that the price list constitutes an offer.

If customers fail to turn up on time, then the table need not be held. Similarly, if the party is only two and not the four previously booked, then restaurants may seek compensation. Alternatively, if the food and drink are not as expected, then the customer can refuse to pay but must provide proof of identity and their home address. Only if fraud is suspected may the police be involved, as fraud is a criminal offence.

However, contracts may be broken if one party is induced to enter into a contract by false statement, e.g. if promised a menu which is not available. In this case there is no obligation for the customer to continue with the contract. Also, if either party is unable to meet the terms of the original contract due to unforeseen circumstances, e.g. illness of customer, or the restaurant burning down, then the contract becomes frustrated as it cannot be fulfilled.

Care should be taken with minors: contracts cannot be made with persons under 18 unless it is for 'goods and services suitable to the minor's needs and his/her station in life'.

Taking orders Taking orders from customers for the food and drink they wish to have, takes time. Limiting the choice can reduce this time but this possibility depends on the particular operation. The order-taking process, though, is part of a longer process which feeds information to the production or bar areas and provides information for the billing method. The three main order-taking methods are:

1. Duplicate: Order taken and copied to supply point and second copy retained for service and billing.
2. Triplicate: Order taken and copied to supply point and cashier for billing, third copy retained for service.
3. Service with order: Taking order and serving to order, e.g. bar service or take-away methods.

In the order-taking procedure it is also important to realize the potential for personal selling that can be carried out by service staff. Personal selling refers specifically to the ability of the staff in a food and beverage operation to contribute to the promotion of sales. This is especially important where there are specific promotions being undertaken. The promise of a particular type of menu or drink, a special deal or the availability of a particular service can often be devalued by the inability of the staff to fulfil the requirements as promised. It is therefore important to involve service staff in the formulation of particular offers and to ensure that briefing and training are undertaken so that the customer can actually experience what has been promised.

However, personal selling does not solely relate to supporting special promotions. The contribution of staff to the meal experience is vital. The service staff contribute to the customers' perception of value for money, hygiene and cleanliness, the level of service and the perception of atmosphere that the customer experiences. Within the context of selling the service, staff should therefore be able to:

- Detail the food and drink on offer in an informative way and also in such a way as to make the product sound interesting and worth having.
- Use opportunities to promote specific items or deals when seeking orders from the customer.
- Seek information from the customer in a way that promotes sales. For example, rather than asking if drinks are required with the meal ask which drinks are to be required with the meal. Or, for instance, rather than asking if a sweet is required ask which of the sweets is required.
- Use opportunities for the sales of additional items such as extra garnishes, special sauces or accompanying drinks such as a dessert wine with a sweet course.
- Provide a competent service of the items for sale and seek customers' views on the acceptability of the food, drinks and the service.

The service of food and drink

The various service methods available are given on pp. 141–2. The choice of service method will depend as much on the customer service specification as on the capability of the staff, the operation and the equipment available. Differing service methods will also determine the speed of service and the time the customer takes to consume the meal which in turn will have an impact on the throughput of customers.

For front-line staff it is particularly important that as well as technical skill and product knowledge they have well-developed social skills and approaches to customer relations. It also requires management to continually reinforce and support front-line workers in the maintenance of good standards of achievement in these aspects. Also the provision of good service is primarily dependent on teamwork, not only among service staff but also staff in other departments.

Billing

The various billing methods found in food service operations are as follows:

- Bill as check: Second copy of order used as bill.
- Separate bill: Bill made up from duplicate check and presented to customer.
- Bill with order: Service to order and billing at same time, e.g. bar or take-away methods.
- Prepaid: Customer purchases ticket or card in advance either for specific meal or specific value.
- Voucher: Customer has credit issued by third party, e.g. luncheon voucher or tourist agency voucher for either specific meal or specific value.

- No charge: Customer not paying.
- Deferred: Refers to e.g. function-type catering where bill paid by organizer.

The actual choice of billing method will be dependent on the type and style of the operation. However, the billing system is also part of a longer process linked first to the order-taking method and second to the revenue control procedures. In managing the billing method, it is necessary therefore to ensure that the method chosen supports both the order-taking method and the revenue control requirements. The range of acceptable payment methods, for example, needs to be predetermined, as well as the discretion which is to be allowed to different individuals or groups of staff. Consideration also needs to be given to the use of electronic point of sale control systems.

Whatever revenue control system is used, it should be able to generate information for a variety of performance measures. These can include:

- seat turnover – the number of times a seat is used in a service period
- average spend per head on food or beverages
- sales mix data
- payment method breakdowns
- sales per member of service staff
- sales per period – can be monitored on an hourly basis in fast-food operations or in bar operation
- sales per square metre or square foot
- reconciliation of total payments against order served

Clearing   The various clearing methods found in food service operations may be summarized as follows:

- Manual 1: The collection of soiled ware by waiting staff to dishwash area.
- Manual 2: The collection and sorting to trolleys by operators for transportation to dishwash area.
- Semi-self-clear: The placing of soiled ware by customers on strategically placed trolleys within dining area for removal by operators.
- Self-clear: The placing of soiled ware by customers on conveyor or conveyorized tray collecting system for mechanical transportation to dishwash area.
- Self-clear and strip: The placing of soiled ware into conveyorized dishwash baskets by customer for direct entry of baskets through dishwash.

The choice of clearing method, whether manual by staff or involving customers, will be dependent not only on the type of operation but also on the nature of the demand being met. In captive situations, for instance, it is possible to have greater customer involvement.

Dishwashing   The capacity of the dishwashing system should always be greater than the operational maximum required. This is because slow dishwashing increases the amount of equipment required to be in use at a particular time and increases the storage space required in service areas.

The various dishwashing systems are as follows:

- Manual: The manual washing by hand or brush machine of soiled ware.
- Semi-automatic: The manual loading by operators of dishwash machine.
- Automatic conveyor: The manual loading by operators of soiled ware within baskets mounted on conveyor for automatic transportation through dishwash machine.
- Flight Conveyor: The manual loading by operators of soiled ware within pegs mounted on conveyor for automatic transportation through dishwasher.
- Deferred wash: The collection, stripping, sorting and stacking of ware by operators for transportation through dishwash at later stage.

Essentially, the potential volume that can be accommodated increases, as well as potential efficiency, from the manual method to the flight conveyor method, and the choice of method will be largely dependent on the scale of the operation. It is also often necessary to employ more than one method. The deferred wash system can be used as a cost-saving approach as wash-up staff do not have to be employed until the end of a service period especially when this is late at night.

Clearing following service   After the service periods, there are a variety of task and duties to be carried out partly to clear from the previous service and partly to prepare for the next. The efficient management of the clearing stage can have a dramatic impact on the potential reuse of an area.

Managing volume

One of the key characteristics of services that is often identified which differentiates the sale of services from the sale of goods, is that the product cannot be stored. The food and beverage product exemplifies this characteristic. For instance, seats in a restaurant which are not sold at one meal-time cannot be compensated for by additional sales at another time. In other words, the sale of food and beverage is limited by the capacity of the operation. Therefore, in food and beverage operations, it is necessary to consider how the capacity of the operation for customer sales can be managed in order that the goals of the business may be achieved.

Business volume inevitably varies throughout any trading period whether this be a year, a month, a week or even an hour. Operating at under full capacity for any period can lead to a disproportionate increase in costs and therefore a reduction in the overall profit contribution. The management of food service operations therefore is also about matching the ability of the operations to provide services to the expected volume of business.

The capacity of a food and beverage operation is measured not only by considering the maximum capacity of customers at a given time but also the capacity that can be achieved over time. For example, a restaurant operation with a maximum seating of 80 covers can achieve a much higher actual capacity for a given meal period if the seats can be used more than once during the period. The potential for this will, however, vary according to the type of operation. A banqueting room, for example, can usually only be filled once during a meal period and therefore the size of the function in terms of covers served will determine the capacity achieved at that time.

Where the actual demand is significantly higher than the capacity of the operation, consideration must be given to methods of limiting the volume of demand. Depending on the type of operation, this issue varies in significance. An à la carte restaurant operating at a high customer service specification will tolerate fluctuations in demand and seek to ensure availability and flexibility to meet all the expected demand. On the other hand, a cafeteria operation will seek to maximize demand during the service period.

Limitations in demand can be achieved through pricing policies. In city-centre hotels for instance, the demand for full breakfast is limited in this way through disproportionately higher pricing for a full breakfast compared to other alternatives. Meal packaging is also a way of reducing the variations in the range of demand being met.

Using queues
In addition though, there is the use of queues to ensure that the operation is working to a full capacity. Examples of this approach are found in, for instance, fast-food operations where although the queue is controlled by a time limit for the customers to queue, it does provide constant demand at the service point. Another example is, for instance, TGI Fridays, where the queue for food service is the central bar area. In this operation, the queue becomes part of the meal experience and also provides for revenue from the queue, through drink sales, while waiting for meal service. In managing the queue requirement there are a number of factors to be taken into account so that the process of waiting in the queue does not become a negative part of the service process from the customers' perspective. The factors which affect customer satisfaction, and some of the actions that the food service operation can consider, are summarized in Table 6.3.

Table 6.3   Service considerations in minimizing queuing dissatisfaction

Factor	Service consideration
Unfair v. fair wait	Try and ensure that the wait the customer undertakes is perceived as fair; design queuing systems to ensure strict rotation
Uncomfortable v. comfortable wait	Consider the impact of the waiting environment; seek to maintain a high level of comfort
Unexplained v. explained wait	Provide reasonable explanations for the wait and update regularly; try and avoid the customer seeing under-used capacity
Unexpected v. expected wait	Accept responsibility; provide reasonable explanations for the wait and update regularly
Unoccupied v. occupied wait	Provide distractions, which either increase the efficiency and effectiveness of the service sequence or involve the customer more in the service sequence
Initial v. subsequent wait	Design the service sequence so that the customer has early contact with the servers; try and spread the total wait time across a number of the stages of the service sequence
Anxious v. calm wait	Assess the general level of anxiety of the customers; be aware of the needs of customers for staff contact and reassurance
Solo v. group wait	Recognize that solo waits feel longer than group waits; consider ways of ensuring that the wait is more pleasant through providing distraction
Valuable service v. less valuable service	Recognize that cusomters will wait longer the higher the value of the service but still try to minimize the wait time

Source: Based on proposals by Davis and Heineke (1994)

Banquet/function operations

In the organization of banquet/function operations, there are special considerations in respect of capacity issues. Clearly the capacity of the function rooms will determine the maximum numbers that can be accommodated at a particular time. However, variations in the service methods and the dining layouts can alter both the maximum numbers which can be served and also the volume which can be achieved over time. Selling functions which are similar in service method and layout, for instance, can reduce the preparation for service and the clearing after service periods.

In addition, the capacity of function rooms is affected by the combination of the bookings taken. The taking of certain types of functions will reduce or preclude the taking of others. Noisy presentations will for instance limit the use of adjoining rooms. If the intention of the operation is to be flexible, then this is inevitable. If operation wants to specialize (and therefore reduce the flexibility) it is possible to increase the volume throughout. This supposes however that the volume of business requiring more standardization is available.

The complexity of managing capacity

Managing capacity in food and beverage operations is not a simple issue. The provision of food and beverages is highly complex with a variety of stages both in the production and the service processes, all of which have an effect on the volume of business which can be met. In addition, the limitations posed by the physical facilities are not always the key determinant of the potential capacity that can be achieved. In many cases the service specification will determine that inefficiency in the use of the facilities will be outweighed by the need to provide a certain level of service. In addition, the control of labour and material costs must be taken into account in determining the potential volume of business which can be handled within the predetermined customer service specification.

Summary

This chapter has considered the difference between the management of food production and service and introduced and explored the concept of two distinct systems being managed within food and beverage service. This approach recognizes the importance not only of the management of the service sequence (or delivery system) but also the customer experience or process. This approach can assist in developing customer service specifications especially where the implications of various decisions are understood in the context of the impact that such decisions can have on resource utilization and efficiency.

Managing the service sequence becomes better informed by taking into account the effects that can be experienced by the customer as well as the need to manage the volume of demand.

References

Cousins J 1988 Curriculum development in operational management teaching in catering education. In Johnson R (ed) *The management of service operations* IFS Publications, Bedford: pp. 437–59

Cousins J 1994 Managing capacity. In Jones P (ed) *The management of food-service operations* Cassell, London: pp. 174–87

Davis M M and Heineke J 1994 Understanding the roles of the customer and the operation for better queue management. *International Journal of Operations and Production Management* **14**(5): pp. 21–34

Lillicrap D and Cousins J 1994 *Food and beverage service* Hodder and Stoughton, London

7 Operations performance appraisal

Aim This chapter aims to identify and evaluate the techniques of measuring and appraising food and beverage operations performance.

Objective The objective of this chapter is to enable you to access a range of performance measures and appraisal techniques and have an appreciation of their application to food and beverage operations.

Introduction

The appraisal of a food and beverage operation is a task which involves the consideration of a range of operational variables, from revenue and costs to atmosphere and image. In order to appraise an operation it is necessary to identify the component parts and appraise them separately before bringing them all together and appraising the whole operation.

The component parts of a food and beverage operations performance appraisal are identified as follows:

- appraisal objectives
- revenue
- costs
- profits
- product
- business environment
- appraisal of the whole operation

Appraisal objectives

Appraisal is the action of placing a value on a measurement or collection of measurements. The measurements taken in a food and beverage operation are predominantly concerned with performance, and are therefore referred to as 'performance measures'. However, a measure alone has no value. In order to be able to place a value on a performance measure an objective needs to be identified. For example, an actual revenue measurement of £1200 has limited value until it is compared with a revenue objective of £1000. The revenue can then be appraised as surpassing the objective by £200, or 20 per cent.

Other measurements and objectives are needed in order to appraise or value the revenue measurement further. If cost objectives and actual costs are known, it is possible to appraise or value the revenue measurement in a more meaningful way, i.e. profits can be measured. Then a profit objective can be applied and a further value placed on the operation.

In order to begin to appraise a food and beverage operation it is therefore a prerequisite to try and determine the objective of the operation. The identification of the operation's objectives will enable the appraiser to focus on those parts of the operation which most significantly impact on the achievement of the identified objectives. However, in circumstances where the operation's objectives are not clear, it is necessary for the appraiser to take a pro-active role. This pro-active role will vary with the appraiser's situation. For example:

- As an owner-operator with unclear or no written down objectives, they should ask themselves what their objectives are. If they think they are unable to do this alone they should invite others to help them with the process; their staff and/or a consultant, for example.
- Area managers, managers, department heads and others with responsibility for revenue, who are unclear as to their objectives also need to be pro-active by consulting with other members of their organization (usually their immediate line manager), in an attempt to establish the objectives.

The formulation of objectives is an important part of any business in order to try and ensure that resources are being efficiently directed. As objectives are dynamic and vary according to circumstances, the setting of objectives is an ongoing process. Appraisal is part of this ongoing process in order to find out whether the objectives are being met. The resultant appraisal will help in making and setting new or revised objectives.

Budgets   Some measurable objectives of a food and beverage operation are commonly expressed in the form of 'budgets'. Examples of measurable 'budget' objectives are revenue, costs, profits, average spend per head, number of customers. These budgets are used in a number of ways:

- Budgets are compared to actual performance and therefore help to appraise that actual performance, e.g. revenue budgets.
- Budgets help effect control over the operation, e.g. cost budgets.
- Budgets help to predict the future, e.g. cash flow and profit forecast budgets.

Operators will use budgets to help place reasoned and objective values on their operation in order to make informed decisions regarding their business. However, budgets can be used for other reasons.

Budgets are often thought to act as a goal. Sometimes the ability to achieve the budget is related to remuneration and bonuses, or if budgets are not met employment of those thought to be responsible may be terminated. This 'stick and carrot' use of budgets can act as a motivator if the budgets are perceived to be achievable, or a demotivator if they are perceived to be unobtainable. For this reason budgets are not necessarily a statement of predicted results, but are very often set with a view to motivate.

Evidence from Shortt (1992, p. 61), identifies this to be the case in the situation where an operations manager for a small group of hotels sets budgets that are more difficult to achieve than the actual desired or possible budget. This was done in order to 'keep managers on their toes'. The argument against this is that management may know that these budgets are being set so as to be too difficult to achieve and the desirable motivation can be negated.

In order to avoid this potential conflict budgets may be set with the agreement of all the participating parties. In large organizations this is clearly impractical, as a board of directors is unable to agree budgets with all the individuals involved in achieving those budgets. Instead budgets are agreed between layers of the organization, for example between the board of directors and the operations director, then the operations director and the regional managers, and so on until agreement between the unit managers and the department heads. In smaller and owner-operated food and beverage operations this agreement between the parties is potentially easier to achieve.

Even with such a 'consultative' approach to budget setting it is still possible for there to be conflict, with one side wishing to increase budget sales and reduce budget costs (the position of the higher-layer manager, the budget setter), while the other party is trying to reduce budget sales and increase budget costs (the position of the lower-layer manager, the budget taker).

Nevertheless, however they are set, it is still possible that budgets may be ill-conceived and badly or falsely communicated. If the desired operational objective is to be identified through the budget, then the setting of the budget itself should be examined for its possible limitations, and how these limitations might affect the use of budgets as an appraisal or valuation of the actual achievement.

Standards Other measurable objectives of a food and beverage operation are expressed as 'standards'. Examples of measurable 'standards' objectives are: portioning, purchasing specifications, staff uniform, temperature, time. These standards are seen to be useful to operators in a similar way to budgets:

*   Standards are compared to actual performance and therefore help to appraise that actual performance, e.g. portioning.

- Standards help effect control over the operation, e.g. staff uniform and hygiene.
- Standards help ensure a consistent product, e.g. the same service, meals and atmosphere, at all times and in all locations.

Some operators will write these standards down in the form of training manuals. Most, if not all branded retail catering operations,* are extremely detailed in this area. The manuals will prescribe precisely each task and duty to be performed with the use of diagrams, photographs, videos and text. These manuals perform three main functions:

1. Manuals enable management to communicate the prescribed performance of all tasks and duties necessary to produce and control their product.
2. Manuals help ensure consistency of product throughout the food and beverage operations in the group or chain.
3. Manuals act as an objective against which to appraise performance.

As with budgets, not all food and beverage operations will have written down standards, and similarly, operators and managers should be pro-active in trying to identify and establish these standards.

This identification and establishment process is also prone to conflict. Staff, as the 'standard takers', are rarely consulted by management, the 'standard setters', resulting in some standards being boycotted or revised. An example would be a standard prescribing the way to answer a telephone: 'Good morning/afternoon/evening, The Royal Hotel, David speaking, how may I help you?', being revised to something with which the person answering the telephone might be more comfortable. Indeed, the staff who perform the standards are often much better placed to understand customer needs. The telephone example above is one with which staff may often feel uncomfortable and customers find insincere and false. However, in general terms standards are seen to be useful to an operation in the maintenance of consistent product delivery.

In summary, therefore, the objectives of a food and beverage operation should be established if effective appraisal is to be performed. These

---

* Chain restaurants have been seen to take a relatively high-profile position in terms of their location (high streets, shopping areas, European ferries, motorway services, hospitals, workplaces and educational establishments), and place great importance on their image through the use of concepts. These catering operations are now more open to the management methods employed by retailers (shops and stores), as are other service industries such as banking and printing, with the change of emphasis being focused on how best to provide an improved customer experience. The branding of catering operations might also be seen to have developed from the retail industry, and provides marketing advantages as well as some economies of scale in purchasing, training (manuals) and distribution. For these reasons the term 'branded retail catering operations' is generally used to describe these types of establishments.

objectives are sometimes written down in the form of budgets and standards, against which actual performance can be measured and appraised. In operations where the objectives are not clear, staff and management should be pro-active in order to identify and establish their objectives. The time and resources devoted to identifying, establishing and communicating objectives will vary between operations, depending on the perceived importance of this process.

Appraising revenue

Revenue is viewed by food and beverage operators as perhaps the most important measure in the operation. Revenue is also called 'turnover', and is often quoted as a measure of the size of a business, but it is not accurate to say that a high revenue equates with high success. Operations with high revenue can fail as well. However, revenue is a prerequisite for success, and most operators would put revenue at the top of their list of objectives.

Revenue is a consequence of two variables: price and volume. When revenue is seen to change over a period of time it is a result of change in either one or both of these variables. Table 7.1 demonstrates how changes in the price and volume variables affect the revenue. Example 1 is the starting-point or base-line. Examples 2–6 result in revenue increasing, with examples 7–11 resulting in decreasing revenue. It should be noted that examples 3 and 5 produce increased revenue even though one of the variables has decreased, and that examples 10 and 11 produce decreased revenue even though one of the variables has increased. Appraising revenue as a single operational variable will therefore include collecting additional information on price and volume variables.

Table 7.1 The effect of price and volume on revenue

Example	Covers/ volume	Price/ASPH (£)	Revenue (£)
1	100	10.00	1000.00
2	120	10.00	1200.00
3	120	9.00	1080.00
4	100	12.00	1200.00
5	80	15.00	1200.00
6	120	12.00	1440.00
7	80	10.00	800.00
8	80	9.00	720.00
9	100	9.00	900.00
10	80	11.00	880.00
11	110	9.00	990.00

Volume Most food and beverage operations will measure volume by the number of customers who consume their product. In a table-service restaurant operation this is a fairly simple matter of referring to copy customer invoices, kitchen order checks or electronic data collection from the cash register. In a counter-service food and beverage operation it is not so easy to know the actual number of customers that have been served, and therefore the number of *transactions* may be recorded, e.g. a fast-food store. In some food and beverage operations it is not seen as necessary to know the actual number of customers or the actual number of transactions, e.g. a bar. In this situation the revenue is still a product of the price and the volume, but it will not be possible to identify the reasons for any revenue variations so accurately.

Price Price can be measured from the menus, wine and drinks lists and other methods of 'product offer' communication. However, price can also be measured by how much a customer spends, and many operations will use 'average spend per head' (ASPH), or 'average check', as a way of determining the price variable. If an operation knows its total revenue and the number of customers or number of checks during the period in which the revenue accrued, then it is possible to calculate the ASPH and the average check. For example:

Total revenue	£1000
Total number of transactions	100
Total number of customers	500

ASPH = £2.00
Average check = £10.00
Average group size = 5

It is possible to calculate the average size of a group of customers, i.e. number of customers divided by number of transactions. In the above example this would be five. It may be important for an operation to know the size of their customer groups. Knowing that large or small parties make up a significant part of their market can help them to plan their restaurant and kitchen layout for example, or to focus their advertising and promotion.

However, the value of such measurements must be considered. An ASPH or average check amount can be misleading because 'averages' do not give the whole picture. An ASPH of £12.50 could be the result of all customers spending £12.50; or half the customers spending £6.25 and the other half spending £18.75. The same misinterpretation can be applied to the average group size measure, and to the average number of customers per hour/day/week. Infinite combinations are possible and it is therefore important to take into account the limitations of averages.

These measurements and others are seen to be more useful when they are used for cross-sectional and time-series analyses.

Cross-sectional analysis   This is to (a) compare one section of an operation with another section of the same operation, or (b) compare one operation or part of an operation with another in the same or similar sector of the food and beverage operations business. For example, comparing the revenue of one steak house restaurant with another in the same chain, or comparing the revenue of one fast-food chain with the revenue of another.

Time-series analysis   This is to compare a measure over a period of time; for example, comparing the revenue of a unit for one week with the revenue of the same unit for the previous week or with the revenue from the same week one year ago. Comparing present with past performance helps place some value on the revenue measure, although it is important to take into account any circumstances that may have changed.

As identified already, a change in revenue is a result of a change of volume and/or price. A restaurant that had a revenue of £10 000 in year one and a revenue of £12 000 in year two, is seen to have increased its revenue by £2000 or 20 per cent. Let us assume that the number of customers has remained static and that prices were increased by 10 per cent. (In this particular example we will assume that the current rate of inflation was 10 per cent, although this by itself may not be the only reason why prices might be increased or changed.) Taking into account the price rise it might be said that the value of the increased revenue is not £2000 but only £1000. In general terms one would have expected the restaurant to increase its revenue to £11 000 in the second year just to remain at the same revenue level, i.e. £10 000 plus the rate of inflation/rate of price increase at 10 per cent, (£1000) would be £11 000. That the restaurant had an actual revenue of £12 000 means that revenue has only increased by £1000 or 9.1 per cent. (Revenue should have been £11 000, revenue was £12 000, the percentage increase is [£1000/£11 000] $\times$ 100 = 9.1 per cent.) When comparing revenues over time, it is important to know if price rises and/or inflation have been taken into account.

Revenue comparisons between food and beverage units should also be made with some caution and in relation to the circumstances. Two roadside restaurants in the same chain will have identical menus and prices, and may even have the same seating capacity, but their revenues may be different. This difference in revenue will still be a product of the volume and price variables, but factors outside the control of the unit management, such as location and spending power of their market, will affect revenue levels, and therefore the revenue budgets need to allow for these differences. Revenue comparisons between food and beverage businesses also need to be made with caution because the objectives and/or costs of the two businesses may be different. One cannot appraise performance on the revenue variable alone.

In order to try and make effective comparisons between food and beverage businesses and units, other forms of revenue measure can be made. Revenue per customer/seat/square metre/staff member, etc. can be measured and compared to similar operations. These measures can also be performed over time on the same business or unit. The real question when these types of measurements and comparisons are made is: 'Are they useful?' It is not always clear if these measurements and comparisons will be useful until they are actually measured and compared. If the time and data are available to make these types of detailed measures and comparisons, then it may be worth doing.

Perhaps the most useful form of revenue appraisal is over time. Average spend per head, average revenue per customer, number of customers, revenue per member of staff, revenue per square metre, etc. can all be measured on an ongoing basis and compared. It will therefore be possible to identify changes and maybe trends, and if any significant changes in these measures are noticed remedial action can be taken.

In summarizing revenue appraisal some key factors are apparent:

- Revenue is a product of price and volume. An appraisal of revenue will need to take these variables into account.
- Inflation and/or price rises need to be taken into account.
- Averages of price, volume and revenue do not always accurately reflect the complete situation.
- Different businesses/operations/units may have different objectives and direct comparisons may be misleading.
- Revenue cannot be fully appraised without reference to other operational variables, such as cost and profit.

Appraising costs

As important as revenue is to obtain, costs are seen as the most important to *control*. Costs are usually divided into fixed, variable and semi-variable costs. Fixed costs remain constant over a set period of time even though the level of business fluctuates, e.g. rent, rates and insurance premiums. Variable costs are proportional to the level of business, e.g., meal ingredient costs and beverage costs. Semi-variable costs are part fixed and part variable, e.g. staff and fuel. However, it is more important to know how and why costs are incurred, and how to measure them accurately, than to argue if they are fixed, variable or semi-variable.

Most fixed (and some variable) costs can be negotiated with the supplier of the service. Rent, insurance and even interest rates (the cost of borrowing money) are services that are supplied within a competitive market and it is therefore worth considering opportunities for alternative, and possibly cheaper, sources of these services. Once the costs of these services are established, they are then fixed for the duration of the contract period, which is usually one year (although interest rates and some other costs can fluctuate more often).

Variable and semi-variable costs can be appraised in absolute terms, but are more commonly appraised as a proportion of revenue. Putting aside the fixed part of the semi-variable costs, (e.g. standing charge for electricity), these variable costs are proportional to the volume of business and therefore revenue. A food and beverage operation will measure these costs as a percentage of revenue, usually on a weekly basis. Costs of food, beverage, staff, linen, disposables, marketing, maintenance and other variable costs can be, and commonly are, measured as a percentage of revenue.

Identifying and measuring costs

Appraising these fixed and variable costs objectively can be performed as follows:

- A cross-sectional analysis can be performed by comparing the costs incurred by one food and beverage operation with similar types of food and beverage operations, thereby allowing a 'value for money' appraisal to be performed. Publications such as Keynote Reports, Mintel Reports, *Caterer & Hotelkeeper*, *Restaurateur* and others, provide useful information in this area, and help comparisons to be made. However, the cost structures of food and beverage operations can vary in a way which makes comparisons difficult. For example, one restaurant may be owned and operated by a family partnership which owns the premises outright (the debt having been paid off over a long period of time), while another restaurant is paying high rent or interest charges. The fixed costs of these two similar restaurants will be very different, resulting in a much lower break-even point for the restaurant with the lower fixed costs. These cost structures are often seen to change over the life cycles of most businesses.

- Relating one cost to other costs is another useful appraisal method. Costs are almost certain to increase in absolute terms year on year, due to inflation and/or the changing cost structure of the business, but by appraising costs as a proportion of total costs, or as a proportion of total revenue, a comparative measure can be established. For example, if fixed costs in year one are 25 per cent of total costs and 7 per cent of total sales, and in year two are 30 and 9 per cent respectively, then a relative dimension is added to cost appraisal. These changes in costs can be calculated to provide a relative measure which helps in their appraisal. This relative measure is sometimes miscalculated as there may be confusion as to how percentage changes are measured. Table 7.2 gives an example of how these measurements are made.

- A time-series analysis can be performed by comparing costs over a period of time, usually year on year. The absolute and the percentage change in these costs can be measured and a comparison made with the previous year's changes. One common budget or standard objective measure in these circumstances is the current rate of inflation or retail price index. Changes in staff costs (rates of pay) are often related and calculated in this way. However, if some costs are seen to rise significantly more or less than the current rate of inflation, or significantly more or less than in previous years, consideration should be given to changing the operating systems of the food and beverage business to take advantage of, or counter, this changing cost structure. Changing from electricity to gas or changing from silver service to buffet service, in order to reduce fuel or staff costs, would be examples of changing operating systems in order to reduce these costs in real and proportional terms.

Reference to Table 7.2 shows how the percentage change in absolute terms is calculated by dividing the difference between the two period's costs (£1200 − £1000 = £200), by the original or last period's cost (£1000), and multiplying by 100:

$$\frac{1200 - 1000}{1000} \times 100 = 20 \text{ per cent}$$

Costs can be said to have risen 20 per cent in absolute terms. However, as a percentage of revenue, costs have been seen to rise from 10 to 10.9 per cent. The percentage change in these cost percentages is calculated as follows:

$$\frac{10.9 - 10}{10} \times 100 = 9 \text{ per cent}$$

Table 7.2

Costs/revenues	£
Last period's cost	1000
Present period's cost	1200
Last period's revenue	10 000
Present period's revenue	11 000
Absolute change in cost	200

Percentages	%
% change in absolute cost	20
Last period's cost as a percentage of revenue	10
Present period's cost as a percentage of revenue	10.9
% change in cost as a percentage of revenue	9

The percentage change in costs as a percentage of revenue is 9 per cent. The percentage change between 10 and 10.9 per cent *is not* 0.9 per cent. It is critically important to know the difference between these measurements, 20 per cent being the absolute cost change percentage, and 9 per cent being the relative change in the cost as a percentage of the revenue. It might perhaps be more accurate to say that costs have risen by 9 per cent, (relative to revenue) than by 20 per cent (in absolute terms).

There is no one standard or budget percentage for the various costs. Food costs of between 28 per cent and 32 per cent are generally seen to be acceptable, as are staff costs of between 20 and 30 per cent and marketing costs of between 1 and 2 per cent. However, these figures should only be used as a guide because the actual percentage of the cost will vary depending on the objectives of the food and beverage operation.

It might be assumed that some sectors of the industry will share similar cost percentages, but there is no evidence to support this assumption. An up-market restaurant with an average spend per head of around £30–£40 may have the same food cost percentage as a roadside food and beverage operation with an average spend per head of around £5. The two operations may also have very similar staff cost percentages. Conversely, two very similar operations may have widely differing cost percentages, e.g. staff cost percentages being low, say 15 per cent of total revenue in an operation run and staffed by a family, and being say 25 per cent of total revenue in an operation which hires staff on the open market. A current theory suggests that new immigrants to a country will start up family businesses with low barriers to entry, like restaurants and take-aways, and are willing to work long hours at rates of pay below what is acceptable to others, resulting in much lower staff cost percentages.

In some sectors of the food and beverage industry, the market is becoming much more competitive and more concentrated in the hands of the large operators. For example, in retail catering prime high street sites have become prohibitively expensive to all but those who can significantly reduce costs and afford the highly expensive mass advertising campaigns and premium rents. The barriers to entry in this 'retail catering' market are becoming higher and therefore restricting the smaller and family-run operations.

This move towards an oligopolistic industry structure is also found in 'contract', 'outside' and 'transport catering', and cost percentage comparisons between them can be made. The chain, or group, food and beverage operations place great value on reducing costs and cost percentages as this is seen as leading to greater profits, and opportunities for a greater market share than their rivals through more competitive pricing. In this highly competitive market, economies of scale, especially in distribution, purchasing and marketing costs, provide advantages over the smaller operator. A greater investment in new technology also provides opportunities to develop more efficient and cheaper operating systems. These large operators see their actual survival as dependent upon their ability to reduce and control their costs, and therefore the value of cost comparisons between them is high.

Apportioning costs   In order to understand the cost structure of a food and beverage operation it is necessary to know why the various costs are incurred, and which costs can, or should be, attributed to the various parts of the operation. As the product is made up from a number of variables comprising the meal experience,* and is therefore not homogeneous – because different customers purchase and value different parts of the experience – apportioning costs requires the identification of the component parts of the product. In a food and beverage operation costs are apportioned to the menu and drinks list, as these lists are the means through which revenue is apportioned.

Direct costs, by definition, can be apportioned directly to the various parts of the menu and drinks list. The ingredient costs of a meal or drink may be calculated accurately and therefore the direct cost for each item on the food and drinks list identified. The use of standard recipes and tailor-made spreadsheets is common among large operators in identifying and measuring these direct costs.

Indirect costs, which comprise almost all the other costs beside the ingredient costs, are much more difficult to apportion. Examples of these indirect costs are: staff, linen, maintenance, cleaning materials, marketing, management, administration, rent, rates, fixtures, fittings, equipment, insurance, training and fuel. In order to overcome the problem of measuring how much of these costs should be apportioned to the individual menu and drinks list items, the costs are commonly apportioned as a percentage of the selling price. This proportion is usually identified as the proportion of the total individual cost to total revenue, for example:

Total food revenue	=	£1000.00
Total staff costs	=	£300.00
Staff cost (per cent)	=	30 per cent
Individual menu item selling price	=	£1.25
Apportioned staff cost at 30 per cent	=	£0.375

All other indirect costs are often calculated and apportioned in this way, and can be formed into groups such as overheads e.g. rent and rates, or operational expenses e.g. linen and cleaning materials. Which costs are included in these different groupings can vary from operation to operation. Many operations will simply group all these indirect costs together under 'overheads'; such apportioning is calculated as follows:

---

* The 'meal experience' (see p. 8) comprises the food and drink, the atmosphere, the service, the cleanliness and hygiene and the price/value for money.

Total food and beverage sales	=	£1000.00
Total overheads	=	£120.00
Overhead cost	=	12 per cent
Individual menu or drinks list item selling price	=	£1.25
Apportioned overhead cost at 12 per cent	=	£0.15

Although this is an uncomplicated way to apportion costs, it is clearly not accurate. If total staff costs are 30 per cent of total revenue, it does not necessarily follow that all menu and wine list items have a labour element of 30 per cent of their selling prices. It is the processes the various ingredients undergo which determine the labour cost, and as various ingredients undergo different processes – some highly skilled and time consuming, others simple and quick – the labour costs for individual menu and drinks list items are quite different. The same inaccuracy is inherent in apportioning other indirect costs, and therefore the value of apportioning costs in this way should be questioned.

In summarizing cost appraisal some key factors are apparent:

- The cost structures of food and beverage operations vary, and change over time.
- Costs can be measured in absolute terms or as percentages of total costs and revenue.
- Changes in the proportional relationship between costs can be measured, helping to identify opportunities for increased efficiency through changing the operating systems. Proportional relationships between costs and inflation also need to be taken into account.
- Cross-sectional and time-series analyses can be used to appraise costs.
- Increased competition among food and beverage operators is leading towards an oligopoly market in some sectors, creating a situation where operators with the lowest costs are perceived as having a key advantage.
- Allocating direct costs is uncomplicated, but methods of allocating indirect costs need to be considered carefully.

Appraising profits

As profits are the difference between revenue and costs, appraising profit requires the identification of the relationship between revenue and costs. The profit and loss account identifies the consequential result of this relationship. Table 7.3 shows an example of a profit and loss account.

In Table 7.3 the profit is £200, but this does not necessarily tell the whole story. If this was an owner-operated food and beverage operation the staff costs may or may not include the owner's salary. If it does include a labour/salary payment for the owner, should this be added to the profit? If it

Table 7.3 Example profit and loss account

Item	£
Income/revenue	1000
Direct costs/ingredient costs	300
Staff costs	250
Operating costs	100
Overheads	150
Total costs	800
Profit	200

does not include it, should this be deducted from the profit? Also, are there any costs still to be deducted from the profit, such as interest payments for a loan? In order to find out the answer to these questions it is necessary *to ask the question* of the person who supplies the information. If the information has been produced by yourself, you must ask yourself the questions to ensure that *you* get the whole picture. Because profitability is expressed in many different ways, and as food and beverage operators use these ways differently, it is important to clarify which costs have, or have not, been included in the profit measure.

Profitability measures The main profitability measures are identified as follows:

1. Gross profit (GP) in food and beverage operations is the difference between the selling price or revenue, and the cost of the food or drink ingredients. Examples are given in Table 7.4.

2. Gross profit percentage (GP%) is the gross profit measured as a percentage of the selling price or revenue. The GP% of the beefburger example is 57.4, the GP% for the soup is 80.6, and the GP% for the operation example is 70. Food and beverage operations use this measure extensively but it is important to recognize that a higher GP% does not always mean a higher GP. The soup has a higher GP% at 80.6 than the beefburger at 57.4, but the soup is less profitable in absolute or cash terms with a lower GP – at £1.41 – than the beefburger at £2.01.

3. Operating profit is measured in different ways by food and beverage operators, but its common usage would be that profit which has been derived solely from the operation, and excluding any profit that might have been made from selling land or buildings for example, which may have been owned by the business. Again, it is necessary to establish if any such 'non-operational' profits have been included in this measure before it can be appraised. It is also necessary to establish if overhead costs have been deducted.

4. Operating profit percentage is the operating profit measured as a

percentage of revenue. As with GP%s, a higher operating profit percentage does not always mean a higher operating profit; Table 7.5 gives two examples. Operation A has a higher operating profit percentage at 20 per cent than operation B at 15 per cent, but operation B has made a higher operating profit at £300 than operation A at £200.

5. Net profit is usually the measure which has deducted all costs from the revenue, including the overheads. However, it is possible that not all costs have been deducted. Sometimes the cost of interest payments, loan repayments and dividends will not have been deducted, and again care must be taken to check this.

6. Net profit percentage is the net profit measured as a percentage of revenue. Again a higher net profit percentage does not always mean a higher net profit. (See operating profit example above.)

7. Net operating profit, net operating profit percentage, both before and after tax and/or dividends, are other measures which are used. Again, it is necessary to check which costs have or have not been deducted, and to appreciate the difference between a percentage measure and an absolute measure.

Table 7.4 Comparison of gross profits

	4oz Beefburger		Bowl of soup		Food and beverage operation	
				Example		
Income	Selling price	£3.50	Selling price	£1.75	Food and beverage revenue	£1000
Expenditure	4 oz burger	£0.50	Stock	£0.07	Food costs	£170
	Lettuce	£0.07	Onions	£0.18	Drink costs	£130
	Dill	£0.05	Oil	£0.05		
	Mayonnaise	£0.09	Croutons	£0.04		
	Bun	£0.15				
Total cost		£1.49		£0.34		£300
Gross Profit		£2.01		£1.41		£700

Table 7.5 Comparison of operating profits

	Operation	
	A	B
Revenue	£1000	£2000
Operating costs[1]	£800	£1700
Operating profit	£200	£300
Operating profit (%)	20	15

[1] These costs would include ingredient costs and staff costs, but maybe not overheads. Therefore the extent to which the other costs might have been included needs to be established.

8. Departmental and unit profitability measures are used to identify the profitability of individual departments or units within a food and beverage operation. Some costs can be directly attributed to a department or unit, such as the cost of staff who only work in that section, and food and drink costs, but other costs such as rates and rent may be more difficult to apportion accurately.

9. Yield profitability measures are used mainly to measure the profitability of the beverage side of a food and beverage operation, although it can also be applied to the food side. Table 7.6 shows how yield is calculated.

At the end of each period, usually a week or month, the amount of beverage stock consumed is identified for each beverage item held in stock. The selling price of each of the beverage items – taken from the price list/wine list – is multiplied by the units of that beverage item consumed, to produce the yield. This yield is then measured as a percentage of the actual revenue.

In operation A the yield was 104 per cent. This happens because:

(a) Drinks have been mixed, as in a cocktail, which realizes a greater revenue than the sum of the parts that have been used to create the mixture.

(b) Customers have been overcharged or short-changed.

(c) Customers have been given short measures.

(d) The yield measure has been miscalculated.

(e) Wastage has not been as high as expected.

In operation B the yield was 95.2 per cent. This happens because:

(a) Wastage or ullage has occurred.

(b) Customers have been undercharged.

(c) Customers have been given a larger measure than necessary.

(d) All the revenue has not been received.

(e) The measure has been miscalculated.

Measuring the yield percentage therefore allows an appraisal of that operation's efficiency in (1) delivering the product and (2) receiving the correct revenue.

Table 7.6 Yield comparisons

	Operation	
	A	B
Total beverage revenue or yield	£1000	£1000
Total selling price of beverages consumed	£960	£1050
Yield percentage	104	95.2

Whichever profitability measures are used it is critical to know which costs have been included in the calculations, how they were apportioned and which costs may still have to be deducted. When this has been established it is then possible to appraise profitability in both absolute and relative terms.

Having identified the most common profitability measures it is possible to examine the way in which they are used.

Gross profit At unit and department level it appears that GP% is considered the most important profitability measure. This measure will be used by the unit manager and his/her immediate managers. In almost 100 per cent of food and beverage operations this is measured weekly although it is perfectly possible to measure GP% as often as is required as long as there are the resources available.

GP% is a simple measure of efficiency but it is important not to confuse efficiency with profitability. On many occasions an efficient operation is also a profitable one but this is not always the case. Food and beverage operations purchase ingredients which are processed into a consumable meal or drink. This process is in fact adding value to the raw ingredients, and the extent to which value is added is a measure of that operation's efficiency at achieving this conversion process. An operation which converts a £2 ingredient cost into an £8 meal or drink might be said to be 400 per cent efficient (£8 – the price, divided by £2 – the cost), and an operation which converts a £1 ingredient cost into a £5 meal or drink can be said to be 500 per cent efficient. The second example is more efficient (500 compared to 400 per cent) but is less profitable (£4 compared to £6).

An operation that has poor purchasing resulting in higher ingredient costs, poor storage resulting in wastage, poor security resulting in pilferage, poor production resulting in high wastage, poor portioning resulting in larger portions than specified and poor pricing resulting in lower revenue, will have a lower GP% than the same operation which improves on these poor performances. The unit and departmental manager is seen to have an influence over how these activities are performed and as such the GP% is thought to measure that manager's performance. It is not usually the case that the unit or departmental manager has any influence over the price, this being determined higher up the organization, and on many occasions they will not have an influence over the purchasing because specified suppliers and negotiated prices are again determined higher up the organization.

The actual GP% figure against which a manager's performance is measured will also be set higher up the organization. In a chain operation these GP%s will be set for each individual operation based on the sales mix of the menu and beverage lists. This sales mix – the amount sold of each menu and beverage list item – will vary from operation to operation depending on the customer profile and the selling techniques of the staff. The selling techniques of the staff can be influenced by the manager, but the manager usually has little influence over the customer profile. Perhaps the most influential factor over customer profile, especially in chain operations, is location. Bearing in mind these factors, an operation will be allocated a 'suitable' GP% to obtain. Achieving this prescribed GP% is seen to be a good performance while not achieving it is seen to be a poor performance.

One way in which to decide upon the prescribed GP% is to run a particular unit or department over a period of time and take an average of the actual GP%s achieved. The individual running the unit during this period should not be someone with a vested interest in being able to achieve the prescribed GP% in the future, but should nevertheless have the necessary skills to operate the unit at a high efficiency level. It is not possible for chain operations to do this with each unit and in many chains it is not done at all. In reality GP%s are set with reference to a desired efficiency level based on what is thought to be achievable (see also potential profitability, p. 173). This GP% is also seen to change as new menus are introduced.

An important factor which influences the introduction of new menus is the opportunity to increase the operation's efficiency and therefore new menus may often come with a higher GP% to obtain. In these situations a chain operation usually pilots the new menus in specifically selected units in order to obtain customer feedback and establish the new efficiency and profitability measure. This measure is then applied to the rest of the group's operations with slight variations for different customer profiles as these will affect the sales mix of the individual units.

Having established the required GP% the unit manager is then measured against the ability to achieve it. The dilemma with this measurement is that it measures a percentage not an absolute figure. Percentages cannot be banked. A higher than required GP% will not necessarily realize a higher than required GP if the required revenue is not achieved (see Table 7.7).

Operation A has a higher GP% than required at 66 (good management?) – but only achieves a GP of £594, £56 below that required, because sales have not achieved their target (perhaps out of the control of the operation?).

Table 7.7 Comparison of GP in relation to revenue

	Operation	
	A	**B**
Required Revenue	£1000	£1000
Actual Revenue	£900	£1100
GP% required	65	65
GP% achieved	66	64
GP required	£650	£650
GP achieved	£594	£704

Operation B achieves a GP% below that which is required at 64 (bad management?) – but achieves a GP of £704, £54 above that required, because sales have exceeded the target (again, perhaps out of the control of the operation?). Operation A could be said to be more efficient than operation B, but operation B is more profitable than operation A.

This is the reason why GP% is often more highly valued than GP itself, because this measure of efficiency will allow for variations of revenue. If operation A had achieved its GP% of 65, its actual GP would have been £584, and although this is below the required GP of £650 the operation can still be viewed as adding value or operating efficiently. That sales are £100 under that which is required may not be directly under the influence of the manager. Indeed it is normal for sales to fluctuate due to the inaccuracies of budgeting and predicting the future. Therefore by measuring GP%, allowances for these sales fluctuations are made. The same reasoning is applied to operation B. Sales are above the required or budgeted amount, but if the operation was running as efficiently as required and achieved its GP% of 65, the actual GP would have been £715, £11 more than actually achieved.

The effect of this measurement on operational performance is worth considering. Many managers of units and departments will perceive the achievement of the GP% as more important than the achievement of the budgeted revenue. As explained earlier in this chapter, revenue budgets may be seen as being too high for the unit to obtain and that even if the revenue budgets are achieved this may only mean that they are set higher next year. However, if the GP% is regularly achieved, the manager can state that the operation is being run efficiently. This thinking takes place at all the operational levels within a food and beverage operation. Regional managers and directors are more concerned with cash profits than with percentage profits, but at the operational level the percentage profits are more highly valued.

The reason for this anomaly is because the GP% measure is seen as a measure for controlling the efficiency of the management and staff rather than addressing profitability. As it is used as a control method, opportunities exist to exploit the system to the detriment of profit. A recent study (Shortt, 1992, p. 86) asked managers at a chain operation which items on their menus and beverage lists were identified for positive selling. (These were the items that managers trained their staff to positively sell.) As it is understood that different menu and beverage items realize different GPs and GP%s, the items identified by the managers for positive selling were always items with a relatively high GP%. Table 7.8 shows an example.

In the theoretical situation in Table 7.8 the two menu items identified by the manager for positive selling would be the plaice and chicken because they yielded a higher GP% than the beef and lamb. By selling these items the manager was aiming to achieve as high as possible a GP% for the individual sale of a menu item, which would in turn contribute positively to the achievement of the required GP% for the whole operation. If, in this situation, the required

Table 7.8   Comparison of GP and GP%

Menu items	GP	GP%	Selling price
Beef	£6.00	50	£12.00
Plaice	£3.50	70	£5.00
Chicken	£4.50	75	£6.00
Lamb	£5.20	65	£8.00

GP% was 68, the plaice and the chicken sales would shift the balance of GP% achievement towards this goal, but any sales of beef and lamb would shift this balance away from the goal. The manager is motivated by an efficiency control mechanism towards achieving a required profit percentage.

A more profit focus examination of Table 7.8 reveals that it is not the plaice and chicken which are the most profitable. With GPs of £3.50 and £4.50 respectively they are considerably less profitable than the beef and lamb at £5.20 and £6.00. A positive selling policy identifying the beef and lamb would realize greater profits than the one identifying the plaice and chicken. However, because GP% is the control measure, the operation is seen to place more value on percentage profitability rather than cash profitability with the result of decreasing potential profit. That a control measure should have this effect (or at least the possibility of this effect) should be of concern to all food and beverage operators.

Potential gross profit and potential gross profit percentage

Some food and beverage operations attempt to avoid the situation described above by the use of a further measure which is termed potential profitability. With the increasing introduction of computerized tills and control systems some operators calculate the GP and GP% that an operation should have achieved in theory for a particular time period. The ingredient cost and price of each menu or beverage item have already been entered into the till system which then automatically records the number of sales of these particular items, and thus a theoretical GP and GP% are calculated.

Recording such data is not new – computerized stock control systems are the main application of such systems – but not all operators are aware that this data can be converted into meaningful sales mix analysis information, of which potential GP and GP% are but two examples. Table 7.9 shows how potential GP and GP% are calculated.

Each of the four items on the menu in Table 7.9 are seen to be achieving a different GP and GP%. After totalling the GP and revenue the potential GP and GP% are calculated at £2075 and 63 per cent respectively. This potential GP and GP% are what the operation should achieve with this particular sales mix. However, if the sales mix were to change from one period to another for any number of reasons (weather, party bookings, change in positive selling routine), then the potential GP and GP% may also change. Using the example of Table 7.9, an increase in the number of plaice sold and a decrease in the number of beef sold, while the total number of covers served remains the same, produce a lower potential (and hence achievable) GP and GP%. Table 7.10 shows the new potential measures to be £1949 and 66 per cent respectively.

In operations where potential GP and GP% are calculated it is possible to measure the operation's performance against that which was actually achievable in relation to the sales mix for that particular period. In the two examples above it is seen that although the operation in Table 7.10 produces a potential GP% of 66 (a potential GP of £1949), it is not as profitable as the operation in Table 7.9 which only produces a potential GP% of 63 (but a potential GP of £2075, £126 more). Operations which calculate potential GP and GP% are therefore more able to measure the operation's efficiency in relation to a changing sales mix. This method of calculating potential GP and GP% not only continues to take account of changing sales levels but also changing sales mixes, and as such is seen as a much *fairer* way of measuring an operation's performance. More importantly, however, is the change in emphasis of this control and performance measure away from purely measuring GP% and towards measuring actual GP (cash). Thus, taking potential GP% and GP into account shifts the appraisal of profit towards cash and away from percentages.

However, in operations where potential GP% is calculated, there is evidence that there is a third GP% which is used to measure and control

Table 7.9   Sales mix example

Menu item	Cost (£)	Price (£)	No. sold	Revenue	GP	GP%
Beef	6.00	12.00	100	1200	600	50
Plaice	1.50	5.00	150	750	525	70
Chicken	1.50	6.00	130	780	585	75
Lamb	2.80	8.00	70	560	364	65
Total			450	3290	2075	63

Table 7.10   Effect of changed sales mix

Menu item	Cost (£)	Price (£)	No. sold	Revenue	GP	GP%
Beef	6.00	12.00	50	600	300	50
Plaice	1.50	5.00	200	1000	700	70
Chicken	1.50	6.00	130	780	585	75
Lamb	2.80	8.00	70	560	364	65
Total			450	2940	1949	66

performance, namely a desired GP%. This desired GP% is set at a level that the operator would like to achieve, in much the same way as the GP% is set in operations where they do not calculate potential GP%. An example of how this might work in practice for a particular time period is given below:

Potential GP%	69
Actual GP% achieved	68.5
Desired GP%	70

In the example above the operator has set a desired GP% of 70. This is the GP% that the operator wants to achieve. From the actual sales mix for that period it was only possible to achieve a GP% of 69 – the potential GP% – and a GP% of 68.5 was actually obtained. The value placed on this performance might therefore be as follows:

> The unit was unable to achieve the GP% desired by the operator. This is a result of the sales mix and may have happened because waiting staff were unable to sell the required high GP% menu and beverage list items. However, the unit was also unable to achieve the potential GP% which is a measure of their inefficiency to add the required value.

Calculating potential GP% and GP, and using them to help appraise food and beverage operations, still allows for fluctuations of revenue – the reason why GP% is used as the main performance measure – but moves the consideration of value in the direction of GP cash and away from GP%. That many operators do not calculate potential GP% and GP, even though they already have the technology to do so, means that they are potentially reducing their ability to maximize cash profitability.

Sales mix analysis Sales mix analyses methods involve identifying the sales relationship between the various menu and beverage list items. By far the most common application of these analyses is to determine the relationship of item numbers sold, i.e. a popularity index. A simple beverage list example is shown in Table 7.11.

From the information shown in Table 7.11 it is observed that Loire wines represent 35 per cent of the total wine sales and as such are the most popular

Table 7.11 Sales mix example

Item	No. sold	% of total
Champagne	20	10
Rhone wines	50	25
Loire wines	70	35
Bordeaux wines	60	30
Total	200	100

customer purchase. Bordeaux wines are the next most popular at 30 per cent. Rhone wines at 25 per cent are the third most popular and Champagne at 10 per cent is the least popular customer purchase. This identification of item popularity is used by many operators to assist with the compilation of new menus and beverage lists. In its most simplistic form the least popular item or items are removed from the listing although this is not always the case. In Table 7.11 it might be considered to retain champagne on the wine list because customers expect to be able to purchase it when required, albeit infrequently. Champagne on the wine list will also contribute to the operation's image.

However, popularity should not be confused with profitability. There is a relationship between popularity and profitability but the most popular selling item is not necessarily the most profitable. In order to examine this relationship it is important to identify which type of profit should be measured. As this is a relationship between individual menu and wine list items, the requirement is that the profit measure must also relate to these individual items. Apportioning costs to individual food and beverage items is difficult. How much of the electricity expenses should be apportioned to each item for example? The same difficulty is experienced when attempting to apportion labour costs. However, direct ingredient costs can be apportioned which will result in a measure of GP for each individual item. A relationship between popularity and GP is illustrated in Table 7.12.

From Table 7.12 it is possible to compare a popularity ranking with a profitability ranking, as shown in Table 7.13. The profitability ranking is clearly different from the popularity ranking, enabling a more focused valuation of the sales mix in relation to how much the individual menu items contribute – at a GP level – to operational profitability.

It is unclear how many food and beverage operators rank their menu and beverage list items in such a way. It appears that most of the large chain operations are using and developing such analysis techniques, as they have marketing departments with the resources required. These techniques have an element of some sophistication; for example, linking with the amount of stock held relative to its profitability, and consideration of a new menu item also

Table 7.12 Example of profitability calculations

Item	GP (£)	No. sold	%	Total GP(£)	% of total GP
Standard burger	0.90	650	31.2	585.00	23.8
4 oz burger	1.20	540	25.9	648.00	26.4
Standard cheese burger	1.08	320	15.3	345.60	14.1
4 oz. cheese burger	1.40	290	13.9	406.00	16.5
Double super burger	1.65	285	13.7	470.25	19.2
Total		2085	100.0	2454.85	100

Table 7.13   Example of popularity and profitability ranking

Popularity ranking		Profitability ranking	
Standard burger	31.2% of sales	4 oz burger	26.4 %of GP
4 oz burger	25.9% of sales	Standard burger	23.8% of GP
Standard cheese burger	15.3% of sales	Double super burger	19.2% of GP
4 oz cheese burger	13.9% of sales	4 oz cheese burger	16.5% of GP
Double super burger	13.7% of sales	Standard cheese burger	14.1% of GP

relative to its profitability. However, these individual company techniques and developments, and their relationship with appraising and improving profitability, are not identified in any literature beyond self-promoting material, which does not critically evaluate the techniques, and makes it difficult to identify their value objectively. However, it is fair to assume that it is assigned some value in order for it to be resourced. The issue here is concerned with the perceived competitive advantage of such relatively sophisticated sales mix analyses techniques and therefore secrecy is observed although the academic world has not been slow to develop and evaluate these sales mix analyses techniques.

It is not intended to critically evaluate these developments here, but it is possible to consider their potential. Shortt (1992, pp. 31–44) has recently attempted to evaluate these sales mix analyses techniques and there is considerable evi-dence that profitability can be and is being improved through the use of such techniques. However, there is also evidence that the UK food and beverage industry is slow to develop and use such techniques, lagging behind its US counterpart, potentially resulting in less profitable and less successful UK operations.

All the various sales mix analyses techniques categorize the individual menu and wine list items and suggest strategies for each category. These strategies are designed to improve profitability but there is considerable evidence that the techniques themselves can be too complex and unproven to be assigned any value by much of the food and beverage industry.

Menu engineering   One approach to sales analysis which has gained some popularity is the technique of 'menu engineering'. This is a technique of menu analysis which uses two key factors of performance in the sales of individual menu items: the popularity and the GP cash contribution of each item. The analysis results in each menu item fitting into one of four categories:

- items of high popularity and high cash GP contributions, which are known as the *Stars*
- items of high popularity but with low cash GP contribution, which are known as the *Plowhorses*

- items of low popularity but with high cash GP contributions, which are known as the *Puzzles*
- items of low popularity and low cash GP contribution, which are the worst items on the menu and are known as the *Dogs*

The advantage of this approach is that it provides a simple way of graphically indicating the relative cash contribution position of individual items on a matrix as in Fig. 7.1.

There are a variety of computer-based packages which will automatically generate the categorization, usually directly using data from the point-of-sale control systems. The basis for the calculations is as follows.

In order to determine the position of an item on the matrix two things need to be calculated. These are:

- the cash GP category
- the sales percentage category

The cash GP category for a menu item is calculated by reference to the weighted average cash GP. Menu items with a cash GP which is the same as or higher than the average are classified as high. Those with lower than the average are classified as low cash GP items. The average also provides the axis separating Plowhorses and Dogs from Stars and Puzzles.

The sales percentage category for an item is determined in relation to the menu average taking into account an additional factor. With a menu

Fig. 7.1 Menu engineering matrix (based on Kasavana and Smith, 1982)

consisting of ten items one might expect, other things being equal, that each item would account for 10 per cent of the menu mix. Any item which reached at least 10 per cent of the total menu items sold would therefore be classified as enjoying high popularity. Similarly any item which did not achieve the rightful share of 10 per cent would be categorized as having a low popularity. With this approach half of the menu items would tend to be shown as being below average in terms of their popularity. This would potentially result in the frequent revision of the composition of the menu. It is for this reason that Kasavana and Smith (1982) have recommended the use of a 70 per cent formula. Under this approach, all items which reach at least 70 per cent of their rightful share of the menu mix are categorized as enjoying high popularity. For example, where a menu consists of say 20 items, any item which reached 3.5 per cent or more of the menu mix (70 per cent of 5 per cent) would be regarded as enjoying high popularity. While there is no convincing theoretical support for choosing the 70 per cent figure rather than some other percentage, common sense and experience tends to suggest that there is some merit in this approach.

Interpreting the categories

There is a different basic strategy which can be considered for items which fall into each of the four categories of the matrix.

Stars There are the most popular items, which may be able to yield even higher GP contributions by careful price increases or through cost reduction. High visibility is maintained on the menu and standards for the dishes should be strictly controlled.

Plowhorses These again are solid sellers, which may also be able to yield greater cash profit contributions through marginal cost reduction. Lower menu visibility than Stars is usually recommended.

Puzzles These are exactly what they are called. Items such as for instance flambé dishes or a particular speciality can add an attraction in terms of drawing customers, even though the sales of these items may be low. Depending on the particular item different strategies might be considered, ranging from accepting the current position because of the added attraction that they provide to increasing the price further.

Dogs These are the worst items on a menu and the first reaction is to remove them. An alternative, however, is to consider adding them to another item as part of a special deal. For instance, adding them in a meal package to a Star may have the effect of lifting the sales of the Dog item and may provide a relatively low-cost way of adding special promotions to the menu.

Some potential limitations

Elasticity of demand   One of the practical difficulties with price level adjustment is not knowing enough about the 'elasticity of demand'. The effect of demand (number of covers) of any one change in the general level of menu prices is usually uncertain. Also, what applies to one menu item equally applies to the menu as a whole. There is an additional problem of 'cross-elasticity of demand' where the change in demand for one commodity is directly affected by a change in price of another. Even less is known about the cross-elasticity of demand for individual menu items than the elasticity of demand for the menu as a whole. Any benefit arising from an adjustment in the price of one item may therefore be offset by resultant changes in the demand for another item. Price level adjustments must therefore be underpinned by a lot of common sense, experience and knowledge of the particular circumstances of the operation.

Labour intensity   In menu engineering the most critical element is cash gross profit. While this may be important the aspect of labour intensity cannot be ignored. The cash GP on a flambé dish for example may be higher than on a more simple sweet, however, when the costs of labour are taken into account – especially at peak periods – it may well be that the more simple sweet is the more profitable overall.

Shelf life   The food cost of an item used to determine the cash GP may not take account of cost increases which are the result of food wastage through spoilage, especially at slack times.

Fluctuations in demand   Another factor is the consistency of the buying of the consumer. The approach assumes that changes can be made in the promotion of various items and that this will be reflected in the buying behaviour of the customer. The approach will work well where the potential buying pattern of the consumer is fairly similar over long periods. However, where the customers are continually changing, as for instance in the restaurant of an hotel, popularity and profitability can become more affected by changes in the nature of the customer and the resultant change in demand rather than as a result of the operation attempting to manipulate the sales mix.

Further applications

While this technique is presented here related to menu food items the same technique can also be applied to wine and drink lists. It is interesting to note, for example, that in many instances the house wine, although having the highest gross profit percentage contribution, often makes a relatively low contribution to the cash gross profit. Additionally, the principles of the technique have also been applied to the selling of hotel rooms and the rates that may be charged, now known as 'yield management'.

It is clear however that although there are some difficulties, benefits can arise since the menu engineering approach requires the following:

- planning for continuous control of cash GP
- giving prominence to, and controlling the determinants of, menu profitability; i.e. the number of items sold, the cash GP per item and the overall composition of the menu
- application of an analytical approach recognizing that menu items belong to distinctly dissimilar groups, which have different characteristics and which require different handling in the context of cash gross profit control

Net profit and operating profit

These profitability measures are used to evaluate more fully the efficiency of a food and beverage operation to add value, because they take account of all or most of the costs incurred by the business. The relationship between costs and revenue to produce net and/or operating profit is not as directly proportional as the GP measure and it is more difficult therefore to identify the relationship between an individual menu and wine list item and total net/operating profit. This relationship has been researched by Pavesic *et al.* (1986–1993) but again the methods appear too complex to be adopted by much of the food and beverage industry. The main relationship for total net/operating profit appears to be with total sales revenue.

This relationship is twofold. As a percentage measure it values an operation's efficiency at adding value. As an absolute measure it values a specific amount of residual utility – usually in cash – which has derived from an absolute revenue. As has already been examined, a high percentage measure may be of less residual utility – cash – than a lower percentage measure. However, as long as the measures are calculated using the same criteria, i.e. they use the same revenue and costs measures, they can be compared. This comparison can help appraise an operation's performance. Table 7.14 states some net/operating profit measures.

Table 7.14   Comparison of net/operating profit measures

	Financial year			
	1991/92	1992/93	1993/94	1993/94 budget
Unit A				
Sales	£1 500 000	£1 600 000	£1 700 000	£1 800 000
N/op Profit	£150 000	£155 000	£145 000	£180 000
per cent of revenue	10	9.70	8.53	10
Unit B				
Sales	£700 000	£750 000	£800 000	£900 000
N/op profit	£70 000	£75 000	£67 500	£90 000
per cent of Revenue	10	10	8.44	10

In the example in Table 7.14 all the measures have been made using the same criteria, year on year, and in both operations. An appraisal of the operation's performance, as individual one-off food and beverage operations, might be as follows.

Operation A

*   Sales have increased by £100 000 year on year representing a percentage increase year on year of 6.67 and 6.25 per cent, and overall by 13.3 per cent. Sales are also £100 000 and 5.88 per cent under budget. The rate of increase in sales has slowed.
*   Net/operating profit increased 3.33 per cent by £5000 in the first year and decreased 6.45 per cent by £10 000 in the second. Net/operating profit is £35 000 and 19.44 per cent under budget. Net/operating profit has declined by 3.33 per cent (£150 000 to £145 000) from 1991/92 to 1993/94; 1993/94 has seen a reversal of profitability.
*   Net/operating profit as a percentage of sales has declined from 10 to 9.7 to 8.53 per cent compared to a required level of 10 per cent. Net/operating profit as a percentage of sales has declined by 12.1 per cent (the difference between 8.53 and 9.7 per cent as a percentage of 9.7 per cent) and is 14.7 per cent under budget (the difference between 8.53 and 10 per cent as a percentage of 10 per cent).

Operation B

*   Sales have increased by £50 000 year on year representing a percentage increase year on year of 7.14 and 6.67 per cent, and overall by 14.3 per cent. Sales are also £100 000 and 11.11 per cent under budget. The rate of increase in sales has slowed.
*   Net/operating profit increased 7.14 per cent by £5000 in the first year and decreased 10 per cent by £7500 in the second. Net/operating profit is also £22 500 and 25 per cent under budget. From 1991/92 to 1993/94 net/operating profit declined by 3.57 per cent (£70 000 to £67 500); 1993/94 has seen a reversal of profitability.
*   Net/operating profit as a percentage of sales was maintained in 1992/93 and has declined by 15.6 per cent (the difference between 10 and 8.44 per cent as a percentage of 10 per cent), in 1993/94. Net operating profit as a percentage of sales has declined by 15.6 per cent since 1991/92 (the difference between 10 and 8.44 per cent as a percentage of 10 per cent), and is also 15.6 per cent under budget (the difference between 10 per cent and 8.44 per cent as a percentage of 10 per cent).

The above evaluation identifies the differences between absolute figures and the differences between percentages. This may appear at times to be fairly tortuous, especially when all the changes are presented together. In reality more value may be placed upon certain measurements than others depending on the message which is to be communicated, and not all the measurements will be communicated at the same time. Using the examples above it might be considered appropriate to say that sales have increased in unit A by over 6 per cent each year, and say nothing about net/operating profit being almost 20 per cent under budget. This is why it is so important to question the presentation of the information which is provided. When it is stated that sales have increased by over 6 per cent each year, the immediate response should be to ask for other performance measures, in this case profit. Questioning is crucial in order to fully appraise an operation.

Many might argue that further value can be placed upon the information in Table 7.14 by comparing these operations' performances with an industry norm, i.e. a measure which suggests a normal performance. Such industry norms are of questionable value. Firstly, food and beverage operations must be categorized into industry sectors before an average or mean net/operating profit can be calculated for that sector. It is possible to categorize food and beverage operations but no two operations are the same (even chain operations differ), and will probably have different objectives resulting in different values being placed upon their profitability. Secondly, the environment in which food and beverage operations operate is dynamic. This environment relates to: consumer behaviour and social/cultural changes; the financial market; the national and international economic position; and political issues and legislation. Different operations will react to these continuing changes in different ways resulting in differing valuations of profitability. The norm therefore may be seen as an arbitrary measure.

However, it is possible to compare an operation's profitability with other similar operations, but care must be taken to establish the value of the norm in such a comparison. Shortt (1992, p. 84) found that food and beverage operations taking part in the research had a required GP per cent in the range 68–72. There is no evidence that certain operations will be at the top or the bottom of the range. The important consideration is the value of the information to the stakeholders, i.e. those with a vested or invested interest in the business. An understanding and declaration of these stakeholder objectives make the appraisal of the operation more objective and of more value.

Inflation is another consideration which may be taken into account as it is a measure of the usually upward movement of prices across a range of commodities and services. For example, if net/operating profit had increased by 10 per cent over the last 12 months, and inflation had been 5 per cent over the last 12 months, it might be considered that in real terms profitability is up only 5 per cent (10 per cent profitability improvement minus 5 per cent inflation). This will be an important consideration for those managing, owning and directing food and beverage operations in the appraisal of profitability. In addition, company taxation and dividends are also an important consideration and will affect profitability, but the complexity of these considerations will not be examined here.

Putting aside industry norms, inflation, taxation and dividends, chain operations with almost identical units across a country or region, can make cross-unit comparisons with some degree of objectivity. If we assume that operations A and B in Table 7.14 are both units which belong to the same chain, a cross-unit comparison may be as follows:

- Sales have increased more in unit B than in unit A, 14.3 per cent compared to 13.3 per cent. However, unit A is only 5.88 per cent under budgeted sales compared to unit B being 11.11 per cent under budgeted sales.
- Net/operating profit has decreased by 3.57 per cent in unit B, but only 3.33 per cent in unit A. Unit A is also only 19.44 per cent under budgeted net/operating profit compared to unit B being 25 per cent under budgeted net/operating profit.
- As a percentage of sales net/operating profit has declined by 12.1 per cent in unit A and 15.6 per cent in unit B.

From these measurements and comparisons it could be said that although unit B has had a greater success than unit A in increasing sales, they have been less efficient at turning those sales into profit. The value placed on this information may form the basis of reward and incentive systems for operational staff and management.

Summary One must always be clear how the profit measure is contrived and ensure that any comparisons made are like with like. Profitability measures themselves have no value, it is only when they are appraised against an objective that they may have some value. Setting the objective, norm and/or budget is difficult and sometimes results in subjective judgements. The ultimate objective is to 'please the stakeholders' who may be a range of different people with a range of different objectives.

Appraising the product

The product that food and beverage operations manufacture is a combination of variables perhaps best identified under the 'meal experience' framework. This framework identifies the component parts of the meal experience under the following headings:

- the food and beverages
- the service
- price
- the atmosphere (including cleanliness and hygiene)

When food and beverage operators develop new and existing products the meal experience variables are changed. Which ones are changed, and what they are changed to, will depend on how the operator considers what will best suit their customers' needs. It is clear that each variable has its own plethora of variables; there are many different ways of producing and delivering many different foods and beverages, in many different atmospheres at differently priced and differently perceived value, in different levels of cleanliness and hygiene. If the objective is to appraise the product, then it is necessary to identify each component part.

Chain operations usually lead the field in this area. With their branded products it is necessary to effect tight control over the meal experience variables. Appraising and controlling revenue and costs are systemized through budgeting and standardized procedures. Appraising and controlling the product are also effected through standardized procedures.

The meal experience variables are specified in training and performance manuals. Appraising and controlling these variables are effected through a 'checking procedure' performed at all the chain units by 'anonymous customers'. These anonymous customers are employed by the chain operation to identify how well each unit is operating in relation to the specified variables. The anonymous customers are provided with a checklist of the variable objectives with some operations having identified and specified over 150 of these. This list will contain objectives covering such areas as:

- the words, demeanour and body language of the welcome
- the information and selling routine
- the time taken to deliver each menu and beverage list item ordered
- the taste, colour, texture, temperature and presentation of menu and beverage items
- the presentation of the bill and concluding routine

Once the 'meal experience' has been evaluated the anonymous customer identifies him/herself to the unit manager and continues the appraisal in non-customer areas. This second part of the appraisal covers such areas as:

- temperature and stocking levels in the fridges and freezers
- cleanliness, security and safety of all areas
- current data collection and collation up to date

Once this product and operational audit has been completed the unit will be given the result as a percentage of objectives obtainable, and this will be communicated to the unit manager detailing the results. This information allows the unit manager to concentrate resources on rectifying specific underperformances. This process is dynamic and as changes are made to the product, new specifications and objectives are drawn up. Operators will have a budget percentage which each unit is expected to achieve, perhaps around 95 per cent. This process itself, and the results of the process, both appraise and control the product.

At the other end of the spectrum one-off and/or owner-operated food and beverage operations take a more subjective and intuitive approach to product appraisal. Because the appraisal process is not so structured and objective, does not mean that it cannot be as, or more, effective. This more subjective and intuitive approach may be more suitable to a one-off operation that does not need to appraise and control its product over a multi-unit structure. However, it is highly dependent on the integrity and skills of its workforce, and therefore can be highly subjective, which will not cause a product problem if the required amount of customers also have the same subjective values and perceptions. It is this intuitive response to customer needs that enables some operators to be highly successful. Much arrogance can be attached to operators' intuition and using some objective measures should be regarded as being responsible and professional. It is good business sense to monitor customer satisfaction in relation to changing customer needs, and objective product appraisal will help in identifying whether the product is matching the operator's and the customer's expectations.

Appraising the business environment

Appraising the business environment enables a food and beverage operation to understand how it relates to the business environment, how the business environment is changing and facilitates an objective view of the future to be taken. The range of resources apportioned to this task is very wide, with large operators employing economists and strategic directors, and small operators relying on instinct and intuition. Appraising the business environment also includes an examination of the competition and what threats that competition may pose.

Several techniques are available to appraise the business environment which are covered in detail in a huge variety of texts and publications (see bibliography at the end of the chapter). Two techniques which can be of use to food and beverage operators are strengths, weaknesses, opportunities and threats analysis (SWOT) and political, economic, social and technological analysis (PEST).

SWOT analyses are useful to the food and beverage operator because they allow a focused identification and evaluation of the issues which affect the operation. Strengths and weaknesses are usually internal to the operation and might include such items as product, staffing, management and operating systems. Opportunities and threats are usually external to the business and might include such items as the existing and potential market needs, interest rates, demographic changes, infrastructure developments and national and local economic outlooks.

PEST analyses are perhaps more sophisticated and would require skills which permit a wider and deeper evaluation of the current and potential business environment. Political influences might include such issues as legislation (hygiene, opening hours, employment contracts and responsibilities, trade descriptions, licensing, etc.), grants and subsidies, and the Monopolies and Mergers Commission. Economic influences might include exchange rates (as they affect tourism), inflation and taxation. Social issues might concern changing market needs, demographic changes and changing patterns of employment. Technological issues might concern the operating systems of a business, channels of distribution (how a business communicates with its customers) and data and information gathering.

The value placed upon these analyses by food and beverage operators will be dependent upon their skills and objectives. To ignore these analyses is imprudent, to include them in appraising an operation's performance, no matter how modestly, is sensible. The process of beginning to use these analysis techniques is a learning process, which will strengthen the operation by making possible a more focused appraisal of how the food and beverage operation complements and matches the environment in which it operates.

Appraising the whole operation

When appraising the whole food and beverage operation it is necessary to consider when an appraisal of the whole operation should take place and how such an appraisal should be performed.

When such an appraisal takes place will be dependent upon the constraints and opportunities perceived by the business, and the rate of change of these issues. It may normally be expected that this appraisal may take place half-yearly or yearly, or when appropriate.

How such an appraisal is structured will affect the outcome of the appraisal process and the value placed upon it. It may be helpful to section the appraisal of the whole operation into three main areas:

1. financial
2. product
3. business environment

These three areas are interdependent, but it would be prudent to evaluate them separately before identifying the interrelationship. The three areas may be summarized for the main issues under each heading. The actual detailed evaluation will have already been completed and it will now be necessary to identify the key issues relating to each of the three areas. An example of these key issues may be as follows.

Financial
- Sales have dropped by 12 per cent over the last year.
- Absolute net/operating profit has declined from £150 000 to £125 000 over the last financial year.
- Costs have been reduced over the last financial year resulting in an improvement of net/operating profit as a percentage of sales from 10 to 12 per cent.
- Average spend per head has increased from £9.90 to £11.50 over the last financial year, while the number of customers has declined by 14 per cent.

Product
- The product has achieved an average of 92 per cent attainment in performing to operational objectives.
- The product has under-performed in the attainment of 'service' objectives, reaching an average of 72 per cent.
- The number of customers buying the product has declined by 14 per cent.

Business environment
- Inflation and interest rates have fallen significantly over the last financial year.
- The opening of the Channel Tunnel and the development of the EU increase the size of the potential market.
- Consumers are becoming more discerning and increasingly rate 'value for money' and 'quality of service' as high priorities.
- The level of business awareness among applicants wishing to be employed by the business, and the number of applications, have both increased over the last few years.

Having identified the key issues under each area it is appropriate to develop alternative strategies over the short, medium and long term. These strategies may be very detailed as in strategies for large food and beverage operators, or very broad and general.

However, it is appropriate to consider the example above and to develop and select alternative strategies. These might be as follows.

Strategy 1

As 'quality of service' is becoming increasingly important to the potential market, and as the operation's 'quality of service' is not performing to the required standard, we must examine the 'service' variable of our 'meal experience' in relation to customer expectations and in relation to operational procedures. We will research food and beverage customers' needs from the general literature available, e.g. Mintel and Keynote reports, and will commission a survey to identify our existing customer needs and how well they perceive these are being met. We will then develop our product better to consistently meet these customers' needs.

Strategy 2

Although we are operating more efficiently than before, we have failed to maintain and expand our customer base. Customers are spending more than before but this is not being turned into the required absolute profit because the number of customers has decreased. 'Value for money' has also become more important to our customers.

We will research food and beverage customer perceptions of 'value for money' and commission a survey of our own customers to identify their perceptions of 'value for money'. We will then develop our product to be perceived as good 'value for money'.

Strategy 3

The potential workforce in our food and beverage operation is increasingly ambitious and skilled. We will research organizational structures of the food and beverage industry and other related industries through subscription to appropriate journals and advice from the local university. We will then develop, initiate and implement an organizational structure which empowers and develops all our staff.

The above broad strategies would then be discussed and debated as proposed by the managers. This may be among all organizational staff, or by selected groups. Issues such as cost and time would need to be considered. After this discussion and debate has taken place, a decision will be made as to which strategies to adopt, and a schedule of implementation will be proposed and agreed. It may be that all three strategies are adopted, and allocated to appropriate management team members to implement.

Summary

This chapter has identified the component parts of a food and beverage operation and examined how their performance may be appraised. Issues concerning 'objectives' of a food and beverage operation have been addressed, as has the importance of being able to appraise objectively.

Appraising overall operational performance has been structured into three key areas: financial, product and business environment, and their interrelationship has been illustrated.

A manager's job is to ask the right questions, not to provide all the right answers.

References

Kasavana M and Smith D I 1982 *Menu engineering: a practical guide to menu analysis* Hospitality Publications, Lansing, Michigan

Shortt D P J 1992 *Pricing and profitability in the restaurant industry* MBA dissertation, University of Brunel, Henley

8 Cases in food and beverage management

Aim To consolidate a variety of aspects of food and beverage management through examples of worked case material.

Objective To enable you to develop a systematic approach to operational business problem identification and problem-solving.

An approach to case analysis and evaluation

At the start of this book it was suggested that using systems approaches meant both that managers should be systematic in their approaches to operational decision-making and that operations should be viewed as systems. The approach outlined below is based on this philosophy.

The basic problem-solving approach being used here is a five-stage process. This is:

1. analysis
2. evaluation
3. identification of limitations in data
4. consideration of short-term action
5. consideration of longer-term action

Analysis This represents the initial stage of the process. This stage has two parts. First is the gathering of information about the operation and presenting this under the various stages of the catering cycle (see pp. 1–2). The second part is the gathering of the trading and other financial data and calculating various performance measures.

Throughout this stage it is important to remain objective in the gathering and representing of the information. This is particularly so in the second part where it is often not until the performance measures have been applied that it can be determined if the information or trends indicated are useful.

Evaluation
This evaluation stage considers the information provided by the analysis and identifies the current strengths and weaknesses of the operation. These should be summarized so that only six to ten key strengths and weaknesses are identified. If the list is too long it merely becomes a restatement of the analysis stage and will not provide much useful direction. The overall approach is to consider what the analysis is telling us about the operation's performance, not merely to restate the analysis, i.e. it is very easy to fall into the trap of providing a précis' of the material rather than an evaluation of it.

Identifications of limitations in data
Inevitably the data on which the evaluation is based will be incomplete. In addition the evaluation stage will also identify areas where additional information will be required in order to make the evaluation more complete. The catering cycle is a useful checklist here. On the one hand it has provided a way of organizing what we do know; however, it also provides for the identification of areas where our information is lacking.

Consideration of short-term action
The difference between short- and long-term action is the difference between putting a fire out and ensuring that there will not be another fire! Short-term action tends to be operationally focused and usually follows directly from the evaluation stage.

Consideration of longer-term action
There are a variety of approaches to this stage depending on the size and sophistication of the operation. Essentially here we are considering the match between the internal achievement and capability of the operation (strengths and weaknesses) and the external opportunities and threats which exist currently and those that might exist in the future.

Using the approach
In presenting these worked cases we are mindful of the difference of approach and interpretation that could exist. Therefore while we have been fairly detailed on the first three stages we have been less detailed or definite at stages 4 and 5. In these stages we have given a statement of the issues for consideration, if possible.

Four cases have been included. These are:

1.   The Osage Avenue Grill – this case provided an example of a complete stand-alone restaurant operation.
2.   The Icham Hotel – this case has been included as a very simple example but which provides an opportunity to demonstrate the use of performance measures.
3.   The Riverside Restaurant – this is another relatively simple case which again provides the opportunity to explore the use of financial analysis.

4.   The Goose Island Marina – this is a more complex case with the food and beverage operation set within a members' club.

These cases are based on four cases previously published by the Hotel and Catering International Management Association (HCIMA) as part of the Part B professional examination in Food and Beverage Management.

The Osage Avenue Grill – the case

The proprietor of the Osage Avenue Grill, Ultratown has appointed you manager. The restaurant is located in the town centre adjacent to the main commercial and shopping centre and caters for business and social entertaining and also attracts an evening-out clientele. Fig. 8.1 shows the layout of the

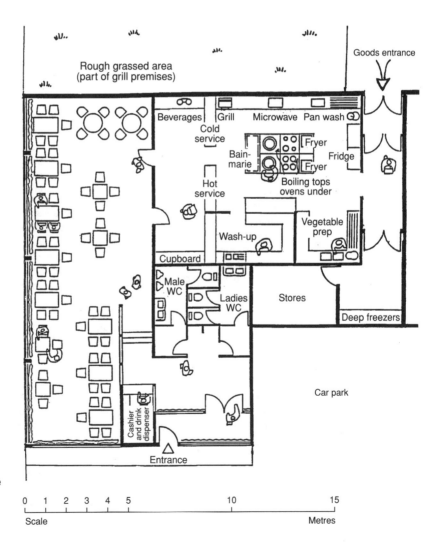

Fig. 8.1 Plan of the Osage Avenue Grill

unit. The menu currently in use is given in Table 8.1 and the budgeted and actual trading results for the last 3 months are shown in Table 8.2.

Table 8.1 Menu for the Osage Avenue Grill

Starters		*Salads*	
Chilled fruit juices	90p	Prawn Marie Rose	£3.25
Minestrone with Parmesan	£1.20	Egg mayonnaise	£2.40
Soup of the day	£1.20	Ham	£2.75
Prawn cocktail	£2.50	Slimmer special (cottage cheese,	
Roll and butter	45p	peach, pineapple	£2.45
Fish platter		*Children's menu*	
Golden fried sole	£2.90	(for under 12s – including drink)	
Golden fried scampi	£3.50	Pirate's platter (fish fingers,	
		baked beans and chips	£1.40
Grills		Banger 'n' beans	£1.40
(with mushrooms, tomato		Cowboy's choice (hamburger,	
peas and french fries)		baked beans, chips)	£1.40
Sirloin steak (6 oz uncooked)	£5.60	Ham and chips	£1.40
Gammon steak	£4.40		
All day special mixed grill		Ice cream	45p
(beefburger, bacon, sausage,			
fried egg, mushrooms, tomato,		*Sweets*	
garden peas, french fries)	£4.40	Knickerbocker glory	£1.50
Chicken grill	£3.45	Banana split	£1.60
		Hawaiian sunset (ice cream,	
All day breakfast		melba sauce, pineapple, cream,	
Traditional breakfast (bacon, egg,		nuts and cherry)	£1.50
sausage, fried bread, tomato,			
buttered toast, marmalade, cup of		*American-style pancakes*	
coffee or tea)	£3.45	Old-fashioned (maple syrup)	£1.20
American breakfast (2 pancakes		Chocolate cream (ice cream,	
with maple syrup, 2 eggs, sausage,		sauce, cream)	£1.35
bacon, cup of tea or coffee)	£3.45	Banana topper (banana, cream	
		melba sauce	£1.40
Omelettes		Cherry cream (cherries and cream)	£1.40
(with french fries and peas)			
Prawn	£2.85	*Beverages*	
Cheese and mushroom	£2.85	Coffee	60p
Ham and tomato	£2.85	Tea	60p
		Milk	60p
Toasted sandwiches		Orange, cola, bitter lemon	
(with salad and relish)		Perrier water bottle	£2.00
Cheddar cheese and tomato	£2.00	Wines – red or white house wine	
Honey roast ham and cheese	£2.30	Carafe: 1 litre	£6.90
Cheese & onion	£2.00	$\frac{1}{2}$ litre	£3.60
		$\frac{1}{4}$ litre	£1.90
		Lager £1.20 pint, 60p $\frac{1}{2}$ pint	

Table 8.2 Budget and trading results for the Osage Avenue Grill for 3 months

Item	Budget			1st month			2nd month			3rd month		
	£	£	%	£	£	%	£	£	%	£	£	%
Food												
Sales	21 600			21 525			21 750			21 375		
Food costs	7 560			7 800			8 220			7 920		
Gross profit		14 040	65		13 725	64		13 530	62		13 455	63
Liquor												
Sales	3 090			3 300			3 345			3 180		
Liquor costs	1 230			1 290			1 305			1 253		
Gross profit		1 860	60		2 010	61		2 040	61		1 927	61
Total sales	24 690			24 825			25 095			24 555		
Total cost of sales	8 790			9 090			9 525			9 173		
Total gross profit		15 900			15 735			15 570			15 382	
Unallocated costs												
Wages and staff costs	6 420		26	7 275		29	7 335		29	7 515		31
Overheads	4 440		18	4 500		18	4 575		19	4 650		19
Total costs		10 860			11 775			11 910			12 165	
Net profit		5 040	20		3 960	16		3 660	15		3 218	13
Stockholding												
Food	3 750			4 125			4 020			4 110		
Drinks	750			795			810			780		
No. of customers	5 410			5 340			5 420			5 340		

The restaurant has been open for 5 years and the menu has remained roughly the same.

The restaurant holds a restaurant licence and is open from 8.30 a.m. to 9.30 p.m., Monday to Saturday. Service is plated and the style of the restaurant is similar to a hotel coffee shop. Staff for the last few years have been easy to find but those new to the area do not want to work full shifts and expect higher rewards for shorter part-time hours.

Ultratown is a modern developing town located in an area of the country with a high concentration of new technology companies, particularly those associated with the computer industry.

The population of the town is dominated by young professionals who have moved into the area within the last 4 years. Market research indicates that these people:

- have a high disposable income
- generally spend their leisure time in outdoor and sports activities
- lead active social lives
- are health conscious

From your own informal research of this area you have noted that:

- Wine bars and themed public houses are being developed including a steak house operation.
- There has been an increasing number of changes in the high street moving towards more up-market shops.

The Osage Avenue Grill – the workings

Stage 1 – Analysis   Table 8.3 gives an analysis of the operations using the catering cycle. Table 8.4 gives the trading figures with a variety of performance measures. Table 8.5 looks at the percentage variance against budget.

Table 8.3   Osage Avenue Grill – text analysis

Consumer and the market	Policy	Interpretation of demand	Convergence of facilities
Adjacent to main commercial and shopping centre Business and social entertaining Eating out clientele Modern town Young professionals: Sporting High disposable income Health conscious Wine bars and theme public houses being developed including steak house	Town centre location Restaurant licence Open Monday to Saturday 8.30 a.m. – 9.30 p.m.	Menu same for 5 years	Style similar to coffee shop 62 covers – bad seating Conventional kitchen
Provisioning	**Production/distribution**	**Control of costs and revenue**	**Monitoring of customer satisfaction**
	Plated service	Budgeting	

Table 8.4 Analysis of the budget and trading results for the Osage Avenue Grill for 3 months

	Budget £	£	%	1st month £	£	%	2nd month £	£	%	3rd month £	£	%
Food												
Sales	21 600			21 525			21 750			21 375		
Food costs	7 560		35	7 800		36	8 220		38	7 920		37
Gross profit		14 040	65		13 725	64		13 530	62		13 455	63
Liquor												
Sales	3 090			3 300			3 345			3 180		
Liquor costs	1 230		40	1 290		39	1 305		39	1 253		39
Gross profit		1 860	60		2 010	61		2 040	61		1 927	61
Total sales	24 690			24 825			25 095			24 555		
Total cost of sales	8 790			9 090			9 525			9 173		
Total gross profit		15 900	64		15 735	63		15 570	62		15 382	63
Unallocated costs												
Wages and staff costs	6 420		26	7 275		29	7 335		29	7 515		31
Overheads	4 440		18	4 500		18	4 575		19	4 650		19
Total costs		10 860	44		11 775	47		11 910	47		12 165	50
Net profit		5 040	20		3 960	16		3 660	15		3 218	13
Stockholding		STO[1]			STO			STO			STO	
Food	3 750	2.01		4 125	1.89		4 020	2.04		4 110	1.92	
Drinks	750	1.64		795	1.62		810	1.61		780	1.68	

[1] STO: Stock turnover.

Table 8.5 Variance percentage against budget

	1st month	2nd month	3rd month	Average
Food sales	−0.34	0.69	−1.04	−0.23
Food costs	3.17	8.73	4.76	+5.56
Gross profit	−2.24	−3.63	−4.20	−3.36
Liquor sales	6.80	8.25	2.91	+5.98
Liquor costs	4.80	6.09	1.87	+5.32
Gross profit	8.06	9.67	3.60	+7.11
Total sales	0.55	1.64	−0.54	+0.55
Total cost of sales	3.41	8.36	0.94	+4.23
Total GP	−1.03	−2.07	−3.25	−2.12
Wage and staff	13.31	14.25	17.00	+14.85
Overheads	1.35	3.04	4.73	+3.05
Net profit	−21.42	−27.38	−36.15	−28.34
Net profit under budget	−£1080	−£1380	−£1822	

Note: variance percentage = [(actual − budget) / budget] x 100

Table 8.6 gives the percentage of food and drink sales to the total sales; Table 8.7 shows the average spend on food and drink; Table 8.8 calculates the seat turnover.

Table 8.6   Percentage food/drink to total sales

	Budget		1st month		2nd month		3rd month	
	£	%	£	%	£	%	£	%
Food	21 600	87.5	21 525	86.6	21 750	86.6	21 375	87
Drink	3 090	12.5	3 300	13.4	3 345	13.4	3 180	13
Total	24 690		24 825		25 095		24 555	

Table 8.7   Average spend

	Budget	1st month	2nd month	3rd month
Food	3.99	3.99	4.01	4.00
Drink	1.40	1.45	1.52	1.48
Total	5.39	5.44	5.53	5.48

Table 8.8   Seat turnover per day

	Budget	1st month	2nd month	3rd month
	3.35	3.34	3.36	3.31

Note: seat turnover = number of meals served ÷ number of seats available

Stage 2 Evaluation   **Strengths**

- Conservative budget and targets for sales are being met.
- Reasonable match between spend and budget with principal problem being costs.
- Clearly an existing market before changes took place in town. (Opportunity exists to meet new customers needs as well as old.)
- Conventional production area thus able to adapt to a variety of menu styles.
- Ground at back and own car park.

Weaknesses

- Overall performance of grill is poor against budget. Net profit is between −21.42 per cent and −36.15 per cent under budget with overall downward trend.
- Food costs are higher in variance than sales resulting in the gross profit running under budget.

- Liquor costs are lower in variance than sales with sales being over budget between 2.91 and 8.25 per cent for the three months. This has also resulted in drink being a slightly higher proportion of total sales (food sales have only varied from −1.04 to 0.69 per cent).
- Stock turnover in food is lower than budgeted possibly suggesting a problem with purchasing.
- Wage costs are between 13.31 and 17.0 per cent over budget with upward trend indicating possible overstaffing.
- Seating layout for the 62 covers is poor and space wasting.
- Kitchen layout is mismatched with menu and also space seems disproportionate to service areas.
- Menu has remained static for 5 years, i.e. before changes in local area started both in customer trends and in other trends, e.g. themed pubs in area. Menu does not now seem to match total market, especially the health conscious element.
- Décor may not match local development.
- Overheads are increasing from 1.35 to 4.73 per cent over budget.

Stage 3   Limitations   The additional information required will include:

- Analysis of sales mix and service period breakdown to show types of clientele and popularity of menu item.
- Examination of purchasing and control system including pricing of food.
- Sales mix information on drink sales to establish reason for costs under budget.
- Examination of production systems and suitability to menu.
- Trading account for last 5 years and budgeting system.
- Staffing information and breakdown of wage costs.
- Information on overheads.
- Examine to what extent is health consciousness important to the customer.

Methods for gathering additional information will include:

- sales mix analysis especially between lunch and evening service to identify if type of clientele is changing
- discussion with proprietor
- discussion with staff
- more specific examination of locality and competition
- survey of existing customers
- 'on the street' survey of potential customers
- analysis of complaints

Stage 4   Short-term action
- Investigate budgeting procedures to identify their appropriateness and accuracy, including examination of overheads.

- Investigate staffing costs with a view to reducing them in line with budget.
- Investigate food costs, purchasing and control in order to meet budget requirements.
- Produce sales mix data for times of day to determine differences in clientele if any – menu is wide and varied, i.e. breakfast through to dinner.
- Investigate drink sales increase and higher profit to determine cause; overages can indicate problems as much as shortages.
- Investigate production systems to determine appropriateness to menu and also to consider reduction in space required.
- Consider alternative layouts for restaurant to increase space usage.
- Consider some healthier changes in menu.

Overall there is a need to reduce costs to budget or increase sales to reachieve net profit target.

**Stage 5
Consideration of
longer-term action**

Opportunities and threats for the Osage Avenue Grill are given in Table 8.9.

Table 8.9   Opportunities and threats

Opportunities	Threats
Prime site	New competition
Possible expansion	Change in market
Could meet a number of markets	Decline in old market
New people in area	Customers changing?

Even though the menu has run for 5 years, sales on food are more or less static on budget while drink sales are over budget. Also the main problems are seen to be cost of food sales and staff costs being over budgets, along with increasing overheads.

Assuming the budget to be accurate and that costs can be brought under control there appears to be little need for change. However, in the longer term the proprietor will have to consider either to remain in this sector or fall in line with apparent trends, e.g. wine bars, steak houses. This change is obviously being taken up elsewhere in the town.

The plan shows apparent scope for development with the grassed area at the back – possibly for a patio extension – and because the production area is currently disproportionately large in comparison to the service area. However the existing conventional kitchen provides for scope to consider alternative menus with the existing kitchen layout.

The actual proposals would follow from the considerations above and clearly state what the proposals would be trying to achieve.

The Icham Hotel – the case

The hotel has bedroom accommodation for 100 guests and two food outlets – the Janus Restaurant and the Gateway Grill each with seating for 60 diners. The restaurant offers à la carte meals six evenings per week and is closed on Sundays. The grill is open from 7.30 a.m. until 10.00 p.m. every day.

The current financial information is given in Table 8.10.

Table 8.10 Financial information of the Icham Hotel

	Last year ending 31 May		This year ending 31 May	
	£000	£000	£000	£000
Restaurant				
Sales	105.0		113.0	
Food cost	35.0		40.0	
Gross profit		70.0		73.0
Wages	35.0		39.0	
Overheads	25.0	60.0	27.5	66.5
Dept profit		10.0		6.5
Grill				
Sales	255.0		282.0	
Food cost	115.0		125.0	
Gross profit		140.0		157.0
Wages	58.0		63.0	
Overheads	36.0	94.0	14.5	104.5
Dept profit		46.0		52.5
Bar				
Sales	85.0		96.0	
Beverage cost	34.8		43.0	
Gross profit		50.2		53.0
Wages	17.0		18.9	
Overheads	10.0	27.0	11.0	29.9
Dept profit		23.2		23.1
Meals served				
Restaurant		9,350		9,149
Grill		48,000		52,000
Average salary per employee		£5,000		£5,500

Prices and salaries were raised by 10% on 1 June last year

The Icham Hotel – the workings

Stage 1   Analysis   Table 8.11 gives an analysis of the operations using the catering cycle. Tables 8.12–14 give a variety of financial analysis and performance measures.

Table 8.11   Icham Hotel – text analysis

Consumer and the market	Policy	Interpretation of demand	Convergence of facilities
Food and beverage based in 100 guest hotel	60-seat restaurant, open 6 evenings per week Coffee shop – 60 seats, open 7.30 a.m.–10 p.m. daily No policy on overheads apportioning Licensed 10% increase prices and in cost of wages last year	A la carte menu for restaurant Coffee shop menu for grill, also serving breakfast	

Provisioning	**Production/distribution**
	
	Staffing estimate
	  Restaurant 7
	  Grill 11+
	  Bar 3+
		Control of costs and revenue
		
		Annual accounts
			Monitoring of customer satisfaction
			
			Spend per head dropping in grill, maintained in restaurant

Table 8.12   Financial analysis

	Last year ending 31 May			This year ending 31 May			Variance this year on last year (%)
	£000	£000	%	£000	£000	%	
Restaurant							
Sales	105.0			113.0			+7.6
Food cost	35.0			40.0			+14.3
Gross profit		70.0	66.7		73.0	64.6	+4.3
Wages	35.0			39.0			
Overheads	25.0	60.0		27.5	66.5		
Dept profit		10.0	9.5		6.5	5.8	−35.0

Note: variance percentage = [(this year − last year) / last year] x 100   *(Continued)*

Table 8.12 *Continued*

	Last year ending 31 May			This year ending 31 May			Variance this year on last year (%)
	£000	£000	%	£000	£000	%	
Grill							
Sales	255.0			282.0			+10.6
Food cost	115.0			125.0			+8.7
Gross profit		140.0	54.9		157.0	55.7	+12.1
Wages	58.0			63.0			
Overheads	36.0	94.0		41.5	104.5		
Dept profit		46.0	18.0		52.5	18.6	+14.1
Bar							
Sales	85.0			96.0			+12.9
Beverage cost	34.8			43.0			+23.6
Gross profit		50.2	59.1		53.0	55.2	+5.6
Wages	17.0			18.9			
Overheads	10.0	27.0		11.0	29.9		
Dept profit		23.2	27.3		23.1	24.1	−0.4

Table 8.13 **Performance measures**

	Last year		This year		Variance (%)
	£000	%	£000	%	
Labour costs percentage of sales					
Restaurant	35	33.3	39	34.5	+11.4
Grill	58	22.7	63	22.3	+8.6
Bar	17	20.0	18.9	19.7	+11.2
Total	110	24.7	120.9	24.6	+9.91
Overheads percentage of sales					
Restaurant	25	23.8	27.5	24.3	+10
Grill	36	14.1	41.5	14.7	+15.2
Bar	10	11.7	11.0	11.4	+10
Total	71	15.9	80.0	16.3	+12.6
Customer spend per head					
Restaurant	£11.23		£12.35		+9.97
Grill	£5.31		£5.43		+2.2
No. of covers per day and seat turnover	*Covers*	*STO*	*Covers*	*STO*	
Restaurant	29.9	0.5	29.3	0.49	
Grill	131.0	2.18	142.0	2.36	

(Continued)

Table 8.13 *Continued*

	Last year	This year
	£000	**£000**
Average daily income		
Restaurant	£336	£362
Grill	£698	£772
Bar	£233	£263
Sales per seat available per day		
(daily sales divided by no. of available seats)		
Restaurant	£ 5.60	£6.03
Grill	£11.63	£12.87

Table 8.14 **Staff utilization measures**

	Results		Variance (%)
	Last year	**This year**	
Average staffing (labour costs divided by average wage)			
Restaurant	7	7	
Grill	11.6	11.4	
Bar	3.4	3.44	
Total	22.0	21.84	
Average annual sales per member of staff			
Restaurant	£15 000	£16 142.8	+7.6
Grill	£21 982	£24 736	+12.5
Bar	£25 000	£27 906	+11.6
Average annual net profit per member of staff			
Restaurant	£1428	£928	−35
Grill	£3965	£4605	+16
Bar	£6823	£6715	−1.6
Productivity index (sales divided by payroll)			
Restaurant	3	2.9	
Grill	4.4	4.48	
Bar	5	5	

Notes on financial analysis

- Prices and salaries were increased at the start of this year. Variance percentages indicate that increases in sales have matched price increases.
- Labour percentage: These have actually risen by 9.91 per cent over the year but with differing percentages in the departments.
- Overheads percentage: There does not appear to be a relationship between apportionment of cost to department sales.

- Customer spend: Restaurant has more or less maintained spend per head, grill is showing reduced spend per head.
- Number of covers/seat turnover: Restaurant is losing custom 0.6 per day. Grill is increasing custom, 11 per day. Seat turnover in restaurant is slightly lower, in grill it is higher.
- Average daily income: This only amplifies figures given on main sheet.
- Sales per seat: Another way of looking at seat turnover and number of covers.

Staffing analysis
- Average staffing: Very rough calculation but gives indication of staffing by department and shows slight changes.
- Average annual sales and variance: Shows bar and grill sales meeting more than 10 per cent price increase and restaurant not.
- Productivity index: As expected: restaurant going down, grill up and bar the same.

Stage 2 Evaluation

Restaurant
- Sales have not kept up with increase (10 per cent) and the lower sales figure is caused by fewer customers, spend per head having been maintained.
- Cost of sales in restaurant have increased by 14.3 per cent, i.e. greater than ability to increase sales resulting in a reduction in the departmental profit.
- On average the restaurant is half-full each night with average seat turnover being 0.5 and now reducing.

Grill
- Sales have increased. This is due to more custom but lower spend per head (customers 48 000–52 000) (average spend £5.31 to £5.43, i.e. less than 10 per cent increase.
- However, cost of sales have decreased at a greater rate so customers may be buying cheaper but more profitable items, or food cost control is better than in the restaurant, possibly because it is open long hours every day and there is a better opportunity to control cost.
- Overheads on grill have increased by 15.2 per cent against overall increase of 12.6 per cent. Profit of grill would be higher if not for this aspect. However, no further knowledge.

Bar
- Sales have gone up more than 10 per cent but costs of sales have increased by 23.6 per cent which accounts for reduction in net profit.

Stage 3 Further information required
- market information
- staffing information – how organized, etc.

- how are overheads apportioned
- production systems, buying procedures, etc.
- control procedures and research
- menu breakdown for both sales mix, etc.
- beverage sales in restaurant

Stage 4 Short-term proposals

- Fully identify market guests/non-guests/competitors, etc. and identify if possible to improve.
- Review grill and restaurant menus. What is customer buying? Possibly revise menus.
- Review costing and control procedures to identify problem areas.
- Review production system to reduce costs.
- Consider not having two 60 seaters if market shares cannot be improved.
- Consider only having coffee shop with wider choice unless market share can be improved.
- Investigate system for apportioning overheads – propose percentage basis or related to turnover percentages.

Stage 5 Consideration of longer-term action

This is not really possible given the limitations of the data.

The Riverside Restaurant – the case

The proprietor of the 50-seat Riverside Restaurant is concerned about the performance and profitability of the business. This unit is open for six days per week and caters to an up-market clientele with an à la carte menu.

The trading results are given in Table 8.5. Table 8.16 gives some information on the food purchases and Table 8.17 identifies the most popular selling items.

Table 8.15   Trading results

	Month			
	1st	2nd	3rd	4th
Number of trading days	24	26	26	27
Average number of meals served per day	108	104	106	109
	£	£	£	£
Opening stock (food)	2 085	2 126	2 221	2 370
plus purchases	8 614	8 925	9 078	9 212
	10 699	11 051	11 299	11 582
Less closing stock	2 126	2 221	2 370	2 392
Consumption	8 573	8 830	8 929	9 190
Staff food cost	1 635	1 680	1 610	1 660
Actual food cost	6 938	7 150	7 319	7 530
Revenue received	19 942	20 039	19 732	19 872
Gross profit	13 004 (65.2%)	12 889 (64.3%)	12 413 (62.9%)	12 342 (62.1%)

Table 8.16   Food costs for commodities purchased in largest volume

	Prices paid per kg (£) [per lb (p)]							
	1st month		2nd month		3rd month		4th month	
Beef (rump and loin)	1.78	[81]	1.81	[82]	1.92	[87]	1.90	[86]
Pork (whole leg)	0.72	[33]	0.71	[32]	0.71	[32]	0.72	[33]
Chicken (oven ready)	0.49	[22]	0.51	[23]	0.51	[23]	0.49	[22]
Dover sole (10/12 oz) (280–340 g)	2.75	[1.25]	2.78	[1.26]	2.76	[1.25]	2.65	[1.20]
Veal escalope	3.70	[1.68]	3.80	[1.72]	4.05	[1.84]	3.85	[1.75]
Scampi (whole)	1.95	[88]	2.20	[99]	2.20	[99]	2.15	[98]

Table 8.17   Sales analysis of the most popular selling lines

	Menu selling price (£)	Average number of dishes sold per day			
		1st month	2nd month	3rd month	4th month
Tournedos rossini	6.95	14	9	8	6
Chef's speciality of the day	4.95	21	21	24	26
Escalope of veal cordon bleu	5.95	12	13	18	22
Chicken Kiev	5.35	n/a	n/a	15	21
Scampi provençale	6.10	17	15	8	n/a

The Riverside Restaurant – the workings

Stage 1   Analysis   Table 8.18 gives an anlysis of the case based on the catering cycle. Table 8.19 provides for a more detailed financial analysis.

Table 8.18   The Riverside Restaurant – text analysis

Consumer and the market	Policy	Interpretation of demand	Convergence of facilities
Up-market clientele		50 seats Open 6 days A la carte menu	
Provisioning	**Production/distribution**	**Control of costs and revenue**	**Monitoring of customer satisfaction**
	Table service Conventional production		

Table 8.19   Financial analysis of the Riverside Restaurant

	1st month	2nd month	3rd month	4th month
No. of trading days	24	26	26	27
No. of meals served per day	108	104	106	109
Seat turnover	2.16	2.1	2.12	2.18
Opening stock (food)	2085	2126	2221	2370
plus purchases	8614	8925	9078	9212
	10699	11051	11299	11582
Less closing stock	2126	2221	2370	2392
Consumption	8573	8830	8929	9190
Staff allowances	1635	1680	1610	1660
Actual food cost	6938	7150	7319	7530
Daily staff food cost	68.12	64.61	61.92	61.48
% of daily consumption	19%	19%	18%	18%
Revenue received	19942	20039	19732	19872
Revenue per day	830.91	770.73	758.92	736
Spend per head	7.69	7.41	7.16	6.75

(Continued)

Table 8.19 *Continued*

	1st month	2nd month	3rd month	4th month
Gross profit	13004	12889	12413	12342
Gross profit %	65.2%	64.3%	62.9%	62.1%
Gross profit per day	541.83	495.73	477.42	457.11
Gross profit per seat per day	10.83	9.91	9.54	9.14
Cost of sales per head per day	2.67	2.64	2.65	2.56
Gross profit per head per day	5.02	4.76	4.50	4.19
Stock turnover per month	4.07	4.06	3.89	3.85

Note: per day averages will be affected by spread of week days to weekends assuming that there is significant difference in trade between these two.

Stage 2   Evaluation

Key Issues

In this case we can only indentify areas of concern as there is insufficient data to identity strengths and weaknesses. Because the months have a differing number of trading days, comparison has been done on a per day basis.

- Overall the restaurant is experiencing a drop in its spend per head from £7.69 to £6.75 as well as a drop in the gross profit from £5.02 to £4.19 (65.2 to 62.1 per cent). This is also reflected in per cover available drop of gross profit from £10.83 to £9.14.
- The stock turnover has reduced from 4.07 to 3.85 times per month. First this indicates a high fresh usage but this is out of line with revenue achieved, i.e. stock turnover is reducing but holding is increasing whereas a drop would be expected. The reduction in gross profit could therefore be partially explained by higher wastage of food.
- Staff food costs seem high at 18–19 per cent of consumption. For a 50-seater restaurant this appears excessive.
- No information is given on staffing, lunch or dinner opening, over-heads, etc. No information given of sales of alcohol.
- No information on some sales suggests poor control system.
- Fluctuation in food prices would also contribute to reduction in GP per-centages. However, fluctuations are not that great. The two further tables of analysis given would seem to be of little help as they stand. There is only an apparent relationship between two items mentioned in both tables (8.16 and 8.17), i.e. scampi and veal escalope. However, the second table does appear to support the drop in spend per head figures with an apparent trend away from more expensive items (steak and scampi) to cheaper ones (dish of the day and veal).
- The dish of the day represents 19.4 to 24 per cent of meals served over the 4 months. This should be investigated to check costing especially as it represents such a high proportion of total meals served.
- Factors like that above together with the drop in spend per head

indicate a possible change in market requirements. This would need to be looked at further.

- GP per cent would more usually be expected to be about 70 per cent.
- Given prices of most popular items, customers do not seem to be spending much on starters, sweets and coffee (£2.75 maximum on figures given).

Stage 3   Additional information required

- Purchasing policies detail including specification and price negotiations. Chef's speciality – what type of dish.
- Full details of menu including sales mix figures and differential GPs for all dishes.
- Complete details of control systems with particular emphasis on revenue. Control and sales analysis information control.
- Information on number of staff and nature of staff food provision and policy on staff meals.
- Opening times for lunch/dinner and trading figures for each session and each day of week.
- Is there a budget?
- What are overhead costs?
- Are there alcoholic beverages sold?
- Details of market served.

Stage 4   Short-term action

- Review staff provision.
- Renegotiate purchasing prices of main items used to avoid fluctuation in month to month prices if possible.
- Investigate immediate control to overcome 'no information available' status.
- Investigate control of food and give specific examples, e.g. define portion specification, weight, for purchasing/and for preparation.
- Establish overall budget.
- Review menu in light of market information.

Stage 5 Consideration of longer-term action

Limitations in information make longer-term considerations impossible.

The Goose Island Marina – the case

You are the newly appointed manager of the Goose Island Marina which is situated on the south coast of Britain about 10 miles from the nearest seaside resort.

The club has been in operation for 25 years and has occupied the same site and club house building. Fig. 8.2 shows the layout of the grounds and a detailed plan of the club house. The boatyard, moorings, advice centre and shop as well as the club house are expected to be financially self-supporting; however, the catering accounts by the club house for the period ending 31 January this year (Table 8.20) represent the first indications to the club committee of a deteriorating financial situation in this area.

Accommodation in the club house comprises dining-room with seating for up to 40 diners, bar with seating for 30 people, lounge, writing room, two committee rooms, games room and Commodore's room (the Commodore is the president of the club). The house also contains accommodation for yourself, four letting bedrooms, kitchen and ancillary areas. At present food and beverage operations are confined to bar service and lunch and dinner service in the dining-room only. The bedrooms are not often let and the need for breakfast service has been met on an *ad hoc* basis by available staff.

Food service is confined to the dining-room using silver service. The kitchen which was designed when the club house opened is of conventional and traditional style. Members are currently advised that advanced booking of meals is recommended. Examples of menus are given in Table 8.21. The present chef has tendered his notice and you will be looking to appoint a new person.

Your own impressions of the club so far are that traditions appear to be dying hard and the club house premises and general atmosphere, which reflect the original 25-year-old-design, no longer appeal to the growing number of younger members. However, the club committee has indicated to you that they are prepared to fund alternatives to the existing operations including structural alterations as required.

At the last Annual Meeting, there was much heated debate about the role of the club house. Many members said they made full and frequent use of the club for yachting and boating pursuits, but felt that the club house just did not provide the kind of amenity or type of catering they wanted. In the summer months many picnicked in the grounds and brought their own food and drink. There was much grievance that club membership subscriptions had to be used this year to prop up an ailing part of the club's activities which was now used by fewer and fewer members. While membership has grown to 1250 over the last few years the management committee felt they had to take seriously the threat of some members resigning. You, however, are concerned to establish more clearly members' needs across the whole membership rather than the views of committee members who are predominantly longer-standing members.

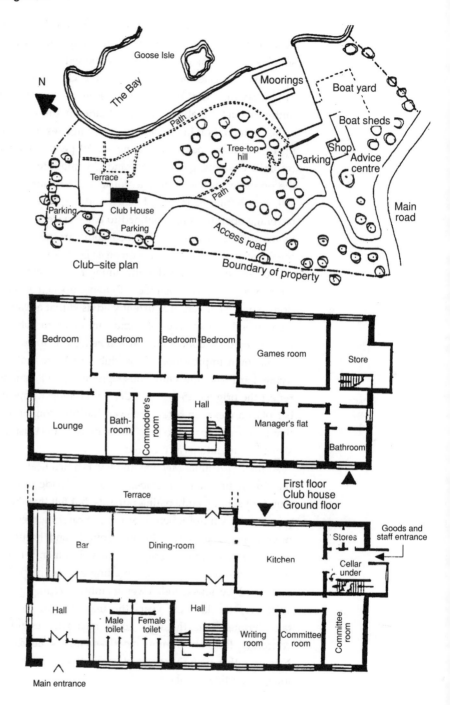

Fig. 8.2 Plan of grounds and club house of the Goose Island Marina

Table 8.20   Club house accounts for the year ending 31 January

Item	Last year		This year	
	£	£	£	£
Income				
Bar sales	48 639		51 957	
Less cost of sales	31 616		34 499	
Gross profit (drink)		17 023	17 458	
Food sales	63 963		65 580	
Less cost of sales	26 097		29 118	
Gross profit (food)		37 866		36 462
Accommodation (gross profit)		1 518		1 202
Sundry sales (bar billiards, magazines, etc.) (Gross profit)		183		234
Gross profit overall		55 590		55 356
Expenditure				
Wages and salaries	35 639		39 951	
Overheads (rent, rates, insurance, fuel, etc.)	20 560		23 186	
Total operating costs		56 199		63 137
Net surplus (deficit)		391		(7 781)
Transfer to main club funds		391		—
Transfer from main club funds		—		7 781

Stockholding (value of stocks at cost price as at 31 January this year)
Drink   £7 314
Food   £4 884

Note: Food and drink prices were increased by 10% on 1 February this year as were wages

Table 8.21 Menu change on a 14-day cycle

Lunch (3 courses priced at £3.75	Dinner (4 courses priced at £5.25)
Chilled fruit juices Egg mayonnaise Oxtail soup	Chilled fruit juices Florida cocktail Paté maison Chef's consommé
Omelette – to choice Lancashire hot pot	Grilled halibut steak Grilled lamb cutlets
Gammon steak and pineapple Cold roast pork or chicken	Roast leg of pork Cold ham or chicken

Boiled potatoes, garden peas,
    buttered carrots
	Roast and purée potatoes,
	    buttered cauliflower, whole beans

Peach Melba Compote of fruit Ices – various	Cherry cheesecake Coupe Enda May Cheeseboard
Coffee	Coffee

The Goose Island Marina – the workings

Stage 1 Analysis

Table 8.22 gives the analysis of the information based on the Catering Cycle. Table 8.23 provides a financial analysis and Tables 8.24–27 give a variety of performance measures.

Table 8.22 Goose Island Marina – text analysis

Consumer and the market	Policy	Interpretation of demand	Convergence of facilities

Club members 1250
Traditions dying hard
Younger members not
    using club
	Self-financing
	Appointment of manager
	Food and beverage
	    service in bar and
	    restaurant only
	Funds available for
	    refurbishment and
	    structural alteration
		Breakfast service met *ad hoc*
		Set menus £3.75 and
		    £4.25
		Accommodation little used
			General atmosphere no
			    longer appeals to
			    younger members
			Dining-room 30 people,
			    lounge, writing room,
			    two committee rooms,
			    games room and
			    Commodore's room,
			    four letting bedrooms

Provisioning
High convenience food
    usage
Low stock turnover
	Production/distribution
	Silver service
	Bar service
	New chef required
		Control of costs and revenue
		High stock levels
			Monitoring of customer satisfaction
			Customers dissatisfied
			    with service of club
			    house, in particular
			    younger members

Table 8.23   Financial analysis for Goose Island Marina

Item	Last year		This year		Variance
	£	%	£	%	(%)
Sales					
Bar sales	48 639	43.3	51 957	44.2	6.82
Food sales	63 963	56.8	65 580	55.8	2.52
Total sales	112 602	100	117 537	100	4.38
Costs					
Bar costs	31 616	65	34 499	66.4	9.11
Food costs	26 097	40	29 119	44.4	11.57
Total costs	57 713	51.3	63 517	54.1	10.22
Gross profit					
Bar	17 023	35	17 458	33.6	2.55
Food	37 866	60	34 462	55.6	−3.70
Accommodation	1 518	n/a	1 202	n/a	−20.8
Sundry sales	183	n/a	234	n/a	27.86
Total gross profit	56 590	n/a	55 356	n/a	−2.18
Other costs					
Wages and salaries	35 639	n/a	39 951	n/a	12.09
Overheads	20 560	n/a .	23 186	n/a	12.77
Total other costs	56 199	n/a	63 137	n/a	12.34
Net surplus deficit	391	n/a	(7 781)	n/a	−20.90
Stockholding					
Drink			7 314		
Food			4 884		
Total			12 198		

Note: Food and drink prices increased by 10% on 1 February at the beginning of this year as were wages.

Table 8.24   Contribution to gross profit

	Last year		This year	
	£	%	£	%
Bar	17 023	30	17 458	31.4
Food	37 866	67	36 462	66
Accommodation	1 518	2.6	1 202	2.2
Sundries	183	0.4	234	0.4
Total	56 590	100	55 356	100

Table 8.25 Stock turnover

Item	Drink		Food	
Cost of sales	34 499		29 118	
Stockholding	7 314	= 4.71	4 884	= 5.96

Table 8.26 Sales per week

Item	Last year	This year
Sales per week	999.17	1261.15

Table 8.27 Wages and overheads

Item	Last year	This year
Wages % on food and beverage sales	32	34
Overheads % on food and beverage sales	18.3	19.8

Stage 2 Evaluation

Strengths

- Captive potential market of 1250 members especially as closest alternative is 10 miles away.
- Good sites and facilities and ability to expand and alter existing services. Funds available for refurbishment and structural alterations.
- Opportunity to appoint new chef to achieve changes.
- Self-financing policy keeps prices down thus potentially encouraging use of facilities.

Weaknesses

- Overall the deficit could largely be accounted for by the massive stocks of food and drink held in comparison with the potential business. The total is £12 198 which represents 2.3 months of sales. If this were about one month (£5301) it would reduce deficit by £6897.
- Food sales and cost: Prices were increased by 10 per cent at beginning of the year. The variance is only 2.52 per cent suggesting there is a loss of business. Cost variance is 11.5 per cent so there is inevitable reduction in gross profit from 60 to 55.6 per cent. For this type of operation a 40/60 ratio would seem reasonable but 50/50 is more desirable especially as it is a non-profit-making venture. Costs are out of line with sales, suggesting lack of adequate control even with standard menus.

- Drink costs and sales: Bar sales have only increased by 6.82 per cent, again indicating a loss of business (price increase was 10 per cent). Costs have risen by 9.11 per cent. Main problems here would seem to be loss of business and low profit margin (33.6 per cent). Again 45–50 per cent would be better. Also increasing costs suggest lack of control.
- Wage costs: These have increased from 32 to 34 per cent of food and beverage sales (the other business only accounts for about 2 per cent of total). This is a variance of 12.09 per cent, i.e. above the 10 per cent increase. This is too high. A maximum of 30 per cent would be appropriate for this type of business.
- Overheads: They have increased by 12.77 per cent (i.e. in excess of price increases).
- Menu: Cyclical and staid, also a large amount of convenience stock being used judging by the low stock turnover (5.96 times per year).
- Members are split between traditionalists and younger newer members. Conflict of requirements.
- Food and beverage services restricted to bar and restaurant.
- Poor general atmosphere.

Stage 3 Additional information required

- Market – membership details/usage, etc./seasonal requirements.
- Policy – how much money available? What flexibility?
- Menus and services usage and last year's bar usage.
- Equipment space allocations.
- Staffing details.
- How customers' satisfaction is, and is to be, monitored.
- Details of overheads.
- Details of sundry sales.

Stage 4 Short-term proposals

- Reduce stockholding to about 2/3 weeks at a time.
- Reduce staffing to 30 per cent cost.
- Introduce bar food (also terrace).
- Carry out survey of club members.
- Complete structural survey of building.
- Introduce monitoring and control procedures.
- Introduce budgeting system and increase drink costs if required.

Stage 5 Consideration of longer-term action

This will include considering the introduction of new services especially on the terrace and over in the boatyard (a kiosk?). Also expected is the replanning of the club house including a reduction in letting rooms, moving kitchens to back on ground floor so as to allow for an extension to the bar and food areas and possibly the letting of rooms upstairs converted into committee rooms (from downstairs).

New chef appointee will have to be able to continue existing services and easily adapt to proposed changes. Person specification should therefore include involvement of new person in proposals and will require variety of previous experience in differing catering operations.

Index